D1568259

If You Love This Game

AN MVP'S LIFE IN BASEBALL

Andre Dawson
with Alan Maimon

TRIUMPH
BOOKS

Library of Congress Cataloging-in-Publication Data

Dawson, Andre.
    If you love this game— : an MVP's life in baseball / Andre Dawson with Alan Maimon.
        p. cm.
    Summary: "The authorized autobiography of Baseball Hall of Famer Andre Dawson"— Provided by publisher.
    ISBN 978-1-60078-700-3 (hardback)
 1. Dawson, Andre. 2. Baseball players—United States—Biography. I. Maimon, Alan. II. Title.
    GV865.D39A3 2012
    796.357092—dc23
    [B]   2012005000

This book is available in quantity at special discounts for your group or organization. For further information, contact:
    Triumph Books LLC
    542 South Dearborn Street
    Suite 750
    Chicago, Illinois 60605
    (312) 939–3330
    Fax (312) 663–3557
    www.triumphbooks.com

Printed in U.S.A.

ISBN: 978-1-60078-700-3

Design by Sue Knopf

Photos courtesy of Andre Dawson unless otherwise indicated

To my family, so many of whom
have been a source of support and inspiration
throughout my lifetime
—Andre

To Angela and the girls—
Dasia, Madison, and Annabelle
—Alan

CONTENTS

FOREWORD
BY GREG MADDUX

BACK IN 1987, I WAS ONE OF THE YOUNGEST PLAYERS IN THE MAJORS AND getting knocked around pretty good my first time through the National League.

It was an exciting and challenging year. I was a 21-year-old kid hoping to prove to myself and everyone else that I could pitch at the major league level. At the same time, I was trying to fit in with my teammates and develop routines that would improve my chances of staying in the big leagues and having a successful career.

Despite going just 6–14 in 1987, I felt I had made positive strides in these areas.

Andre Dawson played a big role in my learning process.

Hawk was a man of few words, so it wasn't anything he said that made an impression on me. It was *everything* he did.

I spent a lot of time simply observing Andre, who was in his first year with the Cubs that season. I watched how he got ready for games. I watched how he worked out after games. I watched how he handled the media. And until we both signed with other teams after the 1992 season, I never stopped doing those things.

As a young player, you pick guys you want to model your career after. Even though I was a pitcher and he was an outfielder, Hawk became one of those guys for me.

Before I ever met Andre, I respected him. The steps he took to get to the Cubs in 1987 were incredible. Rather than staying with an Expos team that took his services for granted, he accepted a pay cut to play in Chicago. By doing so, he stood up for his principles and to owners who had colluded to keep free agents from signing with other teams.

He then went out and established himself as the best player in the National League that season, winning the 1987 MVP Award.

It was an unusual way to do it, but I hope I conveyed my admiration for Andre in a July 1987 game when I hit a Padres player with a pitch in retaliation for Andre getting beaned earlier in the game. It turned my stomach to see Andre lying on the ground with blood streaming down his face.

Coming into that game, I was 5–7 and really could have used a victory. We had a three-run lead when I drilled Benito Santiago in the back during the fourth inning. I was ejected before pitching enough innings to qualify for the win. But that was okay. It was one of those times when doing the right thing took precedence over personal gain. I saw the situation as an opportunity to gain Andre's and the team's trust.

Despite not saying a whole lot, Andre was very much a team leader. He let his preparation, play, and work ethic do the talking.

Here's what I saw nearly every day during the baseball season for six years:

Before games, Andre would take care of his ailing knees, stretch, take outfield and batting practice, and then have his knees worked on again. He'd play the game, and when it was over, he'd take care of his knees again, work out, and then finally, he'd talk to the media.

That last part really impressed me. After very long days, he made time for reporters. But by tending to his body first, he sent a message to me that it's more important to prepare for tomorrow than it is to talk about what you did today.

There were times when I could see Andre was really hurting, but he still maintained his routine every day.

Andre took pride in his performance and wanted his teammates to do the same. He was almost like a silent coach on the field and in the clubhouse. He wanted guys to do things the right way. And if they were smart, all they needed to do was follow his lead.

We had a lot of fun in the Cubs clubhouse during those years. Away from the cameras, guys messed around with each other and pulled pranks. I was a prankster. Andre wasn't. But that didn't keep him from having a good laugh at some of my antics. He was a serious guy, but he also had a sense of humor.

Early in my career, I learned a lot from my Cubs teammates and coaches. Rick Sutcliffe taught me never to try to embarrass a hitter because that would only give him added incentive to want to hit off me. My pitching coach, Dick Pole, instructed me on the finer points of pitching, including all the mental stuff. Goose Gossage helped me learn not to let emotions get the better of me.

Those were lessons I took out to the mound that helped me become a successful pitcher.

Andre's influence on me was different.

Simply put, every day I was around him, he showed me how to play and prepare for the game. And he did that without ever speaking a word.

There were a few times late in my career when I didn't feel motivated to get my work in. Whenever that happened, I'd think, "Hell, if Hawk did it, I can, too."

Andre and I left the Cubs on the same day in December 1992. I signed with Atlanta, where I spent the next 11 seasons. Andre signed with Boston, where he gave American League pitchers a small taste of what he had been doing for years in the National League. Like Andre, I played most of my career for teams other than the Cubs. But the seasons I played with Andre were ones that helped shape my career.

Hawk was a great player and teammate and very deserving of his place in the Hall of Fame.

ACKNOWLEDGMENTS

ANDRE

This book about my trials and tribulations would not have been a story of triumph without my family. As my grandmother, Eunice Taylor, used to tell me, "Trust in the Lord with all your heart and soul. For it is with Him that all things are possible. Count and be thankful of your blessings before you receive them." As a scrawny God-fearing kid in South Miami, growing up to become a Hall of Famer was more than anything I ever could have imagined.

Special thanks to my wife, Vanessa; our children, Darius and Amber; my uncles, John and Curtis Taylor; and my cousin, Donald Napier.

ALAN

Thanks to Chuck Myron for his invaluable help in putting this book together and to Karen O'Brien for preparing the manuscript for publication. Thanks also to Justin Yurkanin, Brett Steidler, and Warren Greene for their support. The insights of Paul Comeau, Warren Cromartie, Shawon Dunston, Greg Maddux, Al Oliver, Tim Raines, and Pete Rose helped make this book better. A final thank-you goes to my family.

INTRODUCTION

AT THE END OF THE 1976 MINOR LEAGUE SEASON, VERN RAPP, THE manager of my Triple A team, took me aside and uttered the words every young ballplayer dreams of hearing, "Congratulations, you're going to the major leagues."

It was hard at first to process the news that I'd be joining the Montreal Expos as a September call-up. Just 16 months earlier, I had been playing baseball at Florida A&M University, hoping to get noticed so that one day I might have a chance to play in the majors. Having just turned 22, my big league dreams were about to become a reality much sooner than I ever expected.

But first I had a job to finish in the minors.

My team, the Denver Bears, had run away with the American Association's West Division, setting up a best-of-seven championship series against the Omaha Royals, winners of the East Division. The Bears' success that season provided hope that the Expos, who were on their way to a 107-loss season in 1976, had the potential to become a competitive team within a few years.

As I waited those extra days to get to the Expos, I tried to stay focused on helping Denver capture the American Association title against the Triple A affiliate of an organization that had passed on signing me out of high school. Throughout the series, I couldn't help but look at Montreal's upcoming schedule to see where and when I might make my major league debut. The thought that my next series would be played in St. Louis, Pittsburgh, or Philadelphia, as opposed to Des Moines, Evansville, or Wichita, was incredibly exciting.

After we beat Omaha in six games, the Expos decided the other call-ups and I would join the team in the middle of a three-game set at Pittsburgh.

On September 11, 1976, I stepped onto a major league baseball field for the first of what turned out to be 2,627 games in my career. I remember my debut well. It was a cold and drizzly Saturday in Pittsburgh. There were fewer fans at Three Rivers Stadium that night than had turned out for our American Association championship games. But there I was, standing on the home turf of stars like Willie Stargell, Dave Parker, Manny Sanguillen, and Al Oliver, alongside a group of young Expos teammates who, like me, were hoping to stick around in the big leagues for many years to come.

A hitless night in Pittsburgh marked the start of my journey in the major leagues. Fortunately, I stuck around long enough to have plenty of successful days and nights in ballparks across America and parts of Canada. Along the way, I experienced a lot—playing with pain, coping with loss, clashing with upper management, and developing as a player and individual.

Having always been a private person, I never really felt the need to talk at length about some of my most personal thoughts and feelings while playing for the Expos and Chicago Cubs, and later, for the Boston Red Sox and Florida Marlins.

Until now.

I've had a lot of time to reflect on my long journey in the majors since I first co-wrote a book about my life and career in the mid-1990s. Back then, I was still an active player and lacked complete perspective on a lot of things that had happened to me on and off the field. I've also experienced a great deal since I retired from the game, including my induction into the Hall of Fame in 2010.

I realized this is a good time to revisit my story, to share details of my life and career that even some of my family members don't know. Because of the subject matter, not all of those experiences are easy to talk about.

It's also important that I have a chance to communicate one of the most important lessons I learned during my career—whether you're a September call-up or a perennial All-Star, it's not possible to get by on ability alone.

It took a lot of work to stay in the majors for 21 seasons. In addition to being the fulfillment of a childhood dream, it was a lot of fun, too.

I hope that when you read my story, you will see how the joy, dedication, and pain that are all part of playing baseball at its highest level led me to fall in love with the game again and again. Baseball has imparted many pieces of wisdom to me over the years. I hope the chance to see the sport through my eyes deepens your love for the game.

1

THE CALL

THERE CAME A DAY EVERY JANUARY THAT STARTED WITH ANTICIPATION and ended with disappointment, beginning with the year my name first appeared on the Baseball Hall of Fame ballot in 2002. In my first year of eligibility, 45 percent of the members of the Baseball Writers Association of America put a check next to my name, signifying their belief that I deserved a place in Cooperstown. That was a far cry from the 75 percent needed to get in. Still, it was an indication that I was a serious candidate. I hadn't really expected to get enough votes that first year. In fact, I was fishing off Key Largo on the day of the announcement. In the years that followed, my hopes grew as I gradually climbed closer to the magic number of votes.

I felt like 2010 was a window of opportunity for me. All the former greats who had gotten more votes than me in previous years, guys like Jim Rice and my former Cubs teammate Rich "Goose" Gossage, had deservedly made it into the Hall. Rice earned his spot in his 15th and final year of eligibility. If you think of it as waiting in line for your turn, I guess you could say there was no one left standing in front of me.

Truthfully, the whole thing was starting to wear on me a little, probably because I had absolutely no control over it. When I hung up my cleats at the end of the 1996 season, I did so having accomplished just about everything I wanted to in the game. I say "just about" because I never did get to play in a World Series in my 21-year career. Nonetheless, I couldn't help but think, "Did I really do enough to earn my place alongside the best to ever play the game?" My advocates spoke of how I played through injuries and was among a select group of players with career totals that included 400 home runs and 300 stolen bases. My detractors pointed out that my batting average and on-base percentage didn't stack up against a lot of the all-time greats. Amid all the talk, I vowed to remain proud of my accomplishments regardless of whether or not I entered the Hall of Fame. At the same time, I was hopeful good things would happen in my ninth year of eligibility in 2010.

When the day of the announcement rolled around, I woke up early at 6:30 AM, to be exact. I wanted to get in a workout, and then I planned to do something I knew would put the day in its proper perspective.

Later that morning, I made the 15-minute drive from my South Miami home to Dade South Memorial Park cemetery. I felt compelled to visit the gravesites of my mother and grandmother, without whose support I never would have realized my dreams of playing a single inning in the major leagues, let alone being enshrined in Cooperstown. My grandmother, Eunice Taylor, died in 1987 after a long bout with Alzheimer's disease. Her passing came during a time of great transition for me. I dedicated the following season, my first in Chicago, to the woman I called "Mamma," and it turned out to be the best of my career. My mom, Mattie, passed away in 2006. She was only 15 years old when I was born in 1954. As a single mother, she worked hard to support my siblings and me and was always a huge supporter of everything I did.

I knelt and thanked these very special women for their unconditional love, for their efforts in raising me, and most importantly, for guiding me along the right path in life. Before I knew it, tears were streaming down my face.

When I got back home, my wife, Vanessa, was waiting on me. "Well, hopefully this is the day," I said. Vanessa had stood by me not only on this day every year but on all other days since we married in 1978. And, believe me, that wasn't always easy for her. Of the many things for which I'm grateful, the presence of strong women in my life is near the top of the list.

Vanessa and I ordered sandwiches from a favorite delicatessen called Roasters 'N Toasters and anxiously hung around the house as the morning turned to afternoon. The official Hall of Fame announcement in New York was at 2:00 PM, and I assumed I'd get a call ahead of time if there was good news to be shared. Although, to be honest, I didn't know exactly how the process worked because my phone had never rung on that day before.

It got to be 1:00 PM and still there was no call—unless you count the one from a family friend who had the misfortune of phoning my wife during our state of high alert. "Can I call you back?" Vanessa nicely asked her. "We're in the middle of something."

It got to be 1:20—still nothing. "Well, I guess it's not going to happen again this year," I said with resignation in my voice. I was tired from my workout and had experienced a lot of emotion at the cemetery, so I decided to lie down in my home office and close my eyes. I asked Vanessa to come get me a few minutes before 2:00 PM, so I could turn on the television and see how the voting went.

A few minutes later, the phone rang.

I shot up into a sitting position. Before picking up the receiver, I glanced at the caller ID and saw it was a call from the New York City area code. A good sign to be sure. At that moment, Vanessa came through the door. Next thing I knew, the president of the Baseball Writers Association of America was congratulating me on *my election to the Hall of Fame*. I flashed my wife a thumbs-up. She put her hands on her face and started to cry. My daughter, Amber, heard what was going on, and she ran in the room. When she realized what was happening, she got choked up, too.

It turned out I got close to 78 percent of the vote, just enough to make it to Cooperstown. I was going into the Hall along with manager Whitey Herzog and umpire Doug Harvey, both of whom were selected by the Veterans Committee.

I hardly had time to process it all. Following the call, everything came at me quickly. There was a full schedule for the rest of the day and the next day. First I was supposed to go to Dolphin Stadium, soon to be renamed Sun Life Stadium, for a local press conference. Then I had to catch a flight to New York for a national press conference the next morning. Before we left the house, Commissioner Bud Selig called to offer his congratulations.

We had packed some bags in anticipation of this happy moment. The Florida Marlins, for whom I work as a special assistant, had also made preparations, sending a limo in case I got the call. But it turned out they were playing it safe. The driver had instructions to park down the street from my house. There was no use sitting right out front if the phone didn't ring. We didn't know about that limo, however, so my wife called another car service to take us to the ballpark. It arrived a short time later and off we went to the stadium. On the way out of the neighborhood, we passed the other limo down the street. I should have put two and two together, but I didn't. "Guess I'm not the only one celebrating something today," I thought as we headed toward the freeway.

It seemed like I was on the phone for the entire 40-minute drive from my house to the ballpark. We decided that my wife and daughter would make the trip to New York with me. My son, Darius, had a college exam the following day, so he wasn't able to go with us. That was hard on him, but we had always insisted he put his academics first. He realized the press conferences were just a prelude to the main event—the induction ceremony in July.

After meeting with reporters at the Marlins' stadium, I did some interviews on the way to the airport. By the time I got there, I had about 50 voicemail messages and just as many text messages. One was from Al Oliver, a good friend and former teammate in Montreal. Al, who was a tremendous player in his own right, had been pulling hard for me to get in the Hall. In his message, he asked a rhetorical question: "Was it worth the wait?"

When we arrived in New York, I went down to the bar at the Waldorf Astoria and met with some Hall of Fame representatives to go over the details of the next day and proceeded to join them for dinner. As if the day hadn't been eventful enough, I experienced an allergic reaction to something I ate. I didn't let on that anything was wrong, though. I had played through a lot of pain in my career, and I was going to make it through dinner no matter what shade of green I turned.

Back in my room later that night, the realization started to sink in. *I was going to be a member of the Hall of Fame.* Was I disappointed that I didn't get in on the first ballot, or the eighth ballot, for that matter? Not at all. I embraced the idea that it's the final destination that matters most, not how long it takes to get there. And finally, I had become a Hall of Famer.

• • •

I had visited Cooperstown a few times before. Once as a member of the Cubs, I was there for the Hall of Fame Game that used to be played annually. On another trip, my kids came along, and we toured the Hall of Fame museum. It was amazing: the plaque gallery, the artifacts, and the various exhibits on the history of the game.

Prior to my own big day, the only time I had attended an induction ceremony was in 2005 when my former Cubs teammate Ryne Sandberg was enshrined. To my surprise, Ryno singled me out in his speech. He said, "No player in baseball history worked harder, suffered more, or did it better than Andre Dawson. He's the best I've ever seen." That was a huge endorsement from a guy I considered the best of the best. For six years, he witnessed firsthand what I had to go through in dealing with chronic knee problems. He saw the treatments I got before and after games. Ryno has always been a man of few words, so the things he said about me in Cooperstown that day meant a lot. In interviews, Ryno said he felt the monster power numbers that other players put up in the steroid era had made my numbers look less impressive and lost me votes.

I started working on my speech almost the moment I came back from the press conference in New York. I tried to prepare myself for that Sunday in July when I would take the stage and address the baseball community. I wanted to talk about the state of the game, reach out to the youth, and have a little fun at the same time. Barry Rozner, a Chicago-area journalist, helped me organize the speech. My daughter, Amber, helped me fine-tune my thoughts.

The toughest part by far was going to be acknowledging my mom and grandmother. I've always been an emotional person, and I struggled with whether I would be able to keep my composure when I honored them. I decided to wait to do that until the end of the speech. That way, if I couldn't get through it, at least I'd be almost finished. Every time I practiced the speech, I broke down when I got to that portion.

A big question prior to induction day was whether I'd enter the Hall as an Expo or a Cub. I had a clear opinion on the matter—my preference was to go in as a member of the Chicago Cubs, the team I played for from 1987 to 1992. I won the National League Most Valuable Player Award in my first year with the Cubs, but more importantly, I felt warmly embraced by Cubs fans and the city of Chicago. While I appreciated the fact that I got my start with the Expos and played more than 10 years in Montreal, I'd be lying if I said I wasn't unhappy about the way things ended there.

When I got to the big leagues, I wanted to be one of those special players who spent his entire career with one organization. I gave a lot to the Expos and their fans, including a Rookie of the Year award, three All-Star appearances, and six Gold Gloves. But in the end, I felt I became a victim of team executives who were far more calculating and business-minded than me. This happened during the collusion era in baseball when major league teams had an unspoken, not to mention illegal, agreement to freeze out free agents from earning anywhere close to what they deserved. For me, that would have meant taking a pay cut to stay in Montreal. Well, with my knee problems becoming increasingly worse on the hard artificial surface of Olympic Stadium, the Expos' decision to do me that way let me know it was time to go.

The events that led me to Chicago were unorthodox to say the least: a blank contract, a game of cat and mouse, and ultimately a new home on a grass field. In retrospect, if I had re-upped in Montreal and continued playing on the turf there, my career might have ended prematurely without any chance of being elected to the Hall of Fame. As it turned out, I finished my career with 438 home runs and nearly 2,800 hits. I credited my years in Chicago as pivotal, and that's why I wanted to be enshrined in Cooperstown as a Cub.

The personalized license plates on my cars show I still identify myself with both teams. One says "HAWK8," a combination of my nickname and the uniform number I wore in Chicago (and Florida in the final years of my career). The other has "HAWK10," a tribute to the jersey number I wore in Montreal and in Boston for a brief time. I had gotten over my grudge against the Expos, but given the choice, I wanted to enter Cooperstown as a Cub.

But the Hall of Fame officials wanted me to reconsider and go in as an Expo. They said they were trying to consider the history of the game. Only one other player, my former teammate Gary Carter in 2003, had entered the Hall in a Montreal uniform. They felt strongly I should go in as a member of the team for whom I played the longest. I agreed to do it.

• • •

I was excited when the Hall of Fame weekend finally came. My family arrived in Cooperstown on Thursday and checked into a suite at the Otesaga Resort Hotel. It had a breathtaking lake view that I would have liked to enjoy more, but we spent hardly any time in the room. Every minute of the next few days featured some kind of event.

The first person I encountered when I went for lunch in the hotel restaurant was Hank Aaron. I had talked with Hank the previous year at a function in West Palm Beach for the Reviving Baseball in Inner Cities program, and it was great seeing him again. Within minutes of that encounter, I crossed paths with another of the game's all-time greats, not to mention one of my idols—Willie Mays. I didn't know Willie had just undergone eye surgery. I went over and started talking to him without telling him who I was. After about a minute, he pleasantly asked, "Who am I talking to?" I introduced myself, and he grabbed my arm and congratulated me on my selection to the Hall. I asked him if he wouldn't mind posing for a photo with my family and me, to which he replied, "You don't have to ask me that, son!"

It was thrilling to see so many legends in one place at one time.

The next day I talked a little to Hall of Famer Dave Winfield, a contemporary of mine, about the weekend. As we were chatting, the great Frank Robinson walked up beside us. "You're not a Hall of Famer yet!" he said with a big smile as he put his arms around me. When I saw Frank in the hotel elevator the next day, he said, "You're getting closer!" I guess that's the nearest thing there is to hazing of new Hall of Fame inductees.

The only negative thing about induction weekend was I didn't get to spend a lot of time with family and friends who came to support me. A lot of relatives made the trip from Miami, including my uncles, who were my male role models as a kid. And a lot of former teammates were on hand, including two of the players I was closest with in Montreal—Tim Raines and Warren Cromartie. Jeff Kay, a guy I played rookie ball with in Lethbridge, Alberta, Canada, in 1975 also showed up. The funny thing was that he hadn't aged a year since I last saw him.

One of the highlights of the weekend was a party the Cubs put on for me, an event where I got to spend a little quality time with people who didn't get the opportunity to go to the private reception that was held earlier. Reggie Jackson and some other Hall of Famers stopped by the event, which was very exciting for my family and friends.

Shawon Dunston, a great friend from my years with the Cubs, was a no-show. Shawon has always been excitable, and boy, was he excited the day he called to congratulate me on my selection. Unfortunately, he let me know a couple days before the ceremony that he wasn't going to be able to make it. Shawon had developed a fear of flying, and the weather forecast for the weekend looked bad. He was in tears when he told me. He said, "Hawk, my daughters are laughing at me for not wanting to fly. I don't know what to do." I said, "Shawon, listen, it's okay. Don't worry about it." He told me he loved me, and I told him to be sure to watch the ceremony because I had something special for him.

As forecast, there was rain on Sunday. There was an emergency plan in place to move the festivities indoors if the rain got too heavy. It got dark and started to storm while a video of Doug Harvey's acceptance speech played. Doug, who was suffering from throat cancer, had recorded his speech ahead of time. At the conclusion of the video, Doug, whose 30-year career as a National League umpire earned him the nickname "God," went to the podium to say a few final words. At that moment, the rain stopped and the sun broke through. We were then blessed with a beautiful afternoon.

When I took the podium, I singled out several peers whose playing careers I had admired. I wanted to pay respect to these guys and hopefully give them the push they needed to get into the Hall. It was similar to what Ryne Sandberg, who was in attendance that day, did for me a few years earlier.

I acknowledged Lee Smith, a former Cubs teammate I believe has earned a place in Cooperstown. He was the premier closer of his era and, at one time, the all-time saves leader with 478. Now that we're starting to see relief pitchers get into the Hall, I think he eventually will get that January phone call.

I also mentioned Timmy Raines. Timmy was like a little brother to me in Montreal, just like Shawon was in Chicago. I always regarded Timmy as the Rickey Henderson of the National League. He accumulated more than 2,600 hits and stole more than 800 bases in his career.

Timmy and I went through a lot together in Montreal. We had a very special and fun relationship. But our friendship really blossomed after Timmy confronted his drug problem early in his career. I was still young myself and naïve about the drugs some players were taking. When I heard Timmy's name and cocaine mentioned in the same sentence, I was like, "Hey, that's my friend you're talking about!" The only way I was going to believe it was if I heard it directly from Timmy's mouth. And that's eventually what happened. It brought us closer together. I was there to support him and to make sure his cocaine habit was something he would quickly put behind him. For me, it was about saving my friend. I wanted him to be able to focus on his career because he was so talented.

After mentioning Smitty and Timmy, I followed through on my promise to Shawon. I told the audience in Cooperstown and those people watching on TV that he was the funniest man I ever met. "Unfortunately, this is a family show, and I can't tell you a single Shawon Dunston story right now," I said.

One good reason to write this book is to finally be able to share some of those stories!

Still, I hadn't gotten to the most personally meaningful part about my mother and grandmother. Earlier that day, I prayed on it and felt the same kind of humbleness I had experienced when I visited their gravesites the morning of the Hall of Fame announcement. It was then that I knew I'd be okay.

Near the end of my speech, I tried to put into words how much these two women will always mean to me:

> My grandmother, Eunice Tayor. I called her Mamma. She helped raise me. She taught me to believe in myself and to believe in God. And without her, I never would have made it through high school, let alone college or the pros. She taught me that if you want respect, you have to give it first. She was an advocate of education. She always reminded people that baseball was recreation. She said education was a stepping stone to my future.... My mom, Mattie Brown, died four years ago. And I miss her today as much as I did then. She was my mom. She was my dad. She was my big sister. My big brother. My best friend. She was my whole world for a very long time in my life. And I only wish she were here to see this. Before she passed, she dreamt of this moment, she dreamt of this day. She promised me it would happen. And my mother never, never broke a promise to us.

That day in Cooperstown was the culmination of thousands of days—from my childhood in South Miami to my two decades in the major leagues. I was shaped by many people and experiences along the way. One common thread that has run through my life is a love for the game of baseball. As I said during my Hall of Fame speech, "If you love this game, it will love you back." So many times during my career, I heard people comment on how I scowled and never smiled out on the field. But those were surface expressions of focus and concentration. In my heart, I felt joy every time I went out and played. My desire to make it to and excel in the big leagues was driven by a love of the game. My decision to play through chronic knee pain was driven by a love of the game. And my views on the future of baseball are most definitely driven by a love of the game.

Life is about seeking out opportunities and making the most of them. There were a lot of times in my life when I could have simply said, "This just isn't going to work out." But I was determined not to let setbacks shatter my will to get where I wanted to be.

2

MY FAMILY, MY DREAM

WITH A POCKETFUL OF JINGLING NICKELS, I RAN AS FAST AS MY 12-YEAR-OLD legs could take me to the general store across the street from my house in South Miami. I had spent the previous hours washing dishes and scrubbing floors for my mom, and now it was time to put my hard-earned 30 cents to good use. I didn't have to think for a second about what to buy. In fact, the man behind the register at U-Tot-Em might as well have started ringing up my purchase the moment he saw me burst through the door. He had witnessed the same routine for a while now. I'd come in, go straight for the paper-wrapped packs of Topps baseball cards, and grab as many as I could afford. As soon as I exited the store, I'd rip off the packaging and aggressively thumb through the deck. Some kids liked the hard stick of bubblegum that came inside each pack. Not me. I threw the gum away. It was the cards I cherished.

It was 1966, and I was growing up in a place hundreds of miles from the closest major league city. It would be another 27 years before the Florida Marlins would join the National League. But the cards might as well have been high-speed jets transporting me to stadiums across America and bringing me face-to-face with players who had the ability to bring tens of thousands of people to their feet with one mighty swing or one blazing fastball. If I got a card with the name Mays, Drysdale, Banks, or any other star of the day on it, I felt like I had discovered rare treasure. I sometimes thought, "Maybe one day *I'll* have my picture and statistics on a baseball card."

I was convinced from an early age that I was going to be a major league baseball player. Even before I started playing the sport competitively, I soaked up as much information as I could about the game. Many sons learn a love of the game from their fathers. That wasn't the case with me. My dad wasn't around when I was a kid, but my mother's three brothers more than filled the void. The oldest of the three, my Uncle Curtis, had been an avid Dodgers fan going back to the team's days in Brooklyn when Jackie Robinson made history by breaking baseball's color barrier. Before I was born, Curtis would go to Miami Stadium to watch the Dodgers play spring exhibition games.

The Dodgers had moved to Los Angeles by the time I was developing an interest in baseball, but they became my team, too. When I was about eight years old, I became the resident authority on the Dodgers, which wasn't an easy task considering their home games in the Pacific Time Zone often weren't included in the sports page of *The Miami News*. Well, I wasn't going to let that get in the way of my need to know how Walter Alston's team performed every night. On mornings following West Coast games, I'd call a phone number listed in the newspaper that provided scores. Then, when the complete box score of that game appeared in the following day's paper under "late scores," I'd pore over every inch of it. That information came in handy when I went to a vacant lot near my house and played imaginary baseball games pitting the Dodgers against their National League rivals.

I didn't have a bat and ball, so I made do with items from around the neighborhood. If anyone left a broom or mop outside, I'd break it and use the stick as a bat. The lot I played on had a rock pile where I found plenty of "balls." The daily games started with a make-believe public address announcer saying, "Now batting for the Los Angeles Dodgers, No. 3, center fielder Willie Davis!" And it went from there. I'd toss the rocks in the air and hit them out into the open lot. Based on how far I hit the rock, it would either be a single, double, triple, home run, or an out. I'd go batter by batter until I finished a nine-inning game. The Dodgers nearly always won.

During the school year, I'd sit in class and plot out the games that would take place when I got home. There were a lot of things to decide: Who would the Dodgers play that day? What two starting pitchers would face off? And who would hit where in the starting lineup?

Though I may have daydreamed a bit during my days at J.R.E. Lee Elementary School, I liked being there. Physical education was my favorite class, but my Aunt Alice, who taught first grade, helped me develop strong skills in academic subjects. Sometimes she'd keep me after hours and have me write words and sentences on the chalkboard. Then she'd have me work on addition and subtraction. At the time, I thought I was being punished, especially because the extra work kept me from playing my games. But I came to realize she was just giving me old-school tutoring. It later dawned on me that my grandmother, who valued education above all else, arranged for these sessions.

I'm sure it came as no surprise to my teachers when I put down "professional baseball player" on the vocational interest forms we filled out in school every so often. Still, they'd never fail to ask, "What's your second choice, Andre?"

I wasn't being disrespectful when I answered, "I don't really have one." I knew there was more to the world than baseball, but I really couldn't think of anything I enjoyed more.

• • •

Growing up in a working-class, all-black section of South Miami, my life revolved around family and baseball. My mom was a high school sophomore when I was born in July 1954. My dad, a man named Floyd Dawson, was a few years older than my mom and didn't stick around after she got pregnant, eventually going off to college and joining the army.

After I was born, my mom dropped out of high school and got a job as a cook at Toby's Cafeteria, a restaurant about 10 miles from where we lived. She took the bus to and from work and earned about $12 a week.

The house I spent my early childhood in was a "shotgun shack," so named because you could see—or shoot a gun—all the way through the wood structure if you stood at the front door. The weekly rent was $5. It had two bedrooms and a kitchen and a back porch. The bathroom was connected to the outside of the house, so you had to go out the back door to do your business.

The neighborhood of shotgun shacks was known as Madison Square because many of the families there had left a small, predominantly black town in Florida called Madison to find better work opportunities in Miami. It comprised a four-by-four-block area right next to Coral Gables and the University of Miami. It was a quiet residential area. The only store right in the neighborhood was the U-Tot-Em where I bought my baseball cards. A short walk would get you to the closest thing the community had to a downtown. There was a butcher, a barber shop, a soul food restaurant, and a pool hall.

My childhood was pretty self-contained on those streets. My mom didn't have a car, so we went most places by foot or by bus. My friends and I rarely ventured out of Madison Square to go to the beach or other sections of Miami. Lee Park, which sat on the fringes of the neighborhood, was our gathering place, and playing sports there was how we passed the time.

Everyone in Madison Square knew each other extremely well. In fact, if a child behaved badly, any adult who witnessed the offending act was free to hand out discipline. You tended not to act up because in that tight-knit setting, a pair of eyes was always watching.

It's no surprise I got caught a few times breaking mop and broom handles for my imaginary Dodgers games. We also used the handles for a form of stickball we called "Stinger Marie." Per the rules of the game, a pitcher would throw the tennis ball, and you got one swing to try and make contact. If you hit the ball, you ran the bases. If you missed it, you still got to run, but the catcher could throw you out by tossing the ball to the first baseman or hitting you with the ball. I was the king of Stinger Marie, probably because of all the practice I got hitting rocks, which helped me develop good hand-eye coordination.

My uncles say my personality hasn't changed much over the years. As a child, I didn't talk much and more or less did what I was told. I didn't get into too many scrapes, but the ones I did get in left an impression on me, both literally and figuratively.

When I was five years old, I got hit by a car in front of my house while playing hide and seek. It happened after I ran out from between two shotgun shacks and into the road without looking out for cars. Fortunately, the car that hit me was moving slowly. The fact I wasn't injured didn't keep my mom from fainting at the sight of me lying in the road.

A few months later, the same thing almost happened again. I had a couple nickels and wanted to go across the street to a gas station to buy some candy. (This was before I discovered baseball cards.) My Uncle Curtis said, "No, I don't want you crossing the street by yourself for a while. If you're hungry, go fix yourself a peanut butter and jelly sandwich." But I wanted candy. Against Uncle Curtis' wishes, I snuck out the back door and went to the gas station. On my way back, I didn't look both ways before crossing the street, and a car almost hit me. Everyone in the neighborhood, including my uncle, heard the screeching of the car brakes. He was livid with me. And even though I was still small, I knew he was right. That incident taught me to listen to my elders, but it was a lesson I would need to relearn from time to time.

• • •

When I was still very young, my mom had a daughter with a man named Clarence Brown who worked with her at the restaurant. They got married and eventually had six more children together. Clarence lived with us off and on, and when I was about eight years old, they got divorced.

Between army assignments around the United States and Europe, my father drifted in and out of my life. I never developed a real relationship with him. When he'd come back to Miami on furlough, my paternal grandmother, Martha Dawson, would call me and say, "Your father is coming home. He'd like to see you." I'd catch a bus to where they lived in the Coconut Grove section of Miami, stay the day with him, and then catch the bus home. When he wasn't around, I'd sometimes spend the whole weekend with my grandparents. My grandmother on my father's side would always buy me a lot of Christmas gifts. I thought some of them might be from him, but I wasn't sure. The gifts were nice, though I'm sure my mom would have preferred at least a little financial support. But she didn't let it faze her. Money may have been tight in the household, but I can never remember wanting for anything when I was a child.

My dad eventually got married and had another son. He and his family lived in a house not far from mine. As time went on, our encounters became few and far between. My grandmother Martha passed away in 1976. After that, my contact with my father was limited to the Christmas parties he and his wife held every year. Later in life, he and I had some unpleasant run-ins. I harbored no ill will toward the man, but I think as he got older, he felt he needed to explain why he ran off after I was born.

As I was finishing up elementary school, my mom moved us to a similar but slightly bigger house a street over. Both of the first two houses I lived in were rentals. It wasn't until I was a junior in high school that my mom had enough saved to buy a three-bedroom brick house in the same neighborhood. It's the house my mom lived in until she passed away in 2006. My sisters live there now. The house is on a street that was renamed Andre Dawson Drive in 1988.

Because my mom worked long hours, I spent a lot of time with my maternal grandmother, Eunice Taylor, who I called "Mamma." She lived just a few blocks from us, and I was at her house almost every day.

Mamma taught me a lot of things, including the power of faith. Her strong sense of spirituality came from her father, Edward Harrell, who had taught himself to read the Bible while living and farming in rural Georgia. He moved his family to Miami in 1933 in search of a better life and became a deacon at the Mount Olive Missionary Baptist Church. I remember as a young child going to my great-grandfather's house for sunrise prayer meetings. He was the most respected man in the neighborhood. Despite only having a third-grade education, he could read and discuss anything put in front of him.

Christianity was also the driving force in Mamma's life. As the spiritual pillar of the family, she arranged for my baptism. Mamma, who worked as a housekeeper, grew up in a time and place where most black women didn't complete high school. I think that was the reason she was adamant that her children and her children's children value education. Some of my earliest memories of her involve her telling me how important school was. "You're talking about your future," she'd say. "Once you get an education, no one can take that away from you." She insisted I not only do my homework but that I show it to her when I was done.

She constantly told me, "Andre, with God, all things are possible." She believed strongly in the power of prayer and encouraged me to show the same commitment to faith. "Count and be thankful of your blessings before you receive them," she'd say. She didn't press me to read the Bible, but she told me a lot about it. Her talks inspired me to pick up and study the Bible when I was older.

I had a mother-son relationship with my grandmother and more of a brother-sister relationship with my mother.

My mom was one of the most loving and caring people you'd ever meet. But she was a hell-raiser, too. She'd be quick to curse you out if she got mad at you, but in the next breath she'd tell you to pull up a chair and feed you a delicious meal. Her motto was always, "Don't screw around with my money or my kids." Everybody in our neighborhood adored her, partly because she would always open up our home to guests. She worked long days but was never too tired to prepare nice dinners for us. During the week, she'd cook things like pork chops and string beans. On Fridays, she'd make fried fish or shrimp fried rice, which was one of her specialties. The Saturday menu featured hamburgers, french fries, and baked beans. Sunday dinners were the main event. She'd make chitterlings, oxtail, beef stew, or baked or fried chicken. She'd also fix collard greens, macaroni and cheese, and potato salad. For good measure, she'd bake a peach cobbler, sweet potato pie, or strawberry shortcake. When she didn't bake at home, she'd always bring me home a slice of cake from the restaurant. I developed a real sweet-tooth when I was young.

Our neighbors knew my mom always cooked big meals, especially on Sundays and holidays, and sometimes they'd drop by uninvited. A lot of times, people would come to our door and say, "What'd you cook today?" I remember thinking that some of them were taking advantage of her, but she didn't see it that way.

• • •

Without my father in my life, my uncles became father figures, and each in his own way contributed to my development as a person—and as a baseball player.

My mom's youngest brother, Theodore Taylor, had the most extensive athletic background of anyone I knew growing up. He played baseball at Florida A&M University in Tallahassee, and when I was in junior high he was selected by the Pittsburgh Pirates in the ninth round of the 1967 draft. He toiled a couple years in the minor leagues before returning home to Miami. Uncle Theodore, who everyone called "Sugar Bo," the result of breaking a sugar bowl as a child, was only eight years older than me. When he played in the Pirates organization, I'd throw him batting practice in the off-season.

Before he went away to college, Uncle Theodore played on a neighborhood baseball team with my great-uncle, Matthew Napier. When I was nine years old, I'd go out and practice with the team, though when I look back on it, I was probably just getting in their way. Uncle Matthew knew I was having fun out there, so he'd give me fielding practice by hitting me ground balls. He was impressed with my defense.

"For a kid your age, you're not intimidated by the ball," he said. "You don't fear the baseball. You attack it like a hawk."

From that day on, he called me "Hawk." That became my baseball nickname, one that stayed with me from the sandlots to the major leagues.

But before I was "Hawk," I was "Pudgy." That nickname was coined by a neighbor who babysat me when I was a toddler. I was never a chubby kid, so I'm not really sure how he came up with it. But it stuck. To this day, I'm "Pudgy" to my family and "Hawk" to my uncles and everybody else.

Uncle Curtis, my mom's oldest brother, played the biggest role in giving me my first opportunity to play organized baseball. He saw how all the white areas of Miami had Little League and wondered what he'd have to do to start one in my neighborhood. Curtis, a schoolteacher who bought me my first mitt, raised funds for equipment by having us sell hot dogs and peanuts. He convinced Dade County recreation officials to give us T-shirts, and the City of Miami supplied the rest of our uniforms. Uncle Curtis and his brother, John, both coached teams. John still accuses Curtis of hoarding all the best players!

I loved being on and around the baseball diamond. I was the youngest player in the league. Some afternoons, I would play my game and then go keep score for the other games.

Curtis was Mamma's son, and on occasion, that became very clear.

One day, when the coach for my Little League team showed up late, Curtis, who was managing our opponent, made out the lineup for both teams. As he did, I looked over his shoulder and questioned some of his decisions. "Why are you hitting Bo Diddley so high in the order?" I asked, referring to the nickname of one of the kids on my team. "That's not the right spot for him," I continued. I guess I considered myself an expert after filling out so many imaginary Dodgers lineups.

Curtis did his best to ignore me, but I kept pressing him. When he finished filling out the batting order, he turned to me and said, "Who are you to question me on who I think should play? Maybe you should hit at the bottom of the order." He paused. "Better yet, you're not going to play today at all." I thought he was kidding, but then he took a pencil and scratched my name off the lineup card.

I couldn't believe it. Was he really going to bench me? I ran back to my grandmother's house and blurted out, "Uncle Curtis isn't letting me play today!" Mamma asked me what had happened, and I told her.

"No, Pudgy, don't question your elders. Respect your elders."

When Mamma gave that answer, I knew Uncle Curtis was right. Curtis, John, and Theodore were the men they were because of the way Mamma raised them. And that's exactly how I wanted to be.

Uncle Curtis also managed an All-Star team comprised of the best players from all the teams in the league. For fun, he took the team into white areas of town to see how it would fare. I was handling the scorekeeping duties and got to watch as my uncle's team soundly defeated the all-white team. That prompted the other team's coach to ask for a rematch. Uncle Curtis happily obliged, but when he brought his team back for another game, he saw the kids warming up on the field were a lot bigger than the ones from a few days earlier. My uncle's team lost that game, but Curtis arranged for yet another. In the third matchup, Curtis brought kids of equally large size.

Unfortunately, the Little League that Curtis started from scratch lasted only a few years. In 1967, when I was 12 years old, he was drafted into the United States Army and shipped off for basic training. He was 25 at the time, college educated, and employed by the county school district. He sought a deferment from the government, but Uncle Sam turned him down. Without my uncle, the Little League folded. Curtis spent 11 months in Vietnam and was there when Martin Luther King Jr. and Robert Kennedy were assassinated in 1968. That bothered him a lot. There he was, thousands of miles away fighting for his country, and back home gunmen had killed two of the men he most admired.

Growing up, I didn't have much contact with whites, partly because up until 1966, many schools in the Dade County School District were segregated. As my uncles would later say, the county back then had a lot of areas that were very much like the Old South, racist views and all. They tried to shield me from this hostility as much as possible. My first experience in an integrated school came at South Miami Junior High. That was also my first experience with racial tensions. But I didn't see the fistfights between black and white kids in the larger context of what was going on in the country at the time. I grew up with friends and family in a tranquil neighborhood. I was 13 years old when Dr. King was assassinated. At the time, I didn't comprehend the significance of his dream that blacks receive the same fundamental rights as everyone else. My uncles would sometimes talk about the news of the day with each other, but I was just a kid who skipped the front page of the newspaper and went straight for the sports section.

It was probably better that way.

• • •

My first love was baseball, but my first priority was family.

By junior high, I had three sisters and three brothers and had learned to take on some of the responsibilities of an adult. If my mom was at work and one of my younger siblings had a doctor's appointment, it was common for me to take them to Variety Children's Hospital. We had to switch buses to get there, but I knew the route well enough to make sure we didn't get lost. I also got a crash course in how to change diapers. And we're not talking about Pampers! These were cloth diapers that needed to be washed and hung outside.

I didn't mind helping out around the house. My mom usually got home from work in the late afternoon, which gave me enough free time after homework and before dinner to go out and play.

If I wasn't at Lee Park playing a pick-up game, I liked to go fishing in the area canals. I attached a line to a sugar-cane pole and fished for bluegill. My friend, Nathaniel Knight, and I would buy a loaf of bread and chum up the water with it. Then we'd cast our line with a piece of balled-up bread on the hook. It blended right in with the chum line, and the bluegill usually took the bait. My interest in fishing kept growing from there. I was about 15 years old when my mom got me my first fishing rod as a Christmas present. I learned to fish for bass. Then I was introduced to salt-water fishing by a family friend who took me down to the Florida Keys to fish off bridges and catwalks. Throughout my life, fishing was where I turned when I wanted total relaxation.

To earn a little extra money to buy baseball cards and lunch at school, I sold *The Miami News* on the street corner. But at 3 cents per paper sold, I found I wasn't making enough money to justify standing out there for so many hours. On some weekends and in the summer, I worked at a cabbage field pulling weeds from cabbage patches.

As I got older, I looked forward to playing school sports. Unfortunately, the only team sport offered at my junior high was soccer. So I played that. The coach put me at goalie because at close to 5'9", I was among the tallest kids on the team.

I also had pretty good lateral movement. I found soccer kind of boring, but it was fun playing with my friends and wearing a team uniform.

My most vivid memory of soccer wasn't anything that happened on the field. It was the day I attended a swimming party at one of my teammate's homes. All my friends were having a good time splashing around in the water. They kept urging me to get in the pool. I told them I was going to sit it out. None of them knew, and I was too embarrassed to admit, that I didn't know how to swim. Well, one of my friends got out and pushed me in the deep end of the water. The next thing I knew I was flailing around trying to get over to the side of the pool. The other kids thought I was just fooling around, but I was really struggling. I swallowed a lot of water and was gasping for air, but I somehow found a way to get to the side wall. When I got there, some of the kids grabbed my arms and helped get me out of the pool. I didn't need any medical assistance, but I had a horrible headache for the next couple of weeks.

Many years later, when I was retired from the major leagues, two women from Miami contacted me about becoming a spokesman for a swimming school not far from where I grew up. The problem was I still didn't know how to swim. But just like at the pool party in junior high, I didn't want to admit it. I told the women I'd think about it and get back to them. A few days later, I called back to say I'd help them on one condition. "First, you have to give me lessons at the school," I said. They happily agreed. I bought some swim trunks and took a week-long course in the school's beginner's pool. That was enough to pick up the basics. At the age of 50, I finally knew how to swim! That experience taught me that you're never too old to learn new things.

As I got ready to start my high school years, my relationship with baseball remained special. Every kid, at some point, learns to throw a football or shoot a basketball, but for me, those acts paled in comparison to the things I got to do on a baseball field. I couldn't imagine an athletic feat more satisfying than hitting a baseball on the nose and driving it to the outfield. I loved how as a hitter you had to make a split-second decision whether or not to swing at a pitch. I loved roaming the field and trying to catch the small white ball in the piece of leather on my hand.

After playing Little League, I graduated to a team for 13- and 14-year-olds. It wasn't an All-Star team, but it did feature the best players from my area. I was the only black player on the team and mostly played shortstop. But I also did a little pitching and catching. Each year I played in the league, I was one of the higher draft picks. I was setting myself apart offensively, hitting the ball harder and more consistently than my teammates.

But after two years in that league, I was forced to take a break from organized baseball. The only option I had upon entering Southwest Miami High School was to play for the varsity team, which was dominated by juniors and seniors *and* didn't have any black players. Only recently had the school become integrated, and white students outnumbered black students by about 30-to-1. There was no junior varsity team. By this time, most of my friends had developed more of an interest in football and basketball, and I would have been the only one in my circle trying to make the baseball team as a freshman. So instead, I spent my first years of high school playing JV basketball. I didn't get much playing time, although I did build a reputation for being a solid defender and rebounder.

At a time when most kids were coming into their own on high school baseball fields, I was returning to my roots of playing on the sandlots. And that's where I continued to hone my game until I felt comfortable going out for the high school team. Because of segregation, my Uncle Theodore hadn't played high school baseball until he was a senior. Yet he still ended up being drafted by the Pittsburgh Pirates. Like him, I had to play catch-up in terms of going out and impressing coaches and scouts.

One thing was for sure—I didn't want race to be a factor in my decision whether or not to play baseball. To me, baseball was something that could rise above the turmoil of the times. Thanks to Jackie Robinson, the major leagues no longer discriminated on the basis of race. To me, that meant baseball was more just than other institutions. My high school experience didn't change my opinion, but it did open my eyes to the fact that many people still saw things very much in terms of black and white. Fortunately, my high school coach wasn't one of them.

3

A WILL TO MAKE IT

BY MY JUNIOR YEAR OF HIGH SCHOOL IN 1970, I WAS HUNGRY TO GET back on the field, any field. On a whim, I decided to play football to pass the time and stay in shape in preparation for going out for the baseball team the following spring.

Unlike me, a lot of my friends had come up through the Pop Warner youth league and really knew how to play the game. My only experience was playing in the sandlots. Still, I made it known to the coach that I hoped to play quarterback. He found that funny. Apparently, five or six players were already vying for the quarterback job. All of them had been groomed to play the position for years. If I wanted to have any chance of cracking the starting lineup, I needed to find another position. And that was free safety. I wound up enjoying the defensive backfield enough to want to return to the team the following year.

When fall turned to winter, it was time to start thinking about finally getting back on the baseball field.

As a first step, I went to see Paul Comeau, a former baseball and football player at Boston College who was going into his first year as head baseball coach at Southwest Miami High School. Coach Comeau put me in the batting cage and had me take some cuts in front of the team. He liked what he saw.

My interest in playing baseball at Southwest Miami came at a time when Coach Comeau was actively trying to recruit black students to integrate a team that had been entirely white. He went as far as to have students from the art department design posters that he hung all over the building. Each poster had a question on it: "Who is Willie Mays?" or "Who is Hank Aaron?" or "Who is

Curt Flood?" His goal was to remind us of all the great black players who had made a mark on the game of baseball.

I had planned to go out for the team anyway, but Coach Comeau's efforts encouraged some of my friends to play, including Cokes Watson, a very talented player from my neighborhood who I ended up sharing a field with for many years to come.

It didn't take me long to figure out I had a lot of work to do if I hoped to excel at baseball in a more formal setting. I was still a growth spurt away from achieving my full height. I didn't have a particularly accurate arm. And I still didn't grasp the fundamentals of the game. In other words, I was green.

But the coach saw I had potential.

Coach Comeau used an 8 mm camera to shoot batting practice. The benefit of that type of camera was that he could do a frame-by-frame analysis of our swings. Every so often, he'd bring us together as a team and have us look at our bat trajectory for possible mechanical flaws. When he got to me, however, he realized there wasn't much to analyze. In the first frame, my bat was on my shoulder, but by the second frame, I had already completed my swing. When Coach Comeau saw that, he shook his head and said, "My God, Andre, you have major league bat speed!"

During my first year on the team, I benefited from a steady regimen of batting and fielding practice. I played mostly in left field and worked on my right-handed hitting stroke. I could feel myself steadily improving.

The team hadn't had much success the previous few seasons, but Coach Comeau and his assistant, Al Hinson, helped turn things around in their first years on the job.

I was too busy trying to improve to realize some of my white teammates weren't happy to share the field with black players.

Late that season, we had an away game against Miami Beach High School, one of the top teams in the county. Back then, the school district didn't provide bus transportation to and from games. The team came in cars driven by coaches or fellow players. None of the black kids on the team had a car, so we got picked up at our homes by the coach, assistant coach, or a teammate. On the day we played Miami Beach, Al and Coach Comeau weren't available to drive us, so he put a couple of his players in charge of getting us to the game. Well, for whatever reason, our rides didn't show up. Coach Comeau suspected we had been left behind on purpose. He filled out the lineup card with the black players in it, and had Al drive the 20 miles back to our neighborhood to bring us to the game.

The 1960s were over, but it was still a tense time in Miami. There were student walk-outs at the high school and calls for racial equality in the community. I was aware of what was going on around me, but I stayed focused on baseball.

• • •

In retrospect, I wish I had skipped playing football my senior year. I trusted Coach Comeau's assessment that I had a future in baseball. I wasn't playing football because I loved the game, but rather because it allowed me to be around my friends.

I knew I could get hurt. And my family knew it, too. They remembered when my Uncle Theodore took a cleat to the throat in a high school game and needed an emergency tracheotomy. My grandmother in particular recalled how scary it was to see a tube sticking out of her son's throat. But she didn't try to talk me out of playing.

Before the 1971 season even started, I learned the hard way about the high risk of injury on the football field. During summer practice, a teammate's cleat came up through the face guard of my helmet and cut me underneath the eye. I needed eight stitches.

Maybe that was a bad sign of things to come.

My senior season lasted just a few games but impacted me for years to come.

During the fourth game of the season, I was playing safety when the opposing team's quarterback heaved a desperation pass downfield at the end of the first half. The ball was overthrown, so I moved myself into position to try and intercept it. When I jumped, the receiver and cornerback got tangled up, and the cornerback went flying into me as I came down with the interception. My teammate's helmet hit my knee, and I immediately collapsed in excruciating pain. As I was being helped up, I was unable to put any weight on my leg.

This was before the days when schools stationed an ambulance around the playing field in case of a serious injury. There weren't cell phones either, so I couldn't call my family to tell them what happened. After a couple teammates helped me off the field, I sat on the sideline until the game was over. Then I rode a bus with the rest of the team back to my school. From there, I got a ride home. When my mother saw me limp through the front door, she said, "I don't know why you wanted to play that damn sport in the first place!" The following morning she took me to the hospital for X-rays. I panicked a little when the doctor said they'd have to perform surgery and keep me there for several days. It was determined I had torn ligaments and cartilage in my left knee.

This was also before the days of arthroscopic surgery, so the doctor just opened up my knee and went in to repair the ligament and remove cartilage. After that, I remained in the hospital for four days. I guess my high school didn't have any idea that I had gone under the knife, because when my head football coach showed up near the end of my hospital stay, he said, "No one told me anything about this." Well that explained why I hadn't had any visitors! He stood awkwardly by my bed and then reached into his pocket for something. "Here," he said, handing me a 24-pack of Lifesavers candy. "Hope you feel better."

After leaving the hospital, I wore a cast for six weeks. I stayed out of school and got home tutoring until I could get around on crutches. I didn't venture out much at all. Being the oldest of eight siblings, my brothers and sisters were very attentive to my needs, despite the occasional argument over whether we should play Rare Earth (my choice) or the Jackson 5 (my siblings' choice) on the record player. I needed all the support I could get. The cast went from the instep of my foot all the way up to my groin, and it was very uncomfortable. I couldn't wait to get it off and was counting the days until it happened. One of the first times I went out in public after the injury was to attend the big Turkey Bowl game against our rival Coral Gables High School. I was on crutches down near the end zone when a pass interference call on one of our players helped Coral Gables score the winning touchdown.

When my cast came off, the doctor didn't prescribe any physical therapy or rehabilitation. He just removed the plaster and told me he'd see me in a week. I needed some kind of rehab considering the way my leg had atrophied. It would have helped me regain a full range of motion. But as it stood, I bought a knee brace from a drug store and limped around in that until I was able to feel comfortable walking on the leg.

Spring wasn't far off, and my biggest concern was how the injury would affect my senior year on the baseball field.

I never regained enough strength in my leg to play the following season without the brace. For a good part of the season, I was hitting around .200. It got to the point where Coach Comeau felt pressure to take me out of the starting lineup. But after awhile, my knee started feeling a lot better, and I was able to finish my high school career on a high note. In the district playoffs, I went 9-for-13, and all nine hits were for extra bases. Based mostly on the determination I showed, Coach Comeau felt I deserved selection to the all-city team, but the fact that I wasn't nearly the most accomplished player on my own team likely dissuaded the judges from picking me.

During my senior year and the years that followed, I tried to push myself and not let my injury get the best of me. I realized I would have to work a little harder than other players to keep pace. Coach Comeau gave me a valuable piece of advice before I graduated from high school. He said, "Don't sell yourself short. You'll go a long way if you stay driven." I didn't know what that meant at the time, but it made more sense to me later. From high school on, I stayed focused on trying to maximize my abilities. I'd hear teammates tell me to loosen up and relax a little, and I think that was their way of commenting about my single-mindedness on the field.

• • •

My strong junior season and late surge my senior year weren't enough to attract interest from major league scouts. Coach Comeau reached out to local junior colleges and the University of Miami on my behalf only to find out their scholarship allotments were used up. He then had a talk with some people at both campuses of Miami-Dade Community College. They didn't seem to have any interest, either.

I wanted a future in baseball, and when the local schools took a pass on me, I looked for other options. I tried out for the Kansas City Royals when they held a camp at a local community college. The Royals had recently opened a baseball academy in Sarasota that was different from anything else offered by major league organizations. It involved going to school during the morning and playing baseball in the afternoon. The idea behind the academy was to nurture the abilities of talented players, some of whom they would sign to free-agent contracts. After only four years, the academy closed shop, but not before helping to produce future major leaguers Frank White and U.L. Washington.

The Royals went around the country searching for talent for the academy. About 70 kids showed up for the three-day camp in Miami. By the third day, there were only six of us left. Before I left for the camp, I asked my grandmother for her input on what I should do if I performed well enough to receive a contract offer. Her opinion was clear. "You're going to college," she said. "If you're talented enough to play in college, then someone will notice. But you can't sacrifice your education." She didn't buy for a second that the Royals academy offered any kind of real schooling to its attendees.

In my heart, I knew she was right, but I owed it to myself to see if I could convince a major league organization that I had what it took to play pro ball. But the Royals weren't convinced I did. By the end of the camp, neither I nor anyone else was offered a contract. The academy put a big emphasis on speed, and I was told I didn't run the 60-yard dash fast enough. They said they were impressed by my hitting and fielding, however.

College it was.

My family had connections to Florida A&M University. My Uncle Theodore had played baseball at FAMU, and my Uncle John was finishing up his degree there. He had enrolled after leaving the Air Force. Having joined the military against my grandmother's wishes, he was making good on his promise to her to get a college education.

I filled out an application with the intention of being a business or physical education major at the traditionally black university. Once the paperwork was done, it hit me that going to college meant being away from home for the first time. I caught a Greyhound bus to Tallahassee, an 11-hour ride with stops. Fortunately, Uncle John helped me as I went through orientation. He also noticed my homesickness. Even though I was still in the same state, it felt like I was a million miles from friends and family. Before classes started, he bought me a plane ticket back to Miami. I really appreciated that, and when I left home to go to Tallahassee for the second time, I felt much more prepared to start the whole college process. I even knew to catch the express bus, which trimmed a couple hours off the travel time. Uncle John ended up being my roommate for the first half of my freshman year.

One of my first steps at Florida A&M was plotting a way to get on the baseball team. The school had a Division II program in the Southern Intercollegiate

Athletic Conference. I felt I was good enough to play there. My old friend Cokes Watson and I both decided to try to make the team as walk-ons at a fall practice in November 1972. We were among just a handful of guys at the practice who weren't on scholarship. One of the assistant coaches was impressed with my workouts. He said he'd talk to the head coach about bringing me onto the team. It all clicked from there. I was given a partial scholarship, and after I ended up winning the starting job in left field my freshman year, I got a full scholarship. Cokes made the team, too.

It was an honor to play for a school that had such a rich athletic tradition. Olympic sprinters Bob Hayes and Althea Gibson were alumni, as were a number of athletes who played in the NFL. Prior to my arrival, the only major league baseball player who came out of FAMU was Hal McRae, who was breaking into the big leagues when I got to Tallahassee. He went on to make three All-Star teams with the Royals and collect more than 2,000 career hits. In the 1980s, a couple more players out of FAMU got to the majors—Vince Coleman and Marquis Grissom, both of whom had successful careers.

My baseball coach at FAMU was Costa Kittles, a very extraordinary man we called "Pop." He was Christian-driven and an amateur psychologist who knew how to make you dig within to find your best. He stressed that education came first, and he became another father figure to me. I was one of six freshmen who started on his team, and we became a pretty tight-knit group.

The team was comprised entirely of black players, which today isn't the case even at traditionally black universities like Florida A&M. I think this is due to the fact that, over the course of several decades, baseball has lost the interest of the black community. After my career ended, I became involved in efforts to get minority kids interested in the game. I always tell parents it has to start at home. Kids need to start playing baseball at five or six years old so they can maintain an interest in it from year to year. That's what happened to me and a lot of other future major leaguers back in the 1960s and '70s. We had our own parks. We played as a community, and we grew up with the sport. Nowadays, a lot of kids are focusing on football and basketball from a young age.

Growing up with the game and getting a chance to play in college was a thrill for me. I wouldn't have traded the three years I spent in Tallahassee for anything. It was important for me to get away from home, grow, and develop new relationships. I knew I'd eventually get over my homesickness, and baseball was the best cure for that. Once baseball season started, everything else fell into place. I became a physical education major and really started enjoying campus life. As a kid, I had heard a lot about The Marching 100, Florida A&M's famous marching band. They practiced right outside my dorm room, and I got to experience them doing their routines every night.

Throughout college, my grandmother and I exchanged letters. The moment I received one from Mamma, I'd pick up a pen and write back. Her letters were a true source of inspiration for me. "Put God first and get on your knees at the end of every day," she'd remind me at the end of each letter.

Looking back, I remember several of my baseball games in college like they were yesterday. Two were during my sophomore year when we played the University of Miami, which was ranked No. 1 in the nation at the time. The Hurricanes were in Tallahassee playing Florida State anyway, so they put us on the schedule, too. Well, we went out and swept them in a doubleheader. After we split a twin bill with them the next season, they decided not to play us anymore! The games against Miami let me know we had a really talented team that could match up with anybody. I faced a few future major leaguers at FAMU, including Al Holland, a left-handed pitcher who threw a couple no-hitters while at North Carolina A&T. When we faced Holland in Tallahassee, we beat him 6–0. That, too, was a confidence boost for me and the team.

When we played outside our conference and region, against mostly white teams, things could get a little tense. One such time was when we went to Georgia to take on Valdosta State University. My teammate, Wayman Winton, got into a confrontation with one of Valdosta's players, and the situation threatened to get out of hand. The umpires called the game and the local police department instructed us to get back on the bus and leave town. I remember Coach Kittles smiling and saying, "You heard the man! Get on the bus! Let's go!"

From a personal standpoint, I wasn't putting up the kind of numbers that got the attention of major league scouts. Part of that was because our home field in Tallahassee was anything but a hitter's park. It was more than 350' down the lines and about 500' to dead center. Needless to say, it wasn't the easiest park to play home run derby in. To hit one, you had to get all of it. In a game against Morehouse College, I hit a ball to left field that sailed over the fence and landed near a gymnasium across the street from the field. The coaches said it was the farthest they'd ever seen a ball hit on that field. My power numbers weren't great, but my average was in the high .300s. I led the team in home runs and RBIs and also stole a lot of bases.

Over winter break my sophomore year, I ran into my former high school baseball coach at an event in South Miami. Coach Comeau was amazed to see that I had sprouted several inches and had really filled out physically. He said, "My God, Andre, keep thinking major leagues! You've got it all now."

I had no idea what the book on me was during college, but I know at least one scout took notice. During my junior year, a scout from the Montreal Expos contacted Coach Kittles and told him he wanted to get a look at my lateral movement on the field. I wasn't aware of their conversation, so when Pop suddenly moved me from left field to shortstop for a month of the season, I thought he was just sending a message to Leon McRae, the starting shortstop and Hal's younger brother. It was a rough month. I hurt my right arm doing double-play drills, and when I went back to the outfield, I had some problems with tendonitis.

The Expos were apparently still interested in me, however. And other teams knew of me, as well. An older gentleman who came to many of our games was not only a scout for the Chicago Cubs but also a legendary former player in the Negro Leagues. It was an honor to learn from Coach Kittles that Buck O'Neil was there to watch me play. I guess he tried without success to get the Cubs to take me.

The only phone call I got from a major league official during college was from Mel Didier of the Expos. He invited me to a tryout camp in West Palm Beach prior to the June 1975 draft. I remember being down there with Clint Hurdle, a Florida high school kid who the Royals took with the ninth overall pick in the draft that year. It was a very informal workout. I threw, ran, and hit, and though the park was smaller than the one at Florida A&M, a gusting wind was blowing in and knocking down balls that might have otherwise gone over the fence. After the workout, the Expos informed me they might be in touch within a couple days.

Sure enough, on draft day, I got a call from Bill Adair of the Expos, who had also been scouting me. Montreal took me in the 11th round with the 250th overall pick.

I still had another year of college eligibility, but I had no doubts about what I wanted to do. I had always wanted to be a major league baseball player, and I realized that meant being a professional baseball player first. I didn't think there was anything left to prove in college. I knew if I played my senior year at Florida A&M that I'd likely be selected in a higher round and make a little more money. But that wasn't my goal. I just wanted to sign. Even though I hadn't yet earned my degree, I felt I had gotten a lot out of college.

Throughout my life, I had been blessed by good advice from the people I most loved and trusted. I sought guidance from Uncle John. He told me I had to trust my judgment and make the decision I felt was best for me. "You're a man now, and this is the start of a dream for you. It's the big break you've always wanted," he said.

Uncle John's own athletic dreams had been dashed as a child when he came down with rheumatic fever. Before that, he was one of the most talented basketball and football players in the neighborhood. But due to his illness, my grandmother wouldn't let him play any sport.

His words confirmed what I already felt. I signed with the Expos for $2,000 and prepared to report to rookie ball in Lethbridge, Alberta, Canada, a town with a population of only about 10,000. I had just a few days to go home and pack for the three months I'd be there.

And with that, the journey began.

• • •

I had never been on an airplane before when I boarded a Denver-bound flight in Miami. But I already felt like a pro at it by the time I made a connection in Denver for a flight to Lethbridge. I remember seeing the snow-capped Rocky Mountains beneath me as the plane made its way up north. I thought to myself, "Where in the world am I going?" Up until then, Atlanta was the farthest I had ever been from home. I had been to bigger places, just not to such a remote one.

I was met at the Lethbridge County Airport by someone in the Expos front office. We immediately drove to the ballpark where I was introduced to a couple of other guys who had just been drafted. Four of us were put with a host family who had converted the basement of their house into a bedroom.

Most of the guys in rookie ball developed a pretty good bond. Some were fresh out of high school, while others had attended college. Even though the odds were that only a few of us would make the big leagues, we were of the mindset that we'd come up through the system together.

Every player was trying to prove himself, but some of the higher-round draft picks walked around like they already had it made. The Expos first pick that year was a teenager from Texas named Art Miles. His story shows that nothing in life is guaranteed. He hit just .230 and after two more subpar years in the minors was paralyzed in a diving accident.

It didn't take me long to realize the quality of play at the college level isn't much different from that in the lower minor leagues. With the knowledge that I was now being paid to play baseball, I went out and tried to enjoy myself and make the most of my opportunity in Lethbridge.

Some of our bus rides to play teams in Montana were close to 10 hours long. The Sony Walkman wasn't out yet, and the only eight-track cassette we had on the bus was "The Beach Boys Greatest Hits." It played over and over again on every trip. It's kind of funny that a bunch of songs about surfers and California girls got to be the theme music for our treks through Canada. In some ways, the bus rides were preferable to being at the stadium in Lethbridge, where the smell from a nearby slaughterhouse couldn't be ignored.

I wound up hitting .330 with 13 home runs and was named Pioneer League Player of the Year. Along the way, I broke some of Steve Garvey's league hitting records. The player development directors must have been impressed with my speed, because they moved me to center field.

My strong season in Lethbridge made it likely I'd be promoted the following year to Montreal's Single A affiliate in West Palm Beach, which was only 90 minutes from my home. But my first stop after Lethbridge was the fall instructional league in St. Petersburg, Florida. I was one of only a handful of players from Lethbridge who were invited to play in the league. I had just finished my month there when I got a call from someone in the Expos front office who said, "Andre, we want you to go play winter ball in Venezuela." When I heard I was going to another foreign country, my jaw dropped. Then I realized what a great opportunity it was to gain exposure and be around Triple A and major league players, even if I didn't get much playing time.

So off I went to Latin America to play for a team called Cardenales de Lara in the town of Barquisimeto. I had been there just a few weeks when one of my teammates got hurt. Next thing I knew, I was in the starting lineup alongside players including Ron Guidry, who made his debut with the Yankees earlier that year. For the next month, I hit .300 and helped our team get to the championship game. In fact, I was at the plate with the winning run on base when that game got called off because of violence in the stands. The game ended in a tie.

My first year of professional baseball had been quite an adventure. First, I played in a small town in Canada, and then I went to a bustling city in Venezuela. It was nice to get back to Daytona Beach for Expos spring training the following March.

It was there I finally crossed paths with Warren Cromartie, a young team-mate who, like me, was from Miami. I had actually known about Cromartie for about five years; I had just never met him. When he starred at Miami-Dade Community College's North Campus, I went to watch him play. He was very talented and had been drafted by multiple teams in the first round before signing with the Expos in 1973. Before being drafted, he had played summer league baseball in Anchorage, Alaska, and on an All-Star team that toured Japan.

Cromartie and I had a lot in common. We were both from poor sections of Miami, him from the Liberty City neighborhood and me from South Miami.

Both of us grew up without our fathers in the home. Our moms raised us, and we both had several half-siblings. To hone my baseball skills at an early age, I hit rocks with a stick. Cromartie did the same thing, except he used cans. As Cromartie said, "We were brought up in the 'hood not having much except for a love of baseball and a desire to do whatever it took to get to the top."

Cro, who had already seen major league action, knew I had been drafted by the Expos. And I of course knew he was in the organization because I had been following his career. But we didn't come face-to-face with each other until spring training 1976. He and I were alone in the batting cage picking up baseballs after batting practice one day. I'd bend over to pick up a ball. He'd bend over to get a ball. We went about the task silently. The only sound was the rattle of balls as we threw them into a nearby bucket. Then we both bent over to pick up the last ball.

"You're Cromartie, huh?" I said.

"You're Dawson," he replied.

As awkward as that first meeting was, it represented the start of a great friendship. Cromartie was as loud and outspoken as I was quiet and reserved. But our personalities complemented each other's perfectly.

My performance in Venezuela helped convince the Expos that I should skip A ball and go directly to Double A Quebec City. I wasn't there long. I put up big numbers just like I had in Lethbridge and Venezuela, and pretty soon I was taking another step up the ladder, this time to Triple A Denver. Part of the reason for that promotion was the ripple effect of injuries to Pepe Mangual and Gary Carter of the Expos. With Mangual and Carter both on the disabled list, a couple guys went from Triple A to the majors, and I went from Double A to Triple A.

I met my new teammates on the road, and by the time we got back to Denver, I had already hit five home runs. I went on to hit 12 in my first 16 games.

I roomed with Cromartie at Triple A, and despite our similar backgrounds, we became something of an odd couple. He kidded me for being so neat. He'd say things like, "Why do you always have to button your shirt down to the last button? Is that what they taught you to do in college?" I'd give him a hard time for bringing tape on the road so he could fasten the curtains to the wall to keep light from coming in the room.

On the field, it was like I was getting better at each stop. I stayed with Denver until the end of the Triple A season, which concluded with us winning the American Association championship. Before the Triple A playoffs, I learned that Montreal was going to make me one of its call-ups in September when major league rosters expand to 40 players. The day after the playoffs ended, Denver manager Vern Rapp told a few of us, including Cromartie and me, that we were being promoted.

After getting the news, I called my mom. "Your dream has come true," she told me. "Make the best of it."

The other call-ups and I went to meet the Expos in Pittsburgh. I would be playing baseball for another month, but this time it would be in the big leagues.

4

ROOKIE OF THE YEAR

IT HAD HAPPENED. I WAS IN THE MAJOR LEAGUES. THE FACT I GOT THERE without having things handed to me on a silver platter made it all the more gratifying. I had overcome a serious injury to make my college team first as a walk-on and then as a scholarship player. And although I wasn't drafted highly by the Expos, I made the most of every opportunity I was given in the minors.

On September 11, 1976, I went 0-for-2 in my big league debut with the Montreal Expos, as we lost the game 4–3 to the Pirates.

Losing was nothing new to the 1976 Expos, who were in the midst of their worst season since coming into existence seven years earlier. The team finished a dismal 55–107. Fewer than 650,000 people showed up for 81 home games at Jarry Park. Two different managers, Karl Kuehl and Charlie Fox, presided over the disastrous season in which no everyday player hit better than .280 and no starting pitcher won more than 13 games or had a winning record. Third baseman Larry Parrish led the team in home runs and RBIs, with only 11 and 61, respectively. The Expos used an outfield-by-committee consisting of players including Bombo Rivera, Ellis Valentine, and Gary Carter, who had yet to become the team's everyday catcher. Under Kuehl, Montreal went 43–85 to start the season. He was fired and never managed in the big leagues again. Fox finished up 12–22 and wasn't brought back for the following season.

By September, the Expos were playing out the schedule without anything really at stake.

But I had a lot on the line in terms of proving I belonged. I didn't have time to contemplate the blur of events that had led me to the major leagues.

My goal that month was to make sure I played well enough to remain with the Expos for the 1977 season. I was in the starting lineup almost every day, and it felt like I was going out and facing a tough pitcher every time I stepped into the batter's box.

Speaking of tough pitchers, my first major league hit in September 1976 came off future Hall of Famer Steve Carlton of the Phillies at Veterans Stadium in Philadelphia. Prior to the at-bat, Expos hitting coach Larry Doby took me aside and imparted some wisdom. "Carlton likes to get ahead early in the count, so be aggressive up there," he told me. Sure enough, I saw a first-pitch fastball and hit it right back up the middle for a base hit. I guess I got caught up in the moment, however, because Carlton promptly picked me off first base.

During my first month with the Expos, I went 20-for-85 with no home runs. I was still adjusting to pitching at baseball's highest level, but I hoped I had impressed management enough to get an opportunity to stay in the big leagues. A lot of prospects get a shot at September call-ups, but not all go on to enjoy long major league careers. The nine players the Expos brought up in September 1976 included Larry Landreth, Roger Freed, Dan Warthen, Joe Keener, Bill Atkinson, and Pat Scanlon, all of whom were out of the majors by 1980.

In Montreal, the Expos had always taken a back seat to hockey's Canadiens, but in the summer of 1976, the team's popularity suffered another blow when Montreal hosted the first Olympic Games ever held in Canada. One of the good things about that event was it positioned the Expos to move into the newly built Olympic Stadium, or Stade Olympique as it was called in French, the following season. The new stadium was supposed to have a retractable roof, but construction problems delayed that for another decade. Even without the roof, I hoped Olympic Stadium, or "The Big O" as it became known to the English speakers in town, would be a little warmer and hospitable than cold, damp, and windy Jarry Park.

• • •

After the season, I went home to Miami and caught up with family and friends. Since joining the Expos organization the year before, I had fallen out of touch with a lot of people. Some of my friends were under the impression I had just finished my senior year of college. They didn't even know I had signed a professional contract. That made me realize how quickly things had happened for me. My journey to the major leagues consisted of a couple months of rookie ball, a winter in Venezuela, and four months in Quebec City and Denver. Thankfully, my Uncle John chronicled many of my early professional experiences in a scrapbook that included game stories from local newspapers in Canada and the Midwestern United States. He told me he went to newsstands and libraries all over Miami before finding the papers he was looking for.

As tempting as it was to rest, I didn't take too much time off when I got back to Miami. I needed to get myself ready for spring training. The more I thought about it, the more I realized that my performance in Montreal the previous September wasn't good enough to assure me a job with the big-league club in 1977. There would be opportunities in spring training to make the team, but a roster spot wasn't going to just be handed to me. During the off-season, I spent a lot of time working out with my cousin, Donald Napier, who would remain my training partner in the coming years.

When spring came, I drove 270 miles up the coast to the Expos' spring training complex in Daytona Beach. After the terrible 1976 season, the team had brought in yet another manager. And it was someone with a track record of enormous success—former Red Sox, A's, and Angels manager Dick Williams. I knew of Williams mostly from his time with the powerhouse Oakland teams that won back-to-back World Series in 1972 and 1973. Between leaving Oakland and coming to Montreal, he managed parts of three seasons with the Angels. I think management's decision to bring him to Montreal was a sign they wanted to field a winning team, which to that point had never happened.

I made a pretty decent showing that spring but was still nervous every time the team made a round of cuts. It was still very much up in the air whether I would start the season in Montreal or land back in the minors. I was always relieved to see my name in the Expos lineup on the days the team released players or sent them down. That meant I wasn't going to get called into Dick's office to receive bad news. By the end of spring training, I was hitting .306 with two home runs and 16 RBIs.

On the day of the final cuts, I was one of the 25 players still left in camp. I stood to make $19,500 for the 1977 season, and more importantly, I would be one of four outfielders in line to get substantial playing time. Three of the four were 23 years old or younger: Warren Cromartie, Ellis Valentine, and me. The "senior citizen" of the outfield group was Del Unser, who was 32.

Dick seemed happy with what he saw during spring training. "There were only a couple of times I had to be a son of a bitch," he told a Montreal newspaper. "You know there are always players who are going to think the manager is an ass. It depends on them how big an ass I have to be."

With all the youth on the team, a great addition to the roster that year was Tony Perez who, like Dick, knew a thing or two about winning. He had been a key member of the Big Red Machine teams in Cincinnati and was fresh off back-to-back world championships. The Expos acquired him before the 1977 season in a trade with the Reds.

I have to look back and laugh when I think about the first time I crossed paths with Tony. It was in the batting cages in Daytona Beach during spring training. Cro and I were waiting our turn when Tony jumped the line and walked right by us up to the plate. As someone who was trying to make the team, I took batting practice seriously, but I decided to let that slide and wait until he was finished.

We were each supposed to get 10 swings, but after Tony reached that number, he just kept going.

"*Diez!*" I shouted to him, using my limited Spanish. "You're on 15. We're only taking 10!"

Tony stared back at me blankly.

Cro has always said that I coil up like a cobra when I get angry, and I guess I was coiling up pretty good at that point. Tony saw how upset I was and walked out of the cage.

After he left, Cro turned to me and said, "You know who the fuck that was, homie? That was Tony Perez from the Big Red Machine!"

"I don't give a shit," I replied. "He has to wait his turn like everybody else."

To this day, Cro and I laugh about the day I ran a legend out of the batting cages in Daytona Beach. It didn't dawn on me at the time that Tony was baseball royalty and could take as many swings as he wanted.

That incident in no way reflected the huge amount of respect I had for Tony, who everyone calls "Doggie." So when the chance came to give him jersey No. 24, the number I wore the previous September and the number he had donned his entire career, I did so without hesitation. For the remainder of my years with the Expos, I wore No. 10.

The more I got to know Tony, the more I liked him.

He mentored the younger guys and made himself very accessible to us. One of the things he inadvertently taught me was not to use such a heavy bat. His bats were 35" long and weighed 33 oz. They worked for him, so I decided to give them a try. But after facing the likes of Nolan Ryan, J.R. Richard, and Tom Seaver, all of whom threw with velocity I had never seen before, I learned to put that big bat down. I started using a bat that was 34½" and 32 oz., and I never deviated from that throughout the rest of my career. I had a tendency to check my swing a lot, and a bat that was just one ounce lighter meant I could much more easily keep my bat from crossing the plate for a strike.

The Expos didn't just have a young outfield. We had a young team. I was one of five starters who were 23 years old or younger. The Expos had a real family atmosphere during my first years in the organization. Doggie, Woodie Fryman, Rudy May, and the other veterans, like older siblings, reminded us rookies we still had a lot of learning to do. I didn't get harassed too much, though probably because I had a quiet demeanor and didn't talk a lot.

It was exciting to start the 1977 season on a major league roster. Montreal wasn't necessarily the place most kids with big-league dreams envision playing, but I came to learn that Jackie Robinson played a season there before breaking the color barrier with the Brooklyn Dodgers. The Montreal Royals were the Triple A affiliate of the Dodgers at the time, and by all accounts the people of Montreal were very hospitable to Jackie and his wife. Black teammates of mine who played minor league ball in the Deep South described Montreal as a much more welcoming place than some cities in the United States.

My rookie season in Montreal coincided with another big-league team coming to Canada—the Toronto Blue Jays. In 1977, the Blue Jays would be as hapless as the Expos had been when they joined the major leagues as an expansion franchise. It didn't seem that Montreal felt at all threatened by the Blue Jays. The Expos, despite their losing ways, had established themselves as "Canada's team" with beat writers from Toronto and other cities covering our games.

• • •

More than 57,000 people came to watch the first-ever game at Olympic Stadium on April 15, 1977. It seemed like every seat in the ballpark was filled, which was hardly the case during my month with the team at the end of the '76 season. Unfortunately, everyone went home disappointed after we lost 7–2 to Carlton and the Phillies. But we made up for that defeat by winning four straight at home. For the first month of the '77 season, Unser and I platooned in center field. As a right-handed hitter, I got the start on days when a left-hander was pitching, and Unser got the call against righties.

I got off to a little bit of a slow start in April and was hitting only about .200 by the end of the month. There were rumblings in the press that the Expos were considering sending me back to Triple A for some additional seasoning.

I hadn't seen much playing time in May when we left for a trip to Atlanta–Fulton County Stadium to play the Braves. I rode the bench when we opened the set against knuckleballer Phil Niekro but got the start against a left-hander in the second game of the series. I already had a hit in the game when the Braves brought in a right-handed relief pitcher named Buzz Capra. Despite the unfavorable matchup, Dick kept me in the game to face Capra in the top of the eighth inning. To that point, I had come to the plate nearly 200 times in the major leagues without hitting a home run. That changed when I put a good swing on a Capra pitch and sent it into the left-field stands. In fact, it hit the tepee where Chief Noc-A-Homa, the Braves mascot, used to sit. One of our bullpen guys got the ball for me, and it was in my locker after the game. My first home run was a thrilling personal moment, but the fact that we lost the game 10–8 took away from it somewhat.

My bat started to heat up, and I tried to make contributions in the field, as well. The early knock on me was that I still hadn't fully developed all my tools. And one of those tools was defense. I prided myself on playing the outfield well, but a lingering injury from college was hampering my ability to throw the ball as well as I wanted to. During the short time I had played shortstop at Florida A&M, I developed tendonitis in my right elbow and shoulder. I found it difficult to get a lot on my throws from the outfield. Still, I only committed four errors in center field in 1977.

The team was much improved over the season before. But after an 11–9 start, we dropped 11 straight games, including a 21-inning marathon at home to San Diego. We never saw .500 again for the rest of the season.

In June, I started getting a lot of good cuts and raised my average by 40 points. That's when the process of easing me into the starting lineup ended. I started playing every day, hitting in either the third or seventh spot in the lineup.

Despite not winning a lot of games, we showed we had the potential to be an exciting team. I became a contender for National League Rookie of the Year. Valentine hit two inside-the-park home runs at Olympic Stadium and made the National League All-Star team. Cromartie put up good offensive numbers and established himself as an outstanding defensive outfielder.

Duke Snider, the former Dodgers great who worked as an Expos television announcer, touted us as not just the best young outfield in baseball but the best young outfield *he had ever seen.* This was high praise coming from a guy who had observed a lot of great players during his Hall of Fame career. From time to time, Duke would come down from the booth and talk to us about outfield play. He was a guy who also suffered from knee problems during his career, so that created an extra bond between us.

One of the highlights of my rookie season came during a four-game series at Wrigley Field in Chicago when I hit three home runs and had nine RBIs. In one of the games, the first part of a doubleheader played on July 4, we crushed the Cubs by a score of 19–3. It helped that the wind was blowing out that day. My home run in that game came in the ninth inning off Larry Biittner, a first baseman who manager Herman Franks sent to the mound in order to save some relief pitchers for the second game of the twin bill. I remember Cro, whose locker was next to mine, summing up the events of the first game as, "Fireworks on the Fourth of July at Wrigley Field!" We went back out and won the second game of the doubleheader. The sweep of the Cubs that day came during a seven-game winning streak, our longest of the season.

My first trips to Wrigley helped me realize how much I enjoyed daytime baseball. During my rookie season, I hit 10 home runs in day games in just 199 at-bats. That was one more homer than I hit in 326 at-bats in evening games. I also hit for a higher average during the day. The lights at some ballparks bothered my eyes to the point where I'd tear up on occasion. I found I saw the ball better in natural settings. My success in day games continued for the rest of my career. I got a good impression of Wrigley Field on that trip. I had always marveled at the ivy on the outfield wall there. It was unlike anything at any other ballpark. And there I was as a visiting player positioned right in front of it. Another thing that jumped out at me was how the Bleacher Bums in Chicago were right on top of you. It was almost like you could hold a conversation with them while standing in the outfield.

Part of my education in the big leagues came simply from observing other players. I faced pitchers like Carlton, Seaver, Ryan, and Richard, all of whom could be flat-out dominating. It didn't take me long to see what set major league pitchers apart from their minor league counterparts. The fastballs were faster, the breaking balls were sharper, and the location of pitches was more precise. In the big leagues, pitchers could put the ball exactly where they wanted and were adept at finding ways to exploit a hitter's weaknesses. If I had any hope of being successful, I knew I had to pay extra attention to what they were doing to try and fool me. It was a battle of wits. I had to adjust to them and force a readjustment on their part. Another big challenge was learning to hit major league sliders. For years, that remained the most difficult pitch for me to handle.

When I was in the dugout, I enjoyed watching a lot of guys I had long admired. My favorite player while in college was Dusty Baker of the Braves, whose games were broadcast on TV throughout the South. By the time I reached the majors, he was with the Dodgers. Like me, Dusty had been overlooked by a lot of major league organizations. I went in the 11th round of the 1975 draft. The Braves didn't draft Dusty until the 26th round of the 1967 draft. Another guy I liked to watch play the game was Dave Parker of the Pirates. He hit for average. He hit for power. He played great defense. Because we were in the same division as Pittsburgh, I got to see a lot of Parker. Then there was Cesar Cedeno of the Astros, who was the five-tool player I hoped to become.

It didn't take me long to identify the guys who got a lot of attention for their animated style of play. That was never how I played the game, but I didn't have a problem with "showboating" as long as it demonstrated excitement for the game and wasn't an attempt to show up an opponent. Pete Rose would spike the baseball after recording an out at first base. But that was Pete showing his exuberance for the game. Willie Montanez, who I played with in Montreal, was another guy known for his antics. His slow home run trots and his showy way of catching fly balls earned him some criticism. I'm not sure why Willie did these things, which just became comical after a while.

. . .

Off the field, the most eye-opening thing about my rookie year was playing in a French-speaking province. It was a whole different culture, and that was a little bit unsettling at first. I'm not sure if being in Canada and having to clear customs every time I went "home" made me more homesick than I would have been if I had been playing in the United States. It wasn't until I started venturing out more that I realized there were a lot of English speakers in Montreal.

Part of the problem I had at the beginning was that I was putting a lot of pressure on myself to perform well. I couldn't just leave the game at the ballpark. I took it home with me, and when that happened, the walls of my apartment felt like they were closing in. That subsided as I got more comfortable in Montreal and especially when I started playing every day. At that point, the season just seemed to fly by.

When we played on the road, it was easy to see what separated the big leagues from the minor leagues. Everything was first class. You got three or four times as much meal money. You rode charter flights. You stayed in the nicest hotels. And you were around the best players in the world, guys you had read about and seen on TV. For whatever reason, I played a lot better in away games my rookie year.

On the road, I roomed with an outfielder named Sam Mejias. Sam was a party guy. After games, he'd hit the town and enjoy the nightlife. He'd always return to the room before curfew, though. If I was asleep when he got back, he did his best not to wake me. It wasn't until after the 1980 season when I signed a six-year contract that stipulated I wouldn't have to share a room that I said goodbye to roommates.

As thrilling as it all was, I couldn't escape a nagging feeling of loneliness during my rookie season. I had arrived in the place I wanted to be only to find that something was missing. I realized I needed female companionship, and not the kind I could have found at hotel bars after games. I was looking for something meaningful and long-term. Exactly how I was going to find that special someone was something I had yet to figure out.

My mood brightened a lot every time my family came to see me in Montreal. My mom came with one of my sisters, and my brothers, uncles, and aunts also paid visits. Although my mom came all that way to see me, she decided not to go watch my games live. She had it in her mind that I might get hurt, and she didn't want to be there if I did. It was a practice she would maintain throughout my career. I accepted that. In fact, it worked out pretty well for me. While I was at the ballpark, she would stay at my apartment and cook dinner. So when I got home after a game on the days she was in town, a home-cooked meal would be waiting for me.

I always prided myself on how hard I worked out, so I treated myself by eating mostly anything I wanted. Dating back to childhood, I had quite a sweet tooth. I'm sure my mom being an accomplished cake baker had a lot to do with that. Thanks to her, I became something of a connoisseur of cakes. My favorite was strawberry shortcake, which wasn't easy to find in Montreal. That was okay because I didn't limit myself when it came to desserts. I also ate a lot of ice cream, cookies, and candy. During my career, I never carried more than 197 pounds on my 6'3" frame. For many years, my waist size was 31". That said, I don't recommend that anyone adopt a dessert diet in the hopes of staying trim. Yes, I ate what I wanted, but I also was fanatical about my work-outs. I did sit-ups, push-ups, and ran to stay in shape.

My apartment on Saint Catherine Street, or Rue Sainte-Catherine, wasn't far from the arena where the Canadiens played their games. Cro lived in the same building with his wife, a woman from Quebec City he met while playing Double A ball there. A couple other guys also lived in that complex, and sometimes we'd all go out to eat together. When we were out, I noticed that a lot of people recognized us. Even though they knew who we were, you could still tell Montreal was very much a hockey town. I'd have people ask me, "What time is tonight's match?" That was when they actually spoke to you. Most of the time you'd walk down Saint Catherine and there'd be a lot of stares and finger pointing.

The language barrier wasn't so bad. At the ballpark, the public address announcer called out our names in French, and the scoreboard showed information both in English and French. In English, I was a center fielder. In French, I was *le voltigeur de centre*. A home run was *un coup de circuit*. There were English-language television stations and newspapers, but most of the restaurants were French-only. At first, I would just point to what someone else was eating and say, "Give me that, please." Some of my teammates tried to learn French, but

I came to the conclusion it was tough enough speaking English. Ultimately, I just memorized my favorite menu items and stuck with those.

. . .

The Expos finished in fifth place in 1977 with a record of 75–87, or 20 games better than the season before. And for the first time in a while, fans came out to see our ballgames. The attendance for the season was 1.4 million, or more than twice what it was in 1976. The new stadium had a lot to do with that, but so did the fact we were showing signs of being a talented club. We still had a lot of work in front of us, however. The Phillies won the National League East in 1977 with a 101–61 record, and the Pirates came in second with 96 wins.

My final tallies for the season included 19 home runs, 65 RBIs, and a .282 batting average to go along with 21 stolen bases. There was continued speculation I would be in the running for the National League Rookie of the Year award. I was hardly a shoo-in, however. Steve Henderson of the Mets had similar numbers to mine. I hit for more power, but he hit for a higher average.

When the results of the voting were announced, I got 10 first-place votes and Henderson got nine. It was an honor to be the first Expos player to ever win Rookie of the Year. The award also eventually helped earn me a pay raise, though the negotiations between my agent, who was the former football player Nick Buoniconti, and the team dragged on for a while.

Satisfied with my first season in the majors and happy to be back home, I spent a good bit of time in the off-season with my new friend, Cro, who was coming off a great season and was also about to get into a contract squabble with the team. He and I would go fishing or watch football games on TV. And just like kids, we'd take batting practice in his backyard. But instead of the rocks and cans he and I hit when we were younger, we now swung at real baseballs in a batting cage Cro set up on his property.

The part of Miami he came from was a lot more volatile than where I grew up. Liberty City had witnessed race riots in 1968 and again in 1980 after white police officers were acquitted in the beating death of a black man. We were trying to win a pennant when the 1980 incident took place. "That's just the ghetto speaking, homie," Cro explained.

Then there was the best thing that happened after the 1977 season—I found an antidote for my loneliness.

I had known Vanessa Turner since high school. She was a couple years younger than me, and we grew up in the same area of South Miami. She used to come over to my house to have her hair braided by my sister Zerelda. She lived right behind Lee Park where I played baseball as a kid. Her father was the neighborhood barber. I had always liked Vanessa.

After I won Rookie of the Year, I was invited to opening night of a theater in Coconut Grove. It was going to be a red-carpet affair with photographers and writers from society magazines. I needed a date and had all but decided to take one of my sisters. Then Vanessa's name came up. I was a little bit hesitant to ask her, but I fought off the butterflies in my stomach and went by her house to see if she wanted to go with me. To my relief, she said yes.

Our first night out went very well. As advertised, the event at the theater was a pretty big to-do, and we had a lot of fun getting dressed up and having a nice dinner. Vanessa and I started dating, and before long, we got pretty serious. Prior to being involved with Vanessa, I hadn't been very active on the dating scene. I dated a girl in Miami the year before and a couple girls in college, but that was it.

Vanessa was a pretty girl. She had been the homecoming queen in both middle school and high school. She also was very smart. She could have had her pick of who she wanted to date. I liked that our families knew each other. Vanessa wasn't much of a baseball fan, but that didn't bother me.

Less than two months after our first date, with a few more butterflies in my stomach, I proposed to her. And again she accepted! I found out later she told a friend something to the effect of, "I'm not going to let him get away this time!" Apparently she had had feelings for me for quite a while. Asking her on that first date was one of the best things I ever did.

We set our wedding date for December 1978. I went back to Montreal to play my second season, and Vanessa returned to Florida International University to complete her journalism degree. It was important to both of us that she graduate.

It felt wonderful to reconnect with Vanessa and fall in love.

From the day I left for spring training, Vanessa and I talked constantly on the phone. It was very exciting to know that I had only one more season of being alone. That kept me upbeat and positive as I headed back to Montreal.

After the 1978 season, we got married at the Mount Olive Missionary Baptist Church, the house of worship we had both attended since childhood. I knew I was ready for the moment, but I was still quite nervous. Even though I had left home to go play professional baseball, I still felt very much tied to my family and the house I grew up in. I had helped raise my brothers and sisters and tried to provide them with as much guidance as I could. Now it felt like I was really leaving home. Vanessa and I were having a house built in South Miami that we were going to live in during the off-season. The day after the wedding, we left for our honeymoon in the Bahamas.

The joy of exchanging vows with Vanessa helped take my mind off what had been something of a disappointing 1978 season.

We knew our team had a good nucleus of young talent. It was just a question of how well and quickly we would gel. The '78 season showed that we weren't quite ready to compete with the top teams in our division, the Phillies and Pirates. We finished the year 76–86, one game better than the previous season. I played 157 games that season, as many as I would play in any future season. I hit for more power, but my batting average dropped 29 points to .253. A lot of pitchers had made adjustments when facing me. I was swinging at too many sliders out of the strike zone. Now the burden was on me to readjust to what they were doing. The battle of wits continued, and the stakes were about to become a lot higher because in the 1979 season the Expos emerged as a true contender.

5

WE ARE FAMILY, TOO

WHEN I CROSSED THE BORDER INTO CANADA IN 1979 FOR MY THIRD BIG-league season, my wife was with me for the first time. I wasn't sure how Vanessa would acclimate to the new environment, especially considering she didn't have much of an interest in the game I played for a living. But a funny thing happened over the next couple seasons, both to Vanessa and the city of Montreal—they both got hooked on baseball.

In 1977 and 1978, Dick Williams' first two seasons as Expos manager, we were still maturing as a team. We finished with a losing record both years, but everyone was starting to see that the building blocks for success were in place. Dick had a reputation for being a tough and mean guy who berated anybody he felt wasn't doing things the right way. I know he clashed with some of my teammates, including Steve Rogers and Warren Cromartie, but I never had a problem with Dick. I felt you could avoid getting on his bad side by keeping quiet and playing hard. What made Dick most happy was winning, which meant he had a lot to be happy about in 1979. Experience was what separated the '79 Expos team that won 95 games from the '78 team that won 76 games. Though we still only had one everyday player over the age of 30, the core of the team had been together a couple of seasons. And we had gelled as a ballclub.

Dick and the coaching staff did a lot of teaching. Jim Brewer, who was the Expos pitching coach my first two seasons with the team, was more than willing to share some of his wisdom with me, even though I wasn't a pitcher. As a coach and former pitcher, he had picked up a lot of insights about outfield play. I felt very comfortable with him, and he as much as anyone helped me work to get my knees in a bent position when charging a ball on artificial turf. Ozzie Virgil Sr. was another member of the coaching staff who helped me develop my skills. He and I would clown around a lot, but while we were having fun, he would find a way to teach me something. Ozzie and Dick made a good team, and that's probably why they stayed together even as Dick made three different managerial stops during the 1980s. With them, it was the old "good cop, bad cop" situation. Ozzie was a player's coach. Dick was a coach a lot of players couldn't stand.

When the coaching staff wasn't working with us, the team held study sessions of its own. After games, we'd sit around a table in the clubhouse and have in-depth discussions about that day's game. Some of the guys would swig beers. Not me, though. I limited my alcohol intake to the occasional pina colada and strawberry daiquiri. Needless to say, my choice of alcoholic beverage earned me some ribbing from teammates. During these meetings, we'd talk about base running, defensive positioning, and how to approach different pitchers. It was mastering details like these that separated losing teams from winning ones.

And in 1979, for the first time in franchise history, the Expos were a winning team.

Unlike in previous years, we got out of the gate fast, going 29–15 in the first two months of the season. A 1–0 win over the Phillies at the end of May gave us a 3½-game lead over second-place Philadelphia. In June, we extended our lead further. To say the Expos were in uncharted waters was an understatement.

The first part of my season had its ups and downs. There was a stretch in April and May when I got a hit in 16 out of 17 games, which pushed my batting average well over .300. But a slump after that dropped it back to around .270 at the end of the first half of the season.

Back then, we didn't really have film to study, so trying to break out of slumps was not an exact science. If I was really struggling, I might experiment with a slightly different batting stance, but I never liked to deviate too much from what felt normal to me. My philosophy was to trust my hands and to keep my feet as quiet as possible at the plate. You don't have to be in the big leagues very long before you learn that there will be times when the baseball looks like a golf ball and other times when it looks like a beach ball. In baseball, which is the ultimate game of frustrations and challenges, everything tends to even out in the end.

The keys to success have always been making adjustments, learning from mistakes, and maintaining a good work ethic. Today, the game's mental component is better understood. I was nearing the end of my career when major league teams recognized that anxiety and stress can affect a player's ability to hit or pitch a baseball. That's when team psychologists entered the picture.

At the 1979 All-Star break, we led the surging Cubs by 2½ games, but the race to the finish looked to be tight. Even the fifth-place Cardinals had a realistic shot to win the division, trailing by only 6½ games at the break.

John McHale had replaced Charlie Fox as the team's general manager before the season, and he oversaw the addition of a couple of players who aided our evolution into a competitive team. The Expos traded outfielder Sam Mejias to the Cubs for outfielder Jerry White and second baseman Rodney Scott, both of whom had already had a stint with the Expos. We got the better end of that deal. Rodney beat out Dave Cash for the starting job at second and emerged as a solid everyday player. His speed at the top of the lineup helped us add a new dimension to our offensive game.

And then there was Bill "Spaceman" Lee, who came over in a trade with the Red Sox. Spaceman was a huge part of our pennant run in 1979. Six of our pitchers won 10 or more games that season, and Spaceman led the pack with 16. He was a big reason the Expos led the league in team ERA that season. And his contributions were even more significant in light of the fact that Ross Grimsley, a left-hander who became the Expos first 20-game winner the season before, won only half as many games in 1979.

Spaceman was great on the field, and off the field, let's just say he earned his nickname many times over. I really enjoyed talking to him, even if I didn't always fully understand the things that were coming out of his mouth. He was smart and seemed to know a little bit about every topic but not in a way that made you feel uncomfortable. In fact, it was just the opposite. He made you feel loose and relaxed as he mused about art or philosophy. When we were on the road, he'd go to museums and tell us about some of the things he saw. Sometimes he got a little deep. When that happened, I'd listen for as long as I could and then just slowly walk away. He didn't seem to mind. He'd just turn to someone else and continue his thought or, if no one else was around, keep talking to himself. One guy who really enjoyed his company was Rodney Scott, who became Spaceman's best friend on the team. They were a little bit of an odd couple, the young black second baseman and the older white pitcher, but they really hit it off.

Gary Carter was another excellent teammate and a guy I considered a real "gamer." His nickname was "Kid" because he played the game with a child's excitement. But that nickname kind of evolved into "Kodak Kid" and "Teeths" for his tendency to flash his pearly whites for the cameras. Unlike a lot of us, Gary genuinely enjoyed talking to the media, especially the television media. He always made himself available for interviews after games. When guys were fed up after a loss and didn't want to address the media, Gary would pop out and do the talking. On days like that, when reporters closed in on us, we would always say, "Go talk to Kid!" Then the flock of reporters would head over to Gary's locker. Every team needs a personality like that in the clubhouse, someone who enjoys the spotlight and acts as the unofficial team spokesman. There are different types of leadership, and that is definitely one of them.

Another type is leading by example on the field. Gary most certainly did that, as well. He was a seven-time All-Star as a member of the Expos and a key part of the Mets team that won the 1986 World Series. Unfortunately, Gary was diagnosed with brain cancer in 2011. I visited him at his Florida home several times during his ordeal, and I hope my visits brought him some comfort in his final months. Gary passed away in February 2012.

Back in 1979, it was nice to have teammates like Spaceman and Kid because the more games we won, the more attention we got from the local media. There were French-speaking reporters, English-speaking reporters, and cameras and microphones constantly staring you in the face. I liked that the media was showing more interest in the Expos. Every now and then, I'd get an odd question, like the time a French-Canadian reporter asked me, "Where did you get the name Andre?" By that point, I knew Andre was a pretty popular French name, but I explained that the name was given to me by an aunt on my father's side and that it had no connection to French culture. That was the first and last time in my entire life I have been asked about the origin of my first name.

I wasn't referred to by my first name very much anyway. My nickname, "Hawk," which I got as a child, stuck with me when I got to the majors. Most of my teammates had nicknames, many of which were thought up in the Montreal clubhouse by Cromartie. Rodney Scott became "Cool Breeze" early in his career.

Tony Perez had long been referred to as "Doggie." And Steve Rogers had been called "Cy" after Cy Young ever since his rookie season. But most of the other nicknames came into being while I was with the team. Jeff Reardon, a relief pitcher who came to the Expos in 1981, was nicknamed "Yak Yak" for the simple reason that he hardly ever said a word to anybody. Bill Gullickson, one of our starting pitchers, was "Sugar" because he was diabetic. Bryan Little, a white player who joined the team in 1982, became known among the black players as "Like Me," because he liked hanging out with us. The few players who didn't have a nickname were referred to by a shortened version of their last name. That included Cromartie, who was Cro.

The fact that the team was vying for the division added to the enjoyment of taking the field every day. It was such an exciting time that I resolved to play through the discomfort I was feeling in my surgically repaired left knee, the one I injured during a high school football game. The constant pounding my knee took on the hard artificial turf at Olympic Stadium didn't exactly help my condition. But nothing was going to keep me from being in the lineup. Whenever I felt pain in my knee, I'd have it drained of fluid and get a cortisone shot. I was still very young, just 24 years old entering the 1979 season, and my youth helped me get through the first couple of seasons. The real problems with both of my knees would come later on.

• • •

As I mentioned, 1979 was also the year my wife, Vanessa, arrived in Montreal. It took her a while to adjust to the new culture and climate in Quebec. Having grown up and attended college in Miami, this was her first time away from home. The first thing she learned was that the clothing she owned wasn't going to cut it in chilly Canada. She went out and splurged on a fur coat, which not only kept her warm but made her feel a little more comfortable in fashion-conscious Montreal.

To get a little bit of a taste of home, she'd hop in the car and go across the border to Plattsburgh, New York, to buy groceries. She liked the scenery on the way to upstate New York, but she also liked the familiarity of the American supermarket. Some of my teammates' wives helped take Vanessa under their wings. Tony Perez's wife, Pituka, and Dave Cash's wife, Pam, were two of the women who made themselves available whenever Vanessa had a question or needed anything. Vanessa was just 21 at the time, so the support of the other wives was invaluable. The organization took care of the wives, too, even offering French lessons to anyone who was interested.

I was only in my third full season in the majors and not making a lot of money, which meant Vanessa couldn't do all the things other players' wives did. Some spouses, for example, might arrange to fly to New York to join the team on a road trip. Vanessa would ask them for their flight information as if she was considering joining them. She'd then hop on a train and meet them there.

Our wives were part of the Expos family, and it was good to see they were hitting it off as well as we were. When you're around the same guys almost non-stop for seven months of the year, you become a tight-knit family. That means you've got to respect each other, have each other's backs, or know when to simply leave a guy alone.

Baseball was what we did every day, but music was where me and my closest friends on the team turned when we wanted to get away from the game for a while. The 1970s was the disco era, and the guys on our team were really into music. A lot of us had our own boom boxes, and it seemed like when we got onto a bus or plane, seven or eight boom boxes would come on board with us. It could create conflict sometimes when a boom box occupied a choice seat.

I had always been a big music fan. I liked everything from Rare Earth to Bootsy Collins. A competition developed between myself, Ellis Valentine, and Cromartie to see who could discover the next big artist or group. We'd sift through each other's collections to figure out what we needed to get. I befriended a guy in New York who ran a record store. When we were in town playing the Mets, he'd invite us in and give us all kinds of music. When we were in other cities, the first thing we'd do is try to find the nearest record store. Valentine was the unofficial disc jockey in the clubhouse. He played a lot of disco and what could be considered an early form of hip-hop by artists including The Sugarhill Gang and Kurtis Blow. Ellis was locked in to what was current.

When you're around the same guys all the time, not every day is going to be a good one. All families fight and have disagreements and shouting matches. Sometimes tension boiled over and we'd have a fisticuff or two. That kind of thing usually happened because of some kind of lingering hostility between two guys. Cro and Valentine went at it in Atlanta before a game. When the team got to the ballpark that day, they both were sitting at their lockers with their heads down. I think that incident cleared the air between them.

• • •

When your team is at or near the top of the standings, you really look forward to getting to the ballpark every day. It's invigorating suiting up to play knowing there's something at stake. In May 1979, as we stood at the top of the standings, Ellis told reporters, "We're the Rolls-Royce of the league right now. This is May, and by August, we could be a bicycle. But I know one thing for sure, we burned 'em up in April."

We didn't turn into a bicycle, but I guess you could say another Rolls-Royce joined us on the road later in the season.

My first pennant race was also the franchise's first. Our fans sensed this was the way baseball was supposed to be played, and my teammates and I fed off their energy. We were 56–25 in games played at Olympic Stadium in 1979. On the road, we had a losing record. Maybe some of the opposing players who came to town didn't get their rest and partied too much at the nightclub Chez Pareé, but more likely it was that we felt so comfortable in our home environment. What once was a cold and somewhat inhospitable park had transformed into a place we loved to play.

The Expos had even gone out and invested in a mascot, Youppi, which meant "Yippee!" in French. Youppi, who today cheers on hockey's Canadiens, is a fuzzy orange creature that would have fit in well on *The Muppet Show*. The fans loved him. You could see him in the stands during games doing his thing, which was to get everybody charged up about the game. He would do things like run and slide across the opponent's dugout. On one occasion, he got a little overzealous and went into a headfirst slide and couldn't stop himself. He slid right off the top of the dugout and down to the ground below. Everybody thought it was just part of the act. But then he didn't get up for a while. For the next day or two, Youppi was nowhere to be found. He was nursing his injuries, I guess. But it wasn't long before he was back on top of the dugout again. Another memorable Youppi moment was when Cro put on the costume and entertained the fans during a rain delay by sliding on the tarp. When he took the Youppi head off, the fans went wild.

After the All-Star break, the front office made a move geared toward helping us compete until the very end of the 1979 season. Rusty Staub was already something of a legend in Montreal, having played for the Expos from their inaugural season in 1969 through 1971. Back then, Staub, or *Le Grande Orange* as the fans called him, was an All-Star in the prime of his career playing for a team that couldn't buy a win. When the Expos acquired him from the Tigers for a player to be named later in 1979, he was a 35-year-old veteran whose best days were behind him but who could give the contending Expos a boost down the stretch. He was going to be mostly relegated to pinch-hitting duties, but he also was going to be another clubhouse presence to help a still-young team make a push for the division crown. Back then, the National League East was composed of the Expos, Phillies, Pirates, Mets, Cardinals, and Cubs. There was no wild-card round of the playoffs, and division winners advanced directly to the League Championship Series.

On his return to Montreal, Rusty wore No. 6, not the No. 10 jersey he donned during his first stint with the team. He offered me cash in exchange for giving up that number, but I had grown attached to it and made it clear it wasn't up for sale.

We started September in second place behind the Pirates and found ourselves in a seesaw battle with Pittsburgh for the remainder of the season. The atmosphere at Olympic Stadium during that final month was unlike anything I had witnessed before. We drew crowds of more than 50,000, a number we only usually saw on Opening Day. That same month we played the lowly Mets in front of only 5,000 fans in New York City!

By this time, Vanessa had turned into a big baseball fan. When she came to games at the start of the season, I'd take a glimpse at where she was sitting to make sure she was paying attention to the game. If she wasn't, I had to remind her to keep an eye on the action and look out for foul balls that might come in her vicinity. Well, by the end of the season, she had learned the game enough to where she not only paid close attention to every pitch but also critiqued my play. She'd ask things like, "Why'd you swing at that pitch that bounced in front of the plate?" I'd laugh and say, "If you think it's that easy, you go grab a bat and try and hit it!"

In late September, we were nursing a half-game lead when we headed to Three Rivers Stadium to play a four-game series against the Pirates. The prize of a division title was staring us right in the face.

The Pirates made a name for themselves that season by adopting the song "We Are Family" as their theme. When we played in Pittsburgh, that's all you would hear. It blared over the loudspeakers when they took the field, when they rallied to take a lead, and when they won a game. They had a lot of great ballplayers, like Willie Stargell and Dave Parker.

The first two games of the set were played as a doubleheader. Because of bad weather in Montreal at the start of the season, it was the eighth twin bill we had played that month. By the time we split the doubleheader, we had played something like 15 games in 10 days.

All those games had to take a toll on our pitching staff. We went on to lose the final two games of the series. That dropped us 1½ games behind the Pirates. We went into the final game of the season needing a win at home against the Phillies and a Pirates loss to the Cubs. Neither happened, and we finished the 1979 season in second place with a record of 95–65. We had shown amazing consistency during the season, playing 15 games over .500 in both the first and second halves of the season.

The Pirates swept the Reds in the National League Championship Series and beat the Orioles in seven games to capture the World Series.

We were good…just not good enough.

• • •

In 1979, I tied a career high in home runs with 25 and set a career high in RBIs with 92. My .275 batting average was higher than in the year before but lower than in my rookie season.

I knew in my heart I could be a .300 hitter if I made a couple of adjustments at the plate. Part of what I needed to do dealt with my general approach to hitting. I felt I could reduce the number of times I struck out, which was more than 100 in 1978 and 1979, if I became a gap-to-gap hitter who put more balls in play and used the opposite field. My biggest weakness was still the slider, which at times would come in with the velocity of a fastball and then make a late break. I had a tendency to chase the slider as it danced off the plate. My goal coming into the

1980 season was to lay off that pitch and force pitchers to elevate the ball. I would try to become more of a high-ball hitter, but that meant being able to demonstrate enough patience not to swing at too many pitches early in the count.

The hope for the team's future was brighter than ever. Our strong performance in 1979 helped increase the popularity of baseball in Montreal.

Now it was up to us to keep that excitement alive.

In 1980, we brought in a player who typified excitement. His name was Ron LeFlore, and he was known to most of us through *One in a Million*, a made-for-television movie starring LeVar Burton about LeFlore's life story, which aired in 1978. After spending several years behind bars for armed robbery, during which time he played on a prison baseball team, LeFlore signed a contract with the Detroit Tigers. He had several very good seasons with the Tigers before coming over to Montreal in a trade for pitcher Dan Schatzeder.

We never called him Ron, Ronnie, or Mr. LeFlore. We called him "Burglar." It was the perfect nickname when you considered he spent time in prison for theft and that he was an incredible base stealer.

He swiped 97 bags in his only season with us. That was more stolen bases than 10 entire major league teams had that year! He helped us go from a team that was in the middle of the pack in stolen bases to one that rivaled for the league lead. The joke around the clubhouse was, "Man, you run the bases like you're running from the cops!" With Burglar at the top of the lineup and Rodney Scott hitting behind him, we had great table-setters who added a whole new dimension to our lineup. For a few months the previous season, I had hit in the lead-off spot. But with LeFlore, we had a bona fide top-of-the-lineup guy.

It was a joy watching him run the bases. Sometimes he'd steal second and third on back-to-back pitches.

On one occasion, he decided on his own to try and steal home. There was no sign from the third-base coach, so Cromartie, who was at the plate, had no idea LeFlore was racing down the line. As the ball was traveling toward home plate, LeFlore yelled, "Cro, don't swing!" Fortunately, Cro heard him. A split second later, Burglar slid in safely to score a run.

We needed the extra boost he provided in 1980 because I was one of several starters who missed time due to injuries.

Prior to the season, I had a second surgery on my left knee and my first since hurting it badly in high school. I hobbled around the entire off-season, and when I reported to spring training in Daytona Beach, it still didn't feel right at all. A doctor drained fluid from the knee, and I just tried to play through it. But back in the cold and damp of Montreal to start the season, the pain returned in a big way. I couldn't figure out what was going on. To my surprise, an X-ray showed I had a fractured bone in the knee. It was a relief to know the exact nature of the problem. It became a question of how we would deal with it. I missed a few games but was determined not to go on the disabled list. When I returned to the lineup, I took the painkiller Darvocet to get through games. I took one pill an hour before batting practice, another before the start of a game, and a third during the game. In addition to that, I had both knees taped. Once the medication wore off, it was back to being in pain until I got to the ballpark the next day.

That was the first time my knee really flared up during my major league career. But it wasn't the last. It seemed like I'd get a few years out of the knee and would then need to go back for a tune-up. I ended up having more surgeries on my right knee, which took the brunt of the extra weight I put on it because I was favoring my left knee.

Injuries to a couple of my teammates in 1980 may have cost us a chance to build a big division lead early in the season. Our third baseman, Larry Parrish, hurt his wrist and missed a good chunk of the season. And we lost the services of Valentine for a month after a pitch hit him in the face and shattered his cheekbone.

Despite our injuries, we again competed for a division title all the way until the final weekend of the season. This time around, it was the Phillies who stood between us and a shot at the playoffs. With Pete Rose, Mike Schmidt, Greg Luzinski, Larry Bowa, and Garry Maddox in the lineup, they were a veteran-laden team. And led by that year's Cy Young Award winner Steve Carlton, the Phillies had enough pitching to compete with anybody.

Though I never learned to speak French while playing in Montreal, there was a French phrase I knew that applied to the 1979 and 1980 seasons: *déjà vu*, or the feeling you're doing something that you've experienced before.

After being in and out of first place since June 1, we entered the final weekend of the 1980 season tied with Philadelphia. And as fate would have it, we finished the season with a three-game series at home against the Phillies. The series started on October 3, making it the first time the Expos had played meaningful games in October. Just like our late-season series against the Pirates the year before, the Phillies series would determine who would get a chance to play for the pennant. Both teams came in riding winning streaks and playing their best baseball of the season.

In the first game of the set, which was played in front of our biggest crowd of the season, we sent Scott Sanderson to the mound to face Dick Ruthven of the Phillies. The game was a nail-biter. Ruthven and two relievers held us to just four hits, and the Phillies came away with a 2–1 win. I knocked in our only run with a sacrifice fly.

We trailed the Phillies by a game and needed to win the next two games to take the division. But Mike Schmidt, well on his way to an MVP season, made sure that didn't happen. In a game that was delayed by rain for several hours, Schmidt's 48th home run of the season off Stan Bahnsen in the top of the 11th inning gave the Phillies a 6–4 win that clinched them the division title and rendered the final game of the season meaningless.

The Phillies went on to beat the Astros and Royals to capture the World Series.

I played through my injury and finished the season with a .308 batting average. Even though I appeared in fewer games than the season before, I got more hits, scored more runs, and took more walks. My home runs and RBIs were down slightly, but I had fulfilled my goal of getting on base more.

Of the three starting outfielders on the team—myself, Cromartie, and Valentine—I was the one who most people thought needed the most work on defense. I was criticized for not charging balls hard enough and not getting rid of balls quickly enough. To my right in the outfield, I saw Valentine, who had one of the strongest arms I'd ever seen. And to my left was Cromartie, who had as much range as anybody. I worked diligently on my defense to bring myself up to an equally high level.

At the end of the season, I was recognized for my defense with my first Gold Glove award.

It provided some consolation that the teams that beat us out for the division title went on to win the World Series in both 1979 and 1980. The Pirates and

Phillies teams that took home the championships were great, but I think if a couple things had gone differently, we might have been the team celebrating a World Series title. The doubleheaders at the end of the season took a toll. The other thing working against us is we never could land that one marquee, big-name free agent to add to the lineup or pitching rotation. On the bright side, although our payroll still lagged behind other teams in our division, the front office was spending more money on the team than in previous years.

I was one of the recipients of that. Before the 1981 season, I signed a five-year contract that was worth about $1 million a year. The deal included an option that would allow the team to keep me for a sixth year. It was not only a huge pay bump but a sign that the Expos considered me worth locking up for several years.

Based on the near misses of the two previous seasons, I was hungrier than ever to help the organization break through.

6

NO BASEBALL, PLAYOFF BASEBALL

FROM THE MOMENT YOU SIGN YOUR FIRST PROFESSIONAL CONTRACT, you realize baseball is more than just a game. It's very much a business, too. Before you even suit up for the first time, a monetary value is placed on you. The mathematics of a first contract are pretty simple—the amount of your signing bonus is commensurate with your probability of making and succeeding in the majors. When the Expos drafted me out of Florida A&M University in 1975, I signed for $2,000. In my rookie year of 1977, I was paid $19,500, a little more than the major league minimum. In order to earn a bigger paycheck, I needed to prove myself. And I did, winning Rookie of the Year. Many other contracts followed. When each expired, I could re-sign with my existing team or try to negotiate a better deal with another club.

Now take my individual experience and roll it together with those of several hundred major leaguers of my era. Taken as a whole, that's what's known as the "economics" of the game. At the end of the day, despite some shared interests, management and players have to look out for No. 1. There is a lot of money in baseball, and neither group can be blamed for wanting to stake a claim to as much of it as possible. The realization that baseball and business go hand in hand didn't affect my love of the game. It was simply a fact I accepted.

Prior to the 1981 season, we major league players were informed by our union that team owners wanted to change the way free agency worked. The owners argued that teams that lost a free agent should be compensated with a player from the signing team's roster. Maybe not a star, but at least someone with major league experience.

This idea was unacceptable to the Major League Baseball Players Association, which had waged many battles over the years to give players the right at certain points in their careers to test the open market through free agency. The union felt the owners' plan would deprive players of the full benefits of free agency. The union's counter-argument went like this: If Team A was forced to give a player to Team B because Team A signed a free agent from Team B, then Team A might decide against signing that free agent in the first place. In effect, the owners' proposal was an attempt to make free-agent signings resemble trades.

I was fully behind the union on this issue. Despite the owners' contention that they deserved compensation for players lost to free agency, neither they nor the game was suffering financially under the existing structure. I felt players had made a lot of strides to get where we were, and if we yielded on this issue, we'd be taking a major step back. As strongly as I felt about the issue back then, I'd gain an even better understanding later in my career of the importance of checks and balances between players and owners.

I didn't think this impasse would lead to a strike, and I started the 1981 season assuming the disagreement would eventually get resolved. I knew the business of baseball never slept, but as far as I was concerned, I had my own business to tend to.

The near misses of the two previous seasons gave us hope 1981 would be the year we broke through and made the playoffs. I wanted to do whatever it took to help get the Expos over the hump. I got the sense that my teammates had started to view me as a leader—not a vocal rah-rah guy, but rather someone who tried to lead by example. If younger players had questions about pitchers, I'd try to answer them. If someone on the team needed counsel or guidance, I'd try to provide it. It wasn't a role I sought out, but it was one I was happy to fulfill.

There were enough exciting moments in the first part of the 1981 season to take my thoughts away from a possible strike.

We started by winning 11 of our first 13 games, a streak that included a three-game sweep at home of the Phillies, our nemesis from the year before. Then in May, Charlie Lea threw the third no-hitter in Expos history and the first since I joined the team. As the potential last out of the game soared toward me in center field, I started celebrating a little too soon and almost turned it into a tougher play than it needed to be. Following that 4–0 win over the San Francisco Giants, beer and champagne flowed in the clubhouse.

Later in May came the first indication that team executives were no longer going to be satisfied with second-place finishes.

It came as a surprise when I heard we had traded my outfield partner Ellis Valentine to the Mets. Losing Ellis brought an end to a four-year period I thought would last a lot longer. Since I became a regular in 1977, it had always been myself, Warren Cromartie, and Ellis roaming the outfield, with the exception of 1980 when Ron LeFlore's arrival moved Cromartie to first base. From the time we played together in the minors, it was said we had the potential to be the best and most exciting outfield in baseball. And after a few seasons with the Expos, I felt we had lived up to the hype. We adopted a have-no-fear attitude that enabled us to compete with the best teams in the league.

However, after a slow start to the 1981 season and some concerns over his attitude and ballooning weight, Ellis was shipped off. In retrospect, I suppose it was a deal the Expos could afford to make because a young second-baseman-turned-outfielder named Tim Raines was about to establish himself as a star. The trade started to look even better when Jeff Reardon, who we got in the trade for Ellis, emerged as an outstanding closer.

Two weeks after Ellis was traded, the baseball season came to a screeching halt after talks between owners and the union broke down. At the time of the strike, we were 30–25 and four games behind the division-leading Phillies. Through 51 games, I was enjoying a fine season that included 13 home runs, 29 RBIs, and a .325 batting average.

For the first time since I was a kid, I wasn't sure if I would be playing baseball over the summer. In the hopes the strike would get worked out quickly, Vanessa and I stayed in Montreal for the entire month of June. I felt the work stoppage would last a week, maybe two, and that it would encourage the sides to reach an agreement.

It was hard to have the season interrupted like that. Since the Expos facilities were closed to us during the strike, I tried to stay sharp by throwing a baseball against the side of my apartment complex. I'd also swing a lead bat to keep my batting stroke from getting rusty.

If there was anything positive about the strike, it was that it gave me ample opportunity to fully explore Montreal for the first time. Our winning brand of baseball over the past few seasons led to increased notoriety around town. The people on the street who recognized me were very cordial, and it never reached the point where the attention was overwhelming. My personal success and that of the team also led to a couple endorsement deals, nothing really high-end, but enough to keep me busy during the strike. I worked with a Chevrolet dealership in suburban Montreal. I wasn't brave enough to do any radio or TV spots in French, however. If anybody was going to do that, it would be Gary Carter, who at one point took a French course. He did a lot of commercials, including a very memorable English-language one with his daughter for 7UP soda.

As June turned to July, I got fidgety. I wanted to get back to baseball.

Finally, at the end of July, the union and owners reached a compromise on how teams would be compensated for losing free agents. At the time, the 50-day strike was the longest in major league history. And it left baseball scrambling to figure out a way to salvage a season that had been gutted of its middle.

My teammates and I went to the Expos new spring training facility in West Palm Beach for a week of workouts before games resumed. As teams prepared to get back on the field, baseball officials came up with a revised plan for that season's playoffs. It involved splitting the season into two halves. In each of the four divisions, the winner of the season's first half would play the winner of the second half in a best-of-five playoff that would decide the teams advancing to the League Championship Series. And what would happen if the same team won both halves of the season? Well, that issue created a few headaches before it was decided that, in this case, the second-place team in the second half of the season would qualify for the playoffs.

In the National League East, that meant the Phillies, the winner of the first half of the season, were guaranteed a spot in the division playoff. It was just a question of who they would face.

• • •

The first major league game played since mid-June was the All-Star Game at Cleveland Stadium. For the first time in my career, I was selected by fans to represent the National League. Carter and Raines were also picked. Timmy was having a tremendous rookie season. Prior to the strike, he had stolen 50 bases in just 54 games and was hitting .322. He had been touted as the best rookie prospect in the Expos system, and he was living up to those expectations.

Timmy, a Florida native like Cro and me, was making a huge impression on the field. But in the clubhouse, he didn't say a whole lot—at least at the beginning. One of our few conversations came when we first met. We shook hands, and then he launched into a story about having watched an Expos spring training game in Orlando his senior year in high school, which was my rookie year. "I asked you for an autograph, and you told me to take a hike," he said.

I couldn't recall ever having done that.

Well, it turned out it never happened. I guess Timmy was nervous and trying to break the ice with a joke. But I didn't pick up on it, and I certainly didn't smile. I think that incident caused him to tone down his big personality until he established himself on the field.

"I decided I wouldn't say anything to Andre unless he said something to me first," Timmy said. "I found him to be a very intimidating guy."

It was great to be back on any baseball field after the strike, but making my return at the All-Star Game was doubly exciting. It was thrilling to share a clubhouse with players I respected, including Dave Parker, Dusty Baker, and Pete Rose.

Other than the game itself, the most exciting part of the All-Star experience was the players' brunch, where every participant received an All-Star ring. Later that day at the ballpark, we had a chance to mix and mingle with the other players and sign some autographs. The whole thing wasn't quite the spectacle it is today with the Home Run Derby and other events leading up to the game.

At my first All-Star Game, I got to meet President Ronald Reagan, who made the rounds of both clubhouses, shaking hands but barely saying a word to any of us. In the hour or so before game time, the chit-chat ended, and we began focusing on going out and beating the American League for the 10th consecutive time.

This was long before Major League Baseball implemented a rule change in which home-field advantage in the World Series went to the league that won the All-Star Game. When I played, we didn't need any incentive to make the game meaningful. It was a matter of pride to show your league was superior. And back then, there was no interleague play, so it was the only time the two leagues faced each other before the World Series.

In 1981, the National League kept its winning streak alive with a come-from-behind 5–4 victory. I played the entire game and went 1-for-4 with a stolen base. But the hero of the game was Carter, who hit two home runs and took home Most Valuable Player honors.

I returned to Montreal knowing a lot was riding on the last 53 games of the season. The second half represented a clean slate for us—and every other team in baseball. Our first half had been good, but we knew the second could be even better. With the split season, every game became that much more important.

Near the end of August, things really started to click. We won five straight games at home against Cincinnati and Atlanta, outscoring the Reds and Braves 34–4. The Phillies meanwhile had no real incentive to win the second half. They were headed for the playoffs regardless of how they performed in the final months of the season. On the day we started our five-game winning streak, the Phillies went into a six-game skid. That turned the race for the second-half crown into a battle between the Expos and the Cardinals, who had been playing consistently well all season.

As we geared up for another pennant race, something unexpected happened.

We were in Philadelphia when news broke that the Expos had fired manager Dick Williams. I knew Dick's combative style didn't always endear him to players, but apparently his gruff style had also alienated general manager John McHale and others in the front office.

Dick had caught flak for not using Reardon enough out of the bullpen. And the fans really turned on him after he put our ace, Steve Rogers, into an extra-inning game as a pinch-runner. Rogers wound up breaking a rib trying to prevent a double play. The criticism from fans signaled Montreal was becoming more of a baseball town.

I could see there was some dissension in the clubhouse, but Dick's firing still came as a bit of a shock. He was not only a guy who had been to the World Series, but after taking over the Expos in 1977, he had helped transform us into a winning ballclub. It was his ballclub. Yes, he rubbed some people the wrong way, but he was still one of the best in the business. I guess his gruff manner combined with memories of two consecutive second-place finishes in the National League East were enough to make the front office think someone else could do the job better.

The person they chose surprised everyone. Jim Fanning, whose most recent managerial job had come nearly 20 years earlier in the minor leagues, took over as skipper. To that point, Fanning had served as the Expos' player development director.

Even though the season was already in its final weeks, the feeling among my teammates was Fanning would manage a couple games and then yield the job to someone with more experience. We were on the brink of making the playoffs, and it didn't make sense to have a rookie manager trying to lead us to a place Dick had already been several times before.

The Jim Fanning era didn't start well at all. We lost three straight games, and I think at that point everyone in the baseball world expected us to unravel. Cro publicly criticized Fanning after he was benched, and Bill Lee, in his unique Spaceman way, described the team to the press as floating on a "river of despair."

Fanning's inexperience as a big league manager really got the better of him in a game that season when a foul pop-up was hit near our home dugout. Carter threw off his mask and followed the flight of the ball until he appeared to have a bead on it. Then, all of a sudden, Fanning leaned out onto the field and started barking instructions at Carter. "You've got room! You've got room!" he yelled. Well, he got a little too excited, because just as the ball was about to fall into Kid's glove, Fanning accidentally bumped him. The ball fell to the ground. Jim's actions cost us an out at a critical time in the season. But it was also about the funniest thing any of us had seen on a baseball field!

Fortunately, Rogers returned from his rib injury on September 12 to pitch six shutout innings in a 2–0 win over the Cubs. That victory broke our long losing streak, and from there, things slowly fell back into place. A seven-game winning streak, our longest of the season, helped us pull ahead of the Cardinals. For the third straight season, we had a chance to win the division title—or in this case, the second-half division title—entering the final weekend of play.

This time around, that's exactly what we did.

On the second-to-last day of the season, we beat the Mets 5–4 at Shea Stadium to clinch the second-half title.

The Cardinals finished with the best overall record in the National League East with a mark of 59–43, but because they failed to win either half of the season, they did not qualify for the playoffs. That was a tough break for them, but the rules were the rules.

Looking back on it, I wish we had been able to celebrate our division title with two people who had recently left us: Dick Williams and Ellis Valentine. I'm sure Dick regretted not being in the dugout when the Expos celebrated a playoff berth. And it had to be hard for Ellis to see us clinch a playoff spot against his new team. He even came into our locker room while we were celebrating. Sadly, his career went into a tailspin after he left the Expos. Some people traced his decline to a game in 1980 when he was hit in the face with a pitch. Others blamed narcotics. After his career ended, Ellis confessed he was already hooked on drugs and alcohol by the time he reached the majors. Fortunately, he got his life together and now runs an organization that helps kids with chemical dependencies.

• • •

Since Major League Baseball implemented the wild-card system in 1995, there have been two rounds of league playoffs every year prior to the World Series. But back in 1981, this was a new concept, and one forced upon baseball by the strike.

If we could take three out of five games against the Phillies in the Division Series, we'd punch a ticket for the National League Championship Series. Our 7–4 record against Philadelphia during the season gave us hope, but we knew we were in for a battle against the defending World Series champions.

The series started with two games in Montreal, the first of which was a matchup of aces named Steve: Rogers and Carlton. During my career, the only pitchers I faced more times than Carlton were Bob Forsch and Rick Reuschel. I knew how good Lefty was and came to understand that if you didn't get to him early in a game, you might not get to him at all.

In Game 1, we pushed a run across in both the first and second innings. Rogers took care of the rest, limiting the Phillies to just one run. We won the first playoff game in franchise history by a score of 3–1.

The second game of the series was nearly a carbon copy of the first. We got a few early runs en route to another 3–1 victory.

We led the series 2–0 and needed just one victory in Philadelphia to advance to the NLCS. That was an attainable goal, even though we hadn't been a very good road team during the season. Unfortunately, our poor play away from Olympic Stadium carried over to the playoffs. Before we knew it, the Phillies had evened the series at two games apiece.

The Phillies had all the momentum going into a decisive Game 5 at Veterans Stadium.

The three All-Stars on our team that season—myself, Raines, and Carter—were all position players. The Expos had built a reputation as an exciting offensive team that beat you with speed and the long ball. Not nearly enough was said about our starting pitchers, especially Rogers.

Steve Rogers was a pitcher I was glad I didn't have to face. He had an unorthodox pitching motion where he'd nearly fall off the mound as he released the ball. His sinking fastball and sweeping curve could make him flat-out dominating at times. From 1977 to 1983, he averaged 15 wins a season, but he never got the attention he deserved. Part of that had to do with playing in Canada. Another reason was he competed in an era when pitchers like Carlton and Nolan Ryan established themselves as among the best hurlers of all time. Rogers was also our player's union representative, a solid presence in the clubhouse and the pitcher who gave us our best chance to win. The rap against Steve was that he didn't thrive in big games, and in the previous couple seasons he had come up on the short end of some important contests. That created a lot of tension between Steve and Dick Williams.

Now with Dick no longer in charge, Steve had a golden opportunity to show he was clutch. In a rematch of Game 1, he opposed Carlton. I had at least one hit in each of the first four games of the series and hoped to keep that streak alive in Game 5. As it turned out, I did, but the offense we needed to win the game didn't come from me or any of the other likely candidates.

In the top of the fifth inning of a scoreless contest, Rogers came to the plate with the bases loaded and one out. Though his batting average of around .150 didn't show it, I knew Rogers could swing the bat. If a pitcher made the mistake of putting one right down the middle, Rogers could slap the ball for a hit. And that's what he did against Carlton, singling up the middle to bring home Larry Parrish and Chris Speier.

Rogers' arm finished the job. He threw a complete-game, six-hit shutout that allowed us to celebrate a 3–0 win and a berth in the NLCS against the Dodgers, who later that afternoon blanked the Astros 4–0 in Game 5 of the other National League Division Series.

The imaginary Dodgers games I played as a kid were about to get very real. It was off to L.A. to play for the chance to go to the World Series.

We dropped the first game of the NLCS at Dodger Stadium but got another great pitching performance, this time from Ray Burris, to salvage a split in Los Angeles. Burris outdueled the Dodgers' young sensation Fernando Valenzuela, who later that year became the first player to win Rookie of the Year and the Cy Young Award in the same season.

We returned to Olympic Stadium needing to win two of three games to earn a trip to the World Series. Rogers beat Jerry Reuss in Game 3 to put us a game away from the Fall Classic. But the Dodgers battled back the next day to tie the series 2–2.

Again, our playoff fate would be determined by one deciding game. But we had to wait an extra day to play it because, in typical Montreal fashion, a cold rain led to the postponement of Game 5 from a Sunday to a Monday afternoon.

Maybe it was fate that Game 5 was played on a Monday because the Dodgers had an outfielder named Rick Monday whose exploits in that game ended up resonating in Montreal for years to come.

It was dry for Game 5 but every bit as cold as you'd expect a mid-October day in Montreal to be. The temperature during the game dipped into the 30s. I had played a lot of games in wintry conditions, but as someone born and raised in Miami, I never tried to be brave by wearing short sleeves. In fact, I tried to bundle up as much as I could without restricting my mobility. I'd go as far as to rub hot ointment and baby oil on my skin. I didn't try to be a hero. I just tried to stay warm.

The final game of the series was another nail-biter that featured Valenzuela and Burris matching each other pitch for pitch. Our best chance to jump on Fernando came in the first inning, but with Expos runners on first and third and nobody out, I grounded into a double play. A run scored, but we missed a great chance to put a crooked number on the board early.

The Dodgers tied the game 1–1 in the fifth, and the score remained that way entering the top of the ninth.

It was then that Fanning made what I and a lot of other people considered a questionable decision. Burris had thrown a lot of pitches, so going to the bullpen made sense. But rather than give the ball to one of our relievers, Fanning called on Rogers, just two days removed from pitching a complete game in Game 3. Not only was Rogers being asked to pitch on short rest, but he was entering the game in an unaccustomed role. Our bullpen had pitched well, especially Reardon, who had given up just six runs in 41⅔ innings since joining the Expos. I thought he should have come in to try to preserve the tie.

Fanning almost looked like a genius after Rogers retired the Dodgers' most dangerous hitters, Steve Garvey and Ron Cey, to start the inning.

That brought up Monday, a left-handed hitter. Fanning stuck with Rogers rather than bringing in a lefty to create a more favorable matchup. We all breathed a collective sigh of relief after Monday hit a towering fly ball down the right-field line. The ball definitely had home run distance but ended up curling foul.

Two pitches later, however, he connected again on a ball to center field. At first, I thought I had a bead on it. But it kept carrying and carrying. The next thing I knew, I was on the warning track looking up as the ball cleared the Olympic Stadium wall.

Now down 2–1, we had three outs to get at least one run.

Valenzuela got the first two outs of the inning before giving up back-to-back walks. At that point, Dodgers manager Tommy Lasorda brought in Bob Welch, who had been a starting pitcher during the regular season, to face Jerry White. With the tying run on second base, White grounded out to end the game and our season.

It was by far the most devastating loss of my career to that point. If I had come through in that final game, we likely would have won. For the series, I was just 3-for-20 without a single RBI. We were all packed and ready to go to New York to play the Yankees in the World Series. I blamed myself for us having to unpack our suitcases. The realization that our season was over hit me right in the gut. The Dodgers proved they were the best team in baseball that season, beating the Yankees in six games.

Despite a major interruption in the middle, a managerial shake-up in the final weeks, and a major disappointment at the end, the 1981 season was and remains a very memorable one, perhaps because all these things happened. By far, the most lasting memory was "Blue Monday" at Olympic Stadium, the afternoon that Rick Monday's home run sent the Dodgers to the World Series instead of us.

7

AMONG THE BEST

FOLLOWING THE 1981 SEASON, I FINISHED SECOND TO MIKE SCHMIDT OF the Phillies in the National League MVP vote and took home a second Gold Glove. During the strike-shortened season, I hit .302 with 24 home runs and 64 RBIs. I learned the Elias Sports Bureau had crunched some numbers and ranked me as the top offensive outfielder in the National League. That was all well and good. I was honored to be recognized for my accomplishments, but at the end of the day, baseball is a team sport. And it nagged at me that I wasn't able to contribute timely hits when we needed them in the '81 playoffs.

As far as I was concerned, the window of opportunity was still wide open for the Expos. The core of the team was still in place. It was just a matter of staying healthy, playing up to our potential, and luring a key free agent or two to cross the border. Our team batting average in 1981 was just .246, so we definitely could have used another hitter.

Making that happen was easier said than done.

The Expos had been trying for years to lure a marquee player. Prior to my rookie season in 1977, Reggie Jackson, a free agent at the time, came to Montreal to discuss signing with the Expos. Reggie hadn't yet achieved "Mr. October" status then but was considered one of the best power hitters and biggest personalities in the game. The local newspapers ran splashy headlines announcing his visit.

I'm not sure Reggie ever had any intention of signing with the Expos, but that didn't stop the organization from rolling out the red carpet and doing everything it could to woo him. And by everything, I mean they offered him a heap of money, something in the neighborhood of $700,000 a year. That was a lot back then even after you factored in the Canadian taxes that the Expos and Blue Jays players had to pay. To put in perspective what Reggie would have earned in Montreal, the three players who ended up playing the outfield for the Expos in 1977—Ellis Valentine, Warren Cromartie, and me—made $85,000 *combined*.

Not surprisingly, Reggie signed with the Yankees, where he earned even more money than that and also got the chance to play in the national spotlight. Montreal, after all, wasn't New York City.

Hopeful the team could come away with a big free-agent prize for the 1982 season, I lobbied Expos president and general manager John McHale to bring in an offensive star. The names I suggested were former Expo Ellis Valentine, who had been shipped to the Mets the previous season, and Dave Parker, a former National League MVP who had enjoyed many good years in Pittsburgh. I guess the price for Parker was too high. That was unfortunate because when he landed in Cincinnati a few years later, he put together some of the best seasons of his career. McHale ruled out bringing back Ellis and told the press that he thought I had "a soft spot for guys who have been in trouble." There were rumors at the time that Ellis had a drug problem. If that was the case, I felt he could benefit from being back in familiar surroundings with his old friends in Montreal.

If a top player had a choice between the Expos or another team, he usually chose the latter, so that meant Montreal had to look to the trade market to add pieces. That's how we acquired veteran players such as Tony Perez in 1977 and Bill "Spaceman" Lee in 1978.

And on the eve of the 1982 season, that's what brought Al Oliver to Montreal. Al was 35 years old when he came over from Texas in exchange for Larry Parrish and Dave Hostetler. A key part of the great Pittsburgh teams of the early and mid-1970s, he was coming off several excellent seasons with the Rangers. I admired Al's game a lot and was looking forward to playing with him in Montreal.

I quickly learned that he and I shared a lot of the same values. My Christian faith had always been a big part of my existence. Al was also faith-driven. During the season, we'd attend the team's Sunday chapel services. Gary Carter was the team leader at the services, which were conducted by a clergyman from Ontario. About 10 or 12 of us huddled before Sunday games to reflect and pray. For me, the services were extremely important, and I tried to apply the lessons of each to my daily life. As part of chapel, I took up a collection that was donated to Baseball Chapel, an international ministry, at the end of the season.

Al and I also got to spend a lot of quality time in the Olympic Stadium training room during the '82 season. I'd be stretched out on one table getting my knees wrapped before games, and he'd be on the other table getting his arm stretched out. Al was playing with a bone spur in his shoulder, an injury that had limited him to the designated hitter's role in Texas. Now that he was back in the National League, he was doing his best to play the field again at first base. During spring training, he was the butt of jokes because some of his throws looked so comical. I didn't know until we took up our almost permanent positions in the training room that he was battling an injury. One of the many things he and I had in common was that even though we were hurting, we didn't feel the need to tell the whole world about it.

As a career .300 hitter, he didn't lack confidence at the plate, and he would say things like, "I could roll out of bed in the morning and get a hit." Or if a guy got jammed at the plate, he'd say, "I never hit a ball that soft." The thing about it was that Al spoke with a stutter that became especially noticeable when he got worked up about something. It became a running joke among my teammates to imitate Al's stutter by going up to him and saying, "I-I-I can hit." Al realized it was all in fun, and over the years he worked with speech therapists to overcome his impediment. Today, he is an ordained deacon and motivational speaker in his native Ohio.

• • •

In 1982, the clubhouse got a lot louder. Cromartie had always talked up a storm. And Al was a very vocal guy, too. And then there was Timmy Raines, fresh off a season in which he finished second to Fernando Valenzuela in Rookie of the Year voting. He came out of his shell in a big way in '82.

By making the All-Star team in each of his first two full seasons, Timmy had shown he was a player with unlimited ability. In my mind, he had the potential to not only be the best leadoff hitter around but one of the best players in the game, period.

Timmy and I clowned around a lot. His nickname "Rock" referred to his solid physical build, but we joked that it also applied to his brick-like hands out in the field. A couple error-filled seasons at second base in the minors had prompted the Expos to switch Timmy to the outfield.

Standing only 5'9", Timmy barely came up to my shoulders, but that didn't keep him from challenging me to a few rounds of slap boxing. I had gained a reputation for having some of the quickest hands in the clubhouse, and Timmy begged me for a title shot. "Let's do this!" he said one day. "I'm tired of people being afraid of you. I'm going to take you right now!" I looked at him skeptically but decided to silence him once and for all. But before I could get my hands set, he jabbed me in the face. "I knew if I didn't get that one punch in, I was gonna get killed," he later said of his sucker punch, after which he took off running immediately. I had speed, but I didn't have Timmy's kind of speed! He got away, but for weeks afterwards, I could tell he was looking over his shoulder to see if I was coming.

Timmy, who as a kid shared a bedroom with his four brothers, kept the messiest locker I've ever seen. Mine was next to his, which gave me a good view of the extreme disorder. Timmy wasn't going to win the Good Housekeeping Award, but even his messes were funny. On one of the few occasions he cleaned out his space, he found several crushed hard-boiled eggs wedged in the back.

"How long have those been in there?" I asked him.

"I have no idea," he said laughing. "I don't remember putting them in there."

I really enjoyed spending time with Timmy. We went out to dinner, rode to the ballpark together, and our wives were best friends. He was extremely upbeat and never seemed to let anything bother him. He became like a little brother to me.

There was more going on in Timmy's life than I knew about, though.

A lot of things concerning the team played out in public. The media glare of Montreal wasn't as bright as in most major league cities, but with each passing year the local press got savvier. When the team started winning, the national media also started to pay more attention to the once-forgotten Expos. When Dick Williams began clashing with his players and upper management, the beat writers knew about it. When players grumbled about Jim Fanning, they eagerly reported it.

There was one type of story you rarely saw in print, however. And it wasn't an accident, either. It was fairly easy at the time for players to hide their use of marijuana and amphetamines, the most popular drugs of the day. No one popped pills or smoked dope out in the open, and there was no drug testing. It never even crossed my mind to dabble in any of that stuff. The only "drug" I took was an occasional Advil or Darvocet, which was legal at the time, to ease the pain in my knees.

When cocaine entered the picture, the equation changed. The destructive nature of the drug made it more difficult for players to hide their addiction.

Cocaine was a social drug, a party drug, and the drug of choice for Timmy.

He had managed to keep his habit under wraps for a while, but then warning signs started to emerge. He failed to show up to the ballpark one day late in the '82 season and was discovered passed out in his apartment. I didn't ask too many questions about that incident, but the Expos organization apparently did.

I wouldn't find out the scope of what Timmy was dealing with until after the season.

It was then that Timmy publicly acknowledged the extent of his cocaine problem in an article in *The (Montreal) Gazette*. He revealed he had been in a 30-day drug treatment program for his addiction and spared no details in telling the story of how the drug had taken hold of him. He talked about snorting $50,000 worth of cocaine during the previous season. And he admitted keeping a vial of cocaine in his uniform pocket during games.

Timmy wasn't the first athlete to experience the pitfalls of achieving fame at a young age. After dark, he was hanging around with the wrong crowd—and he may not have been the only Expos player in that group. As he later explained, "My goal was to make the majors. And once I made it, I got sidetracked. Montreal was one of those party towns, and I was young and playing well and probably got big-headed. That led me to stray from what I was supposed to be doing."

His situation concerned me deeply. It was more than a matter of how his addiction might affect his play. He had a young son, Timmy Jr., who he loved dearly and who depended on him. I didn't want to see drugs ruin Timmy's life and decided I needed to do something. I just wasn't sure exactly what. This was new to me. I had never been close to anybody who was trying to beat a drug problem.

I thought about the situation before going to talk to Timmy. I told him, "I don't look down on you for this. Not at all. I'm here for you. And if there's anything I can do, don't hesitate to ask. I know you can beat this."

Timmy welcomed the offer and took it a step further.

"You're probably the best player I've seen play, and I want to pattern myself after you," he told me. "From this point on, I want you to show me the way. I'm going to be in your back pocket. Wherever you go, I'm going. Whatever you do, I'm doing."

I think what he needed most at that point was what I had already given him—loyal friendship. I tried to be supportive and make myself available to him whenever he wanted to talk. Timmy beat his drug problem. A couple years later, he named his second son after me and made me the baby's godfather. Andre Raines and I share the same birthday—July 10. Where once I admired Timmy as a ballplayer, I came to admire him as a man for the courage he showed in beating his problem. He cleaned up his act, and his string of consecutive All-Star appearances that started in 1981 continued all the way through 1987.

• • •

On the personal front, Vanessa and I celebrated our third wedding anniversary after the 1981 season. Everything was good between us, and we had started thinking about starting a family. I enjoyed watching my teammates interact with their kids, and I realized I was ready to be a father. I had no doubt that Vanessa would be a great mom.

Well, for us it didn't happen nearly as quickly or as smoothly as we hoped. Over the course of several years, we tried and tried, but Vanessa didn't get pregnant. We wondered what was going on, but we decided to be patient and wait. Only much later did Vanessa get a medical diagnosis that explained the problem.

Vanessa and I got to experience a lot of great things together while I was playing for the Expos. An off-season trip we made to Asia ranks right up there. I had some endorsement opportunities over there, and we traveled for 10 days to Taiwan, Japan, and Hong Kong. During the season, Vanessa came to games and became comfortable in her role as a homemaker. From time to time, we went out and enjoyed Montreal.

For me, an ideal night out was dinner and a movie. I remember watching *One Flew Over the Cuckoo's Nest* starring Jack Nicholson when it was showing. I loved the end of the movie when the character named Chief, acting on the inspiration of Nicholson's character, busted out of a psychiatric hospital.

I didn't try out for my high school baseball team until my junior year. My coach at Southwest Miami High School was impressed with my bat speed and helped me improve my fundamentals.

When I was 13, I joined a traveling team that featured the best baseball players from my area. I mostly played shortstop, but I also did a little pitching and catching. In the team picture, I was wearing catchers' gear.

The baseball team at Southwest Miami High School had been all-white prior to Paul Comeau, far left, becoming head coach my junior year. He and his assistant coach, Al Hinson, far right, turned Southwest into a winning team. There I am as a senior in the front row, second from the left.

My grandmother, Eunice Taylor, who I called "Mamma," was the spiritual pillar of my family, a strong believer in education, and a tremendous influence in my life. She always reminded me to believe in myself and to believe in God. She succumbed to Alzheimer's disease in 1987.

My mom, Mattie Brown, was just 15 years old when I was born in 1954. She was a wonderful cook and one of the most loving and caring people you'd ever meet. She passed away in 2006.

My father didn't stick around after I was born, but my uncles Curtis, John, and Theodore Taylor made sure I had strong male role models growing up. Here I am later in life standing between John, left, and Curtis, right. Theodore, who played minor league baseball in the Pittsburgh Pirates system, passed away in 1985.

Al Oliver was a great friend and teammate, not to mention an outstanding hitter. He and I both won Silver Slugger Awards for our offensive accomplishments during the 1982 season.

On July 13, 1982, the All-Star Game was played at Olympic Stadium in Montreal. It was the first time the Midsummer Classic was held outside the United States. I joined teammates Gary Carter and Tim Raines for a photo before a game the National League won 4–1.

My Cubs teammate Shawon Dunston and I shared a lot of laughs together. This picture was taken at a magazine shoot in the Arizona desert during spring training. I was hesitant to do the shoot because I was afraid I might stumble upon a snake!

The Dawson family before a game at Wrigley Field in 1992. My wife, Vanessa, is holding our daughter, Amber. I'm holding our son, Darius. Both of our children were born in Chicago.

After the 1992 season, I became a member of the Boston Red Sox. It was difficult leaving Chicago, but Vanessa and I enjoyed our time in Boston. Unfortunately, a player's strike wiped out the last two months of my second and final season there and led to the cancellation of the 1994 World Series.

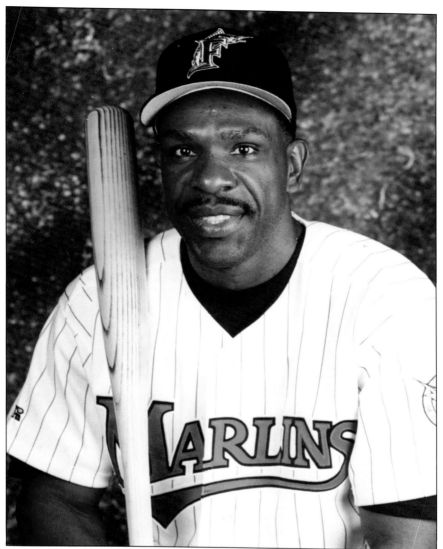

After 11 seasons in Montreal, six in Chicago, and two in Boston, I returned home to finish out my career with the Florida Marlins. It was a thrill to play in front of my family and friends for two seasons. In 2000, I went to work for the Marlins as a special assistant.

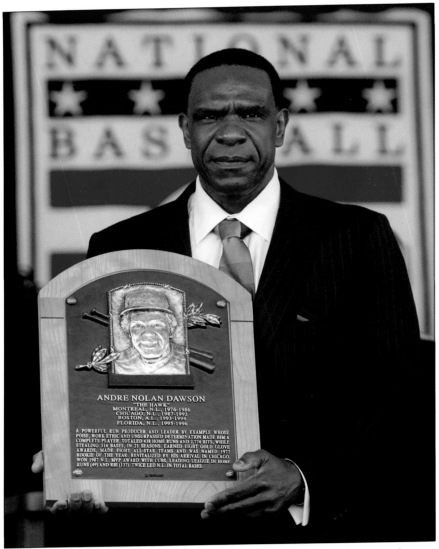

My selection to the Baseball Hall of Fame in 2010 was the culmination of a childhood dream. As I said during my induction speech: "If you love this game, it will love you back." I felt a great sense of joy every time I took the field during my career and am honored to be among those enshrined in Cooperstown.

While I liked sitting in darkened movie theaters, Vanessa had a good time going to discos with the other Expos' wives. In fact, she became such a regular at a Montreal club called Oz that a photo of her on the dance floor ended up in a gossip column in the local paper. The story claimed Vanessa and her friends were being treated like VIPs because their husbands played for the Expos. That didn't sit well with her, nor did she like seeing her picture in the paper. That's when she decided to cut back on her visits to Oz.

My new contract that kicked in before the previous season meant I had more disposable income. I had gotten my driver's license when I left college in 1975 but didn't own a car during my first years in the majors. The first vehicle I bought was for my mom, who didn't have a car either. That was in my rookie year. I then bought myself a Ford van that I had customized.

My $1 million salary from the Expos freed me up to splurge a little, and in the following years, I bought a Mercedes and a Ford Bronco.

Another place my money went was toward my wardrobe. I loved hitting the clothing stores with Cro and Al Oliver. My favorite thing to shop for was shoes. Al would join me on trips to places like the Brass Boot in Chicago, a real high-end shoe store, even though he was a self-described "pants and sweater guy."

One place Al wouldn't step foot, however, were the hair salons a few of us periodically visited to get our hair Jheri curled, which was a popular style at the time among African Americans. When I came into the clubhouse after visiting the salon, I was always afraid that a teammate would do something to mess up my hair. That led to a stern warning: "Whatever you do, do not touch my hair!" Looking back on it, I'm not sure anybody really intended to touch our chemically treated curls. And if someone had, I'm not sure it would have messed it up any more than a baseball cap did.

My hairstyle led to a funny moment in Pittsburgh that season. Cro, Al, and I were eating lunch when a young man excitedly approached us. He pointed at me and got really excited. I was used to being recognized in Montreal, albeit with less fanfare, but I had no idea I was so well known in other cities.

I could tell he was having a hard time containing his enthusiasm. "Well, I'll be, if it's not *Lionel Richie!*" he blurted out.

I guess I wasn't that big of a celebrity outside of Montreal, nor was I the only black man my age with Jheri-curls in Pittsburgh that day. We later learned Lionel was in town for a concert.

My teammates laughed all night long over that one.

· · ·

Another case of mistaken identity that year wasn't the least bit funny. In fact, it led to one of the scariest moments of my life.

In May 1982, my teammate Jerry White and I were out looking for a stroller for his daughter at Eaton's department store in Montreal. We had just gotten off the escalator when we were confronted from behind by two men. Next thing we knew, they were pushing us up against a wall. "Put your hands up and don't move!" one of them shouted in French-accented English.

All I could think at that moment was that a teammate was playing some kind of bad joke on us. Then I felt something cold and metallic press into the back of my head. Out of the corner of my eye, I saw the men behind us. I wasn't sure, but they appeared to be plainclothes police officers.

If this wasn't a robbery attempt, what in the world was it?

As I stood there with a gun to my head, they instructed me to kick a shopping bag I had been holding away from me. I did as I was told and waited helplessly for whatever was going to happen next.

Luckily at this point, one of the officers got a better look at us and recognized who we were—or more accurately, who we *weren't*. "These aren't the guys we're looking for," he told his partner.

Apparently the detectives had been stalking two robbery suspects, and wouldn't you know it, Jerry and I fit the description. By that, I mean we were young, black, and male. To this day, I'm thankful I didn't turn around to confront the officers. That might have been disastrous. The guys apologized to us profusely and went on their way.

Jerry was much more upset than me about the incident. Later that week, we saw the same officers walking on Saint Catherine Street, and Jerry shouted out to them, "Stick a gun to anybody's head lately?!"

It was reported in the press that I was very bitter about what happened at the department store. In reality, I tried not to let it affect my positive feelings toward

Montreal. It was the only incident I experienced there with racial overtones. My black teammates and I agreed Montreal was a very open-minded place. As I said, Jackie Robinson played a season of minor league ball in Montreal before making history with the Brooklyn Dodgers. He was well-received by the locals back then, and we were treated equally well nearly a half-century later.

That's not to say every black player or coach was happy with the Expos organization. After being traded from the Expos to the Angels in 1984, utility man Derrel Thomas accused team management of racial insensitivity. "Black players on the team have to wonder about their future here," he told a reporter. Felipe Alou, a coach in the organization from the Dominican Republic, chimed in by saying, "Maybe one day the Expos will hire a black as manager, but I won't live to see it. Maybe it will happen in the next century or the century after."

Felipe was proven wrong when the Expos hired him as manager in 1992. He remained in that position for 10 seasons, managing more games than any other skipper in Expos history.

I always felt the Expos were good to black players. And there were always a lot of us around. I remember being out on the field with Al before a game and commenting, "It's kind of dark out here, ain't it?" At the time, we had something like 10 black players on the roster. Unlike some teams, the Expos looked for and nurtured young black talent. Al seemed to think so, too. And he was an authority on the subject, having been part of the first all-black starting lineup in major league history for the Pirates on September 1, 1971.

• • •

As a team we had spent several years building to where we could field a team that could compete with Pittsburgh and Philadelphia, the clubs that perennially vied for supremacy in the National League East. Our division title in 1981 showed we had achieved that goal. But we weren't the only team that had turned itself into a contender. Despite not making the playoffs in the strike-shortened season, the Cardinals owned the division's best overall record in 1981. With Lonnie Smith and Willie McGee at the top of the lineup, the Cardinals were dangerous on the basepaths even before champion base-stealer Vince Coleman arrived on the scene in 1985. Keith Hernandez and George Hendrick could be counted on to knock in runs. And Joaquin Andujar, in his first full season in St. Louis, had ace potential.

In short, the Cardinals had added themselves to the mix of teams that could battle for a title. An already competitive division had become that much more so.

I didn't expect Jim Fanning to be managing the Expos at the end of the 1981 season, and I was doubly surprised when he was brought back as skipper the following season. Yes, he had overseen our playoff run that abruptly ended in the National League Championship Series, but in the eyes of the players, he was still very much a front-office guy. I thought the brass shared that opinion and would return him to his position as player development director once they had time to conduct a search for a more experienced manager.

But that search didn't take place.

The sentiment in the clubhouse was that Jim lacked the leadership qualities necessary to take the team to the next level. Whereas Dick Williams was criticized for being too mean, Fanning, or Gentleman Jim as he was nicknamed, had a reputation for being too nice. Even when he tried to be tough, like the time he challenged any player in the clubhouse to a fight, it didn't quite ring true.

Jim was okay with me, though, and I had no reason at the time to question the motives or decision-making skills of the front office or ownership.

The team's majority owner, Charles Bronfman, had been around since the team's inception in 1969. He kept a fairly low profile, occasionally popping up at spring training but otherwise staying out of sight. He wasn't nearly as hands-on as owners like George Steinbrenner in New York or Charlie Finley in Oakland. I imagine Mr. Bronfman spent most of his time tending to the family liquor business, the Seagram Company, which was one of the biggest and most successful in the world.

John McHale was the "suit" players saw on an almost daily basis, and I felt really comfortable when he came around the clubhouse. He rarely criticized his players publicly and seemed to trust in us. I also admired the job he did overseeing the Expos scouting and player development systems. The "homegrown" talent that came up through our farm system was a testament to his ability to spot and nurture young players. When my relationship with others in the front office later deteriorated, I always remained on good terms with John.

Before the 1982 season, the organization took a big step toward the future when it tried to lock up Gary Carter for many years by signing him to the most lucrative contract in team history, a seven-year deal worth more than $14 million.

I was quoted in the press at the time as saying that the contract was excessive and perhaps not good for team morale. That may have been the prevailing attitude in the clubhouse, where Gary wasn't universally liked, but looking back, I realize Kid was worth every penny. He was the game's best young catcher who had made several All-Star appearances and finished second in MVP voting in 1980. In baseball, it's not easy to just go out and replace a star catcher. By signing Gary to a big contract, the organization was showing a commitment to keeping the team moving in a positive direction.

Too bad they reversed course on that a couple years into Gary's contract.

The 1981 season gave us a taste of playoff baseball that we wanted to experience again.

On Opening Day in Philadelphia, I hit a home run off Larry Christenson in the first inning of a game we won 2–0. The shut-out victory by Steve Rogers was his first win in a season opener in seven tries. What was remarkable by today's standards was that Rogers went the distance in his first start of the season in near-freezing temperatures.

But the season was only a few weeks old before Fanning and the front office had to deal with a minor revolt. As I said, not every player was thrilled with how Fanning ran the team. One player who definitely had problems with him was Bill Lee. I remember the time Fanning held a team meeting to get us fired up. When he finished, he asked if anyone had questions. Space's hand shot up. But he didn't really have a question. He just wanted to express some of the anti-establishment views he was famous for.

The incident that put an abrupt end to Space's tenure in Montreal resulted from a decision by the front office to release his best friend on the team, Rodney Scott, who was a favorite of former manager Dick Williams but less well-liked by Fanning. When Space got to the ballpark and saw Rodney cleaning out his locker, he absolutely lost it. He protested the move by ripping his jersey down the middle, writing a nasty note, and bolting from the stadium to a local bar. Next thing we knew, he had joined Rodney as an ex-Expo.

Still, Fanning managed not to lose the clubhouse, and we got off to a good start in 1982, stringing together three consecutive winning months that put us in a first-place tie with the Cardinals in late June. Gentleman Jim was once again exceeding expectations by simply letting a good team go out and play.

By the All-Star break, however, we had fallen to fourth place behind the Phillies, Cardinals, and Pirates. The second half looked to be a four-team race. I went into the break with 11 home runs and 45 RBIs, a .305 batting average, and 21 stolen bases, pretty good numbers considering I had battled a wrist problem most of the season.

Four of my teammates and I were selected for the All-Star Game that season. What made the honor even more significant was that the game was played at Olympic Stadium, the first Major League Baseball All-Star Game ever held outside the United States. Carter, who led all players in fan balloting, Timmy, and I were voted in as starters. Steve Rogers was tapped as the starting pitcher. And Al, who at 35 was putting up career numbers, made the team as a reserve.

Getting to represent the Expos organization and the country of Canada was a great thrill. With the Toronto Blue Jays struggling, we had even more firmly established ourselves as Canada's team in the early 1980s. Attendance at Toronto games was steadily dropping, while ours was on the rise. We had five All-Star representatives in 1982. The Blue Jays had one.

More than 59,000 people packed Olympic Stadium for the game. And for the 11th straight year, the National League beat the American League, this time by a 4–1 score. Dave Concepcion of the Reds took home the Most Valuable Player award, but the Expos delegation left its mark on the game. Four of the National League's eight hits, including one from me, were supplied by Expos, and Steve Rogers pitched three innings of one-run ball to pick up the win.

The All-Star Game had come to Montreal. Now we wanted to bring another division title, and hopefully, a World Series to Olympic Stadium for the first time.

But it wasn't to be.

Nobody dominated the division in 1982, but the Cardinals emerged on top with a 92-win season. We finished 86–76, a fourth straight winning season but one that only earned us third place. In a complete reversal from previous seasons, we struggled to win games at home while putting together a winning record on the road. That was disappointing considering the team drew 2.3 million fans to Olympic Stadium, the most in franchise history. If we had been able to string together just a few more home victories, it's safe to say we would have gotten back to the playoffs for the second consecutive year. As it turned out, for the third time in four seasons, the team that came out on top in the National League East went on to win the World Series.

A lot of guys had good seasons, including myself, Carter, Raines, and third baseman Tim Wallach. I hit .301 and put up decent power numbers. But my career-high 39 stolen bases were especially gratifying. Coming out of high school, I was close to catching on with the Kansas City Royals, but they passed on me because they felt I lacked speed. I was proud of the fact that I had become an accomplished base stealer at the major league level.

Only two Expos had great seasons in 1982: Steve Rogers, whose 19 wins and league-best 2.40 ERA made him the runner-up in Cy Young voting, and my new friend, Al Oliver, who did just about everything he could to put us over the top. In his 15th year in the majors, he led the league in average, hits, RBIs, and total bases.

It's a shame that players like Al, who had more than 2,700 hits in his career to go along with a lifetime average of .303, never got real consideration for the Hall of Fame. In 1991, the first year he was eligible for the Hall, he got less than 5 percent of the vote, which meant he never again appeared on the ballot. A guy like Al deserved more serious consideration for his longevity and consistency. But his chances weren't helped by his reputation for being unfriendly to the media. It's the writers, after all, who largely control whether or not a player gets to Cooperstown.

Al talked about seeing Roberto Clemente get his 3,000th hit in 1972 when they both played for the Pittsburgh Pirates. He admired Clemente greatly and vowed one day to follow in his footsteps by reaching that milestone. He had a chance to do that near the end of his career, which would have guaranteed his enshrinement in Cooperstown. But after leaving the Expos in 1983, he couldn't find a ballclub willing to let him play every day. I know it bothers him that he didn't get a chance to fulfill his goal of 3,000 hits. Of not making it to Cooperstown, he has said, "It wasn't me. It was baseball. I had a lot of gas left in the tank. I could still run and hit, but I was thrown around like I was trash."

• • •

After the 1982 season, Fanning finally returned to the front office. He was replaced as manager by Bill Virdon, a veteran skipper who had taken the Pirates and Astros to the postseason. Virdon was the fourth Expos manager since I came up in 1976.

More so than his predecessors, Virdon was very hands-on and personally oversaw a lot of our drills. That was fine with me. I always felt it was up to players to adjust to the style and personality of the manager and not the other way around. I didn't have a problem with how hard Virdon worked us at spring training because I always got myself into good shape before camp started. My off-season regimen was strenuous. I took October off to let my body regenerate from any nagging injuries. But in November, I'd start working out with my cousin, Donald Napier. I would go to the gym in the morning and lift weights. In the afternoon when Donald got off work, we'd do batting practice. Then we'd run a couple miles and do sprints. We'd finish the day by throwing. All in all, it was about five hours of working out a day.

One of Virdon's favorite drills was standing about 120' from the outfielders and smoking line drives right at our feet. On the grass field at spring training, you had to be mindful of whether the ball was going to skip past you or take a bad hop and hit you. The objective of the drill was to get us to stay low and try to read what a ball would do. It was a challenging exercise, but one I benefited from.

In a game against the Dodgers in 1983, I fielded a ball near the wall in center field and threw it on a line to third base to nail Steve Sax, who was trying to stretch a double into a triple. After the game, Virdon said it was the best throw he had ever seen.

In 1983, we again competed for a division title well into September, but after the Phillies swept us in a make-up doubleheader with 10 days left in the season, our fate was sealed. On the last day of the season, we had a twin bill against the Mets. I came into the day hitting .301, and because the Phillies had already clinched the division, Virdon gave me the choice of sitting out the game so that I would be guaranteed to finish with a batting average over .300 for the fourth straight season. There was no way I was going to skip games in order to preserve my average. I went 1-for-8 in the doubleheader to finish the season at .299.

Although I didn't hit .300, I still felt great about the 1983 season. It was another All-Star year, albeit one in which the American League broke its 11-game losing streak against the National League. I really found myself as a hitter that season and was able to combine the best assets of a contact and power hitter.

I finished second to Dale Murphy in National League MVP balloting. I also led the National League in hits with 189 and established new career highs with 32 home runs and 113 RBIs. I accomplished these feats by embracing my tendency to be a free swinger or "bad ball" hitter. I realized I was never going to be a patient hitter, so I didn't even try to work the count. I walked only 38 times that season. If a pitcher came in with a first pitch that was up in the zone, I'd hack at it and usually make contact.

The best part of 1983 was that my knees felt good. But that would not be the case for much longer.

8

A TURN FOR THE WORSE

AS ONE OF MY GOOD FRIENDS, TIM RAINES, WAS WORKING TO TAKE BACK control of his life from drugs, another was contemplating a huge change of scenery.

Warren Cromartie, a .280 career hitter and great defensive outfielder, was a free agent at the end of the 1983 season. He had established himself as an important part of our team, but when it came time to negotiate a new contract with the Expos, the team didn't expend much effort in trying to re-sign him. They made an offer somewhere in the neighborhood of $400,000 a season, which was roughly the average annual salary for major leaguers at the time. As a proven veteran, Cro deserved more.

Figuring he could do better elsewhere, he tested the market and found some teams, including San Francisco and Boston, that were willing to pay him more. He told me he liked the idea of playing at Fenway Park, which was a good ballpark for lefties like him. But he wasn't so sure the Red Sox were the best organization for him. A lot of black players were aware of the fact that Boston was the last major league team to integrate, and Jim Rice was one of the few blacks who played for the Red Sox in the early 1980s.

Well, if Cro had reservations about the diversity of the team in Boston, I'm not sure what he expected to find in Japan. But when the Tokyo Yomiuri Giants offered him a three-year, $2.5 million contract, he decided he had no choice but to go. He said, "If they'll pay me that kind of money, I'll go and play, homie. I'm not going over there to eat sushi."

So Cro packed his bags and took off for Asia. His departure caused me to reflect on how much things had changed since I joined the Expos in September

1976. That team was in the midst of a 107-loss season that typified the organization's failures to that point. At the time, there wasn't much else to do but look to the future. In my first full season in the majors, we had five everyday players, including myself, who were 23 years old or younger. Cro, Ellis Valentine, and I comprised the starting outfield. And it didn't take long for the three of us to get the attention of the league. We were one of the reasons the team shed its reputation as a perennial loser.

Other players were also on the move following the 1983 season, including Al Oliver, who had one excellent and one very good season in Montreal. Following Al's departure, several players kept the first-base job warm until a prospect named Andres Galarraga established himself as an everyday player in 1987.

Despite all the changes happening around me, I was still committed to playing out my career in Montreal. I didn't know how many years I'd play in the majors, but in the back of my mind, I had set a goal of about 15.

Going into the 1984 season, I needed to get used to a change of my own, one the organization believed would help prolong my career. Based mostly on concerns about my knees, the decision was made to move me from center field, where I had won four consecutive Gold Gloves, to right field to fill the vacancy left by Cromartie. The thinking was that there would be less running and general wear and tear on my knees in right. Timmy took my place in center for the '84 season.

I didn't have any reservations about the switch, but it required some work to get used to the new position. I found that the ball gets on you quicker in right field and sometimes slices away from you.

The best thing about 1984 was that I got to play alongside one of baseball's all-time great players, competitors, and personalities when the Expos signed 43-year-old Pete Rose, who the Phillies had let go after a five-year run with the team that included two World Series appearances. Following his release, the Phillies flew Pete to Philadelphia for a farewell press conference, an unusual event for a player who had just been shown the door. But Pete was a legend in Philadelphia, just as he had been in Cincinnati earlier in his career, and the decision to cut him loose was delicate from a public relations standpoint.

Pete tested the free-agent waters and discovered that a player his age, even one on the brink of 4,000 hits, wasn't a sought-after commodity. So he went home to Cincinnati and got into the best shape of his life. Then his agent made calls to a bunch of different teams. Only one, the Expos, expressed real interest. In January 1984, Montreal signed him for $700,000.

Pete had established himself as a very good first baseman with the Phillies and hoped to win an everyday job with the Expos. During spring training, manager Bill Virdon took a poll of his coaches and instructors, asking them whether they thought Pete should play first base or left field, his position for many years in Cincinnati. Pete would have preferred to play first, and all of Virdon's underlings agreed that was the better position for him. Virdon, however, cast his vote for putting Pete in the outfield. And a single vote from the manager was enough to overrule everyone else. Pete wasn't real happy with Virdon. Eventually, they reached a compromise, and Pete played both positions during his time with the team.

Terry "Tito" Francona, who later went on to manage the Red Sox to two World Series championships, got most of the starts at first base. Many years later, Pete, always a very outspoken guy, remarked at how surprised he was to see Francona managing a team. "If you had taken a survey in the Expos clubhouse of the player who was *least* likely to become a manger, Tito Francona would have won," Pete said. "He was a prankster. He was goofy."

On that topic, I played with a lot of guys who later became skippers, Joe Girardi, Lloyd McClendon, and Brad Mills, just to name a few. Would I have pegged any of them as future managers? The answer is no.

Pete was a jolt of fresh air. What a character! He knew baseball in and out and, like me, was always one of the first guys to arrive at the ballpark. By the time most players wandered into the clubhouse, he was already suited up and walking around with his bat. He'd have one-on-one conversations with players about the finer points of the game. He was also an amateur statistician who would take teammates aside and say things like, "You're hitting .450 over the past two weeks. Keep it up." He played the game with every ounce of his being and at the same time was its biggest fan.

It was with the Expos that Pete collected his 4,000[th] career hit early in the 1984 season against the Phillies. He also set baseball's all-time games-played record while playing for Montreal.

Pete's fiery personality was also on full display that season. In one memorable incident, he got into a clubhouse scuffle with a radio reporter he thought had been overly critical of him and other players. Pete and Doug Flynn, a friend of Pete's on the team, chased the reporter from the clubhouse, with Flynn shouting, "You'd better get out of here before I take a punch at you, too!"

Pete battled elbow and heel injuries in his months with us. He talked about how the cortisone shot he got after hurting his heel in Philadelphia was the most painful thing he had experienced in his career. Pete was hitting better than .300 into June, but after that, his average started to drop. Then his playing time was cut. In mid-August, the Expos dealt him to Cincinnati for a young infielder named Tom Lawless. Just like that, Pete's brief Canadian adventure was over. The trade went down while the Expos were in San Francisco. Pete left the clubhouse before any other players even arrived. He got to say formal goodbyes when we played Cincinnati later in the season.

With the Reds, Pete served as player-manager. It didn't matter to him that he was the one making out the lineup. If he didn't think he deserved a starting spot, I'm sure he would have benched himself. But playing every day for the Reds, Pete hit .365 during the last seven weeks of the 1984 season. "Even though I was 43 years old, I was playing like I was a kid who was brought up from the minors in September," he said. "If that kid does well, you're going to give him a shot the next season. That's why I had a chance to keep playing in 1985."

Pete broke Ty Cobb's all-time hit record of 4,191 the following season. He continued as player-manager until 1986 and then retired as a player. He continued managing the Reds for a few more years after that.

To this day, Pete remains a good friend of mine. Based on his accomplishments on the baseball diamond, he obviously should be in the Hall of Fame. He was an outstanding player, but that doesn't mean he was without flaws. After initially denying he gambled on baseball games while managing the Reds, he eventually admitted his mistake. Despite that apology, he remains officially banished from baseball and ineligible for the Hall of Fame. His critics say his actions hurt the integrity of the game, but it's not as if everybody in the Hall was an ideal poster boy for the game of baseball. It's just Pete has always been judged by a higher standard.

• • •

The chance to play with Pete was a highlight of an otherwise disappointing 1984 season. Just a year earlier, I had turned in my best season in the majors so far. But I followed it up with my worst.

Though I won another Gold Glove in my first year playing right field, my numbers were down in nearly every offensive category. My batting average was a career-low .248. The explanation for the decline wasn't hard to figure out. Between the off-season surgeries and in-season treatments, my knees were really starting to bother me.

The move to right field had helped reduce some of the pounding on my knees, but the Olympic Stadium turf was still the Olympic Stadium turf. And every time I moved on that hard surface, it surely did more damage to them.

I had responded well to an operation on my left knee after the 1982 season, but an arthroscopic procedure the following year to clean up damaged cartilage and shave down bone spurs in my right knee didn't take as well. And that affected my play.

Hitting is all about timing, rhythm, and feeling comfortable at the plate. Even the slightest change in routine can influence your overall mechanics. I liked to put my weight on my back leg when hitting, but that became hard to do during periods when my right knee felt weak. To help cope with the pain, I started wearing one cleat and one turf shoe when I hit. It was the only way I could dig in at the plate. If I got on base, I'd change into the other turf shoe.

In 1982, I stole a career-high 39 bases. Two years later, I stole just 13. The Canadian press, seizing on a comparison it knew the country would understand, wondered if I was the next Bobby Orr, a hockey player whose career ended prematurely due to injuries.

I resolved to battle through the pain, but I think the Expos were starting to worry I had transformed from one of the top players in the game to someone whose career was on the downturn.

I didn't share that view.

I maintained the same everyday post-surgery routine with each operation. I'd work with team therapists to get my knees as strong as possible. Then I'd have them iced down and taped up. If I was in pain, I'd take an Advil, as long as my stomach could tolerate it. Sometimes if one of the knees flared up, I'd have it drained and miss a couple games. Based on my past problems and history of surgeries, I knew

I'd never be 100 percent healthy. But if I was 75 percent, I wanted to be in the lineup, even if that meant I wasn't going to be able to do some of the things I had done earlier in my career, like play center field or steal a lot of bases. It created some mental stress to know I was more limited than before. But if I adapted to what my body would allow, I knew I could remain a very productive player.

I struggled in 1984, and so did the Expos who, with a lot of fresh faces in the lineup, finished with a losing record for the first time since 1978.

The National League East continued to get tougher as the Cubs became the fifth different team in six years to win the division. For the Cubs, it was their first trip to the postseason since 1945. They went on to lose the 1984 National League Championship Series in five games to the Padres, who were managed by former Expos manager Dick Williams.

• • •

While our competitors were building teams capable of winning right away, Montreal was taking a different approach.

After the '84 season, the Expos traded Gary Carter to the Mets for third baseman Hubie Brooks and three young players. Two years after signing Gary to the biggest contract in team history, the Expos unloaded him in what most people viewed as a salary dump. The team also got rid of other veteran players over the next couple of years, including Bill Gullickson and Jeff Reardon.

When the Expos let go of Steve Rogers in May 1985, I became the last remaining player on the team who had come up through the Expos system in the mid-1970s. Rogers, who had been the ace of the pitching staff for many years, had struggled with arm problems, prompting his release and early retirement.

It wasn't just players who were coming and going. The team also decided to switch managers again. Bill Virdon didn't make it through the 1984 season. And in a repeat of 1981, Jim Fanning came down from the front office for the season's final stretch. But unlike his first stint, Fanning's second go-around as manager was brief. General manager John McHale was also relieved of his duties, though he stayed on with the organization as team president. Murray Cook, who I would get to know well in the coming years, took over as GM.

One of Cook's first orders of business was to hire Buck Rodgers as manager. Buck had managed the Expos Triple A affiliate in Indianapolis. I came to respect him, mainly because I felt he respected me.

The Carter trade in particular got me thinking about my own future with the team. Up until that point, Nick Buoniconti, a former NFL star with the Miami Dolphins, had represented me in contract negotiations. He wasn't a big-time agent like some others out there, but we hit it off when I was introduced to him by Cromartie, who was one of Nick's clients. Nick helped me negotiate a six-year, $6 million contract after the 1980 season. But with storm clouds brewing in Montreal, I felt I needed a premier baseball agent in my corner.

That's why I replaced Nick with Dick Moss, who represented players including Carter and Nolan Ryan. "I want to be a career Expo," I told Dick at our first meeting. Maybe I was daydreaming when I said that, but I felt like I had earned a chance to negotiate in good faith with the organization about continuing my career in Montreal. I hoped the top front-office guys—McHale, Cook, and former Expos pitcher Bill Stoneman—would give us a straight answer on whether they thought I had a future with the team. If the Expos planned to continue going in a more youthful and less expensive direction, then I would consider other options. I still had two years left on my contract and hoped everything would get worked out well before it expired.

Unfortunately, I turned in another subpar season in 1985. My power numbers were okay, but I finished with an average in the .250s.

On a positive note, I felt I was making positive contributions in the clubhouse. Being surrounded by mostly young players in 1985 thrust me into a position where I took more of an overt leadership role. I tried to lead by example and give advice, just as Tony Perez and Dave Cash had done for me earlier in my career.

There were some fun days at the ballpark in 1985. One came at Wrigley Field when I hit two home runs and had six RBIs all in the same inning. It was the second time in my career I hit two homers in a single inning. (The other time was in 1978 in a 19–0 win against the Braves.) At the time, Willie McCovey was the only other player to have done that. We built a big lead against the Cubs that day and hung on to win 17–15.

My sense of awe at Wrigley Field grew with each visit. It was electrifying to observe the excitement of a city so hungry for a winner. The atmosphere of the place when the Cubs won the division in 1984 was unlike anything I had seen before. As a visiting player, I had always been the recipient of harsh treatment from the Bleacher Bums. That usually took the form of heckling and beer showers. Maybe this was my imagination, but in 1985 I sensed the Chicago faithful had developed a different opinion of me. The females in the stands shouted words of affection. And their male companions started giving me a break on the beer showers. I started contemplating what it would be like to play in that ballpark and city every day, and how it would feel to be a friend and not a foe to those fans.

• • •

After the 1985 season, I started hearing trade rumors, and I kept hearing them for the next 10 months. The Yankees and several other teams seemed interested in me. Some local reporters were writing stories all but guaranteeing I'd be dealt before Opening Day in 1986.

At one point, it looked like I was headed to the White Sox in exchange for outfielder Daryl Boston. When that story hit the papers, a member of the Expos grounds crew, who happened to be a native Chicagoan and White Sox fan, approached me before a game.

"Word out of Chicago is you might be going to the White Sox," he said.

"Oh, really?" I replied, not having read the paper that day.

He took off his White Sox cap and handed it to me. Without really thinking about it, I put it on.

"How do I look?" I joked.

There were reporters milling around while this was going on, and word got back to Cook that I had been on the field wearing another team's cap. Cook wasn't amused. In his mind, I had disrespected the Expos with my actions. This incident marked the beginning of my stormy relationship with Cook.

The White Sox trade didn't come to fruition, and in 1986 I acquired the power to veto any would-be deals by achieving 10-and-5 status, meaning I had played 10 years in the league and the last five with the same club. Still, I decided I wouldn't nix a trade. If the Expos wanted to deal me, that meant they didn't view me as part of their future. I saw no reason to stay with a team that didn't want me. There was still persistent talk that the Yankees coveted me. The Expos never asked me to give them a list of preferred teams. But if they had, I don't think the Yankees would have been on it. Based on what I knew about how Dave Winfield and Reggie Jackson clashed with management there, I wasn't sure it was the best place for me. As the trade talk got louder, I realized that the 1986 season was almost certain to be my last in an Expos uniform.

There was a complicating factor, however.

None of the top free agents on the market after the 1985 season, including Kirk Gibson of the Tigers, got offers from anyone other than their own clubs, which prompted the players union to file a charge of collusion. The complaint had a lot of merit considering Commissioner Peter Ueberroth had been encouraging owners to drive down players' salaries. The owners blamed the lack of interest in free agents on clubs' skyrocketing payrolls and not on a coordinated effort to keep players from signing more lucrative contracts with other teams.

I played the '86 season thinking I might get traded at any time. For the first time in my career, I wasn't at ease at the ballpark. That was also the first season that an injury landed me on the disabled list. It was a source of pride for me to have played through all my knee problems, but it was a hamstring injury that sidelined me for about a month that season.

When I returned to action, I felt more than ever that my days in Montreal were numbered.

Dick and I heard through the grapevine that Charles Bronfman, the Expos owner, had okay'd making more funds available to re-sign me but that Cook had convinced him that wouldn't be necessary. I think Cook had the attitude that I would eventually sign for anything they offered. Dick was also hearing rumblings that Cook and other Expos executives were spreading word around the league that my knees were shot and that I couldn't play anymore. A decade's worth of positive feelings about the organization were starting to go down the drain.

We were nowhere close to agreeing on terms for a new contract. With baseball owners colluding to keep players from signing big free-agent deals, this was probably to be expected. Another of Dick's clients, Jack Morris of the Tigers, was in the same boat as me.

In a last-ditch effort to personally appeal to the owner, we arranged to meet with Bronfman at Olympic Stadium on a Sunday before a game. Vanessa and Dick got to the stadium early to have brunch, which was one of Vanessa's favorite things to do on a Sunday. The two of them had a nice meal and a couple glasses of champagne before heading up to meet me in Bronfman's suite. The four of us exchanged small talk for a couple minutes, and then Dick got to the point. He looked Bronfman in the eye and matter-of-factly said, "The only thing I ask is that you don't fuck Andre when he files for free agency. We don't need anybody spreading lies about his health." Bronfman looked shocked, as if nobody had put anything to him that bluntly before, which they probably hadn't. Some speculated that it was the alcohol talking, but Dick didn't need any liquid courage to say what was on his mind. And I think he summed up our point of view pretty well.

The incident only deepened management's suspicion toward Dick, who had been an attorney for the player's union before becoming an agent. But I think our anger at the Expos for bad-mouthing me to other teams was justifiable. With this, the battle lines were drawn.

I guess the Bleacher Bums got wind of the fact that the Expos and I might part ways. On visits to Chicago, fans shouted, "We want you here!" That made an impression on me. So did the day games and soft outfield grass at Wrigley Field.

As I worked to regain my form on the field, I was dealing with some bad developments back home in Florida concerning my grandmother's health. The woman who had been my biggest source of inspiration and guidance was suffering from Alzheimer's, a disease that was eating away at her physically and affecting her ability to think clearly. I saw this firsthand every time Vanessa and I returned home.

This was a hard time for my family. In 1985, we lost my Uncle Theodore, who had a history of heart problems, after he suffered complications from a knee injury. Bo, as everyone called him, along with his brothers, Curtis and John, were father figures to me. Bo was also an athletic role model, having played several years in the Pittsburgh Pirates farm system. Now he was gone. And Mamma seemed to be going down the same path.

For the first time in seven years, I neither made the All-Star team nor won a Gold Glove in 1986. I hit .284 with 20 home runs and 78 RBIs, respectable numbers for most players but not the type of performance I knew I was capable of.

During another losing season in Montreal, attendance at Olympic Stadium continued to drop. It seemed the excitement was gone, both for me and the fans.

• • •

I entered the off-season ready for a last gasp at negotiations with Expos management.

As I said, McHale had ceded the general manager job to Cook, which was too bad because I had always gotten along well with John. Everything Cook did and said communicated the message that I'd be the next veteran heading out of Montreal.

Dick and I had met with Cook during the '86 season in hopes of working something out before the off-season. But it soon became evident to us that the Expos had a warped sense of my worth. They were offering a two-year, $2 million contract, which equated to roughly the same yearly salary I had been paid during my six previous seasons with the team.

I wasn't the only Expo caught up in collusion. My teammate and friend, Timmy Raines, who had established himself as one of the best players in the game, drew no real interest from other teams when he filed for free agency at the end of the 1986 season. This was a guy who had just led the league in hitting and had made the All-Star team and stolen 70 or more bases in six straight seasons! Finding no place to go and with the 1987 season already underway, Timmy went back to negotiating with Montreal. He finally signed a three-year, $5 million contract with the Expos.

At 32, I felt like I had many good years ahead of me. I simply needed to be somewhere I was respected and where the game could be fun again. I didn't feel welcome in Montreal anymore. The message I got both silently and verbally from management was that my best days were behind me.

It was funny to me that the same team that had been trying to raid another team's minor league system by trading me was now saying I was damaged goods. That was the dagger. Wherever I ended up, I resolved to prove the Expos wrong in their assessment that I was washed up. My sense of pride depended on it.

I told Timmy of my plans to go elsewhere, and he wished me well. "You're finally going to get off the fucking Astroturf," he said with a smile. Timmy had come a long way in just a few seasons. He was no longer the young man I had tried to steer in the right direction when he admitted his drug problem. He was a leader now and more than capable of playing the role I had once filled.

I had one last meeting with McHale in the late winter of 1986. I made it clear to him that the team's offer was a slap in the face and that I had no desire to return to Montreal for another season.

"I appreciate the years I've played here, John," I said. "You've been a friend and always treated me well. But it's time to move on."

"You've given a lot to this organization, Andre, but if it isn't going to work out, all I can do is wish you the best," he responded. "You've represented the Expos well in every way."

John had always been a class act, and that final conversation with him allowed me to achieve a sense of closure. After 10 full seasons in Montreal, I left as the club's all-time home run leader with 225, a record that would later be broken by Vladimir Guerrero. I also had the most hits and RBIs in franchise history at the time I declared for free agency.

• • •

At the same time I was facing great uncertainty about my baseball future, I was trying to stay strong as my grandmother's health continued to deteriorate at a nursing home in Ocala, Florida. Back home in Miami for the off-season, Vanessa and I frequently made the five-hour drive to visit with her. On our final trip to the nursing home, her doctors told us that she was in the late stages of Alzheimer's disease and didn't have much longer to live. We huddled as a family and decided that we wanted Mamma to spend her final days with us.

Back at my mom's house, I saw my grandmother's body grow weaker with each passing hour. It was agonizing to watch this once strong woman struggle to eat gelatin and sip water. I could tell the end was near when she curled up into a fetal position.

I was at home with Vanessa when my mom called and told us to come over right away. Vanessa later told me I started moving in slow motion after hanging up the phone. There was no urgency in my step, and I seemed in a daze. When we drove up to my mom's house, a fire and rescue team was parked out front.

I knew Mamma was gone.

By the time we arrived, the paramedics had already covered up her body, but they told me they could arrange for me to go in the bedroom to take one last look at her. I stood motionless in the living room for about 10 minutes before I went back to her bed.

My grandmother had been a lot of things to me: a confidante, a spiritual pillar, and in many ways, a second mom. That's why I called her Mamma. As the oldest child of a young mother who worked a lot, I spent a lot of time with Mamma. Her reminders to always trust in God and myself were lessons I always lived by.

My family wanted me to close her coffin after the viewing at our church. I was the one they thought should give the last goodbye. When the time came, I stood in front of her coffin for a few minutes, trying to call up the strength to close it. Finally, I did.

I took a week to mourn Mamma's death. Then I tried to get focused again. One thing was for sure—wherever I ended up playing baseball, I vowed to dedicate the season to her.

For a moment, I toyed with the idea of joining Cro in the Japanese League. Every time we spoke, he told me what a great time he was having, both on and off the field. But when I mentioned Japan to my wife, she gave me a very direct response: "Are you crazy?" Vanessa didn't go as far as to threaten me with *Sayonara* if I decided to go to Asia, but that was the implication.

I was faced with two questions: Where did I want to play? And how was I going to overcome collusion to get there?

If at all possible, I hoped to stay in the National League. I had a lot of reasons for that. I was comfortable playing in certain cities and familiar with a lot of the pitchers in the league. Another major factor was that despite my knee problems, I still felt I had a lot left to offer defensively. If I went to the American League, I was pretty sure my new team would be tempted, at least on occasion, to make me the designated hitter. It made sense that managers would view putting me at DH as a way to lessen some of the stress on my knees. But I didn't want to sit and watch any portion of the game. I wanted to be as much a part of the team as I could, and that meant being out on the field.

That said, my circumstances didn't allow me to rule anything out. If an interested American League team had called, I would have listened. But that didn't happen.

The Cubs and Braves were the two teams I decided to target. Both were in the National League, and both played on grass. I liked Atlanta because, at the time, it was the closest major league city to my home in Miami. I had always enjoyed playing in Atlanta. But the Braves were a somewhat distant second in my heart to the Cubs. My career average at Wrigley Field was close to .350, not entirely surprising considering I always hit better in day games. And I loved the atmosphere there. The more I thought about it, the more I wanted to play day baseball in front of the Wrigley Field faithful.

Spring training had already started when Dick and I met at his California home to discuss how we would go about trying to interest the Cubs in my services.

That's when the idea of the "blank contract" entered the picture.

9

MVP SEASON

THE WRITING WAS ON THE WALL. ALMOST NO PLAYERS WERE GETTING fair offers from their own teams after the 1986 season, let alone from other teams. With that in mind, my agent, Dick Moss, and I decided to take a risk.

We set up a meeting with Cubs general manager Dallas Green at the team's spring training facility in Mesa, Arizona. In the current climate, we knew it would be futile to go in and try to negotiate a deal the traditional way. The situation called for a little creativity.

The plan Dick and I cooked up at his California home was to force the Cubs to tell us what they thought I was worth. Depending on their response, we were willing to go even a step further by proposing that I try out for the team as an unsigned player.

Dallas didn't have warm feelings toward my agent, stemming from Dick's days as an attorney for the player's union. For that reason, we knew our plan could backfire. A week before the meeting, Dallas called out Dick in the press by saying, "In my opinion, Dick Moss seems more interested in nailing baseball to the cross than he does in taking care of his player and getting him signed. Andre should fire him."

The next day, Dick and I took his "dog and pony show," as Dallas would later call it, to Mesa. As we entered the complex, we could feel the stares of reporters looking for any shred of spring training news. For that morning and the days to come, I was it.

From the get-go, Dallas tried to take control of the meeting. He launched into a speech about how he felt loyalty to some of the younger players in the

Cubs organization who deserved a chance to win jobs with the team. This was another way of saying that cost had nothing to do with the Cubs' lack of interest in me. He made what I hoped was a joke about possibly signing me for the major league minimum salary of $60,000.

Undaunted, I shared our idea with Dallas.

"It's a standard contract," I told him, handing him the document with empty spaces where the salary figures should go. "You just fill in the blanks."

I think Dallas was surprised. In fact, I know he was. After a few moments of silence, he said he appreciated my interest in the Cubs but that he couldn't guarantee that the interest would be mutual. We told him we would give him a day or so to consider our proposal. If we didn't hear back, our plan was to make the same offer to the Atlanta Braves.

When the story of my visit hit the papers, Cubs players, including Jody Davis, Keith Moreland, and my former Expos teammate, Scott Sanderson, all spoke up publicly in favor of the Cubs signing me. Rick Sutcliffe went as far as to offer $100,000 of his salary to help bring me to the team.

I left Arizona and returned home to Miami. Vanessa was eager to know where we would land, and I told her about the meeting with Dallas.

"A blank contract?" she asked skeptically. "How is that supposed to work?"

"Don't worry," I replied. "They don't want to embarrass themselves by offering me peanuts."

"Well, they're not going to offer you the moon, either," she correctly surmised.

The next day, Dallas Green called with a proposal.

"I'm not sure how far I'm going to get with this, but I can offer you a one-year contract for $500,000."

He probably expected me to hang up the phone at that point. Montreal had wanted me to take a pay cut, but their offer was still twice the amount the Cubs were proposing.

But there was no way I was going back to Montreal. Faced with taking a pay cut regardless of where else I played, I figured I might as well go to a place I truly wanted to be.

"That's fine," I told Dallas. "I'll take it."

I waited for a response but didn't get one.

"Are you still there, Dallas?"

"I'm here," he replied. "Can I call you back in about an hour?"

"Sure, I'll be expecting your call."

I guess he needed time to get his arms around the fact I was willing to accept his offer. He also probably had to check in with the commissioner's office.

When the phone rang an hour later, Dallas sounded a lot more cheerful. "Welcome aboard. We're glad to have you as a member of the Cubs."

In publicly announcing my deal with the team, Dallas put a positive spin on the previous few days.

"Andre and Dick were willing to sacrifice salary and principle in 1987 in Wrigley Field for the Cubs," he said at a press conference. "He was willing to bet that his production on the field would better his salary for 1988 and the future, something rather unusual in itself in these wild days of free agency."

The official terms of my deal included the $500,000 base salary and a $150,000 bonus if I stayed off the disabled list until the All-Star break. I could also earn another $50,000 if I made the All-Star team in 1987.

After the phone call from Dallas, I packed my bags for Arizona and joined my new teammates the following morning.

"Where are you with your conditioning?" Cubs manager Gene Michael asked me when I arrived at camp. It seemed he wanted to be a little cautious with me because of my history of knee problems. It hadn't helped that the Expos had led people to believe my body was shot.

I told him I'd been working out all off-season and was ready to play. That afternoon, he put me into a spring game as a pinch-hitter. I started the at-bat by smashing a long foul ball down the left-field line. Then I got a base hit. After my hit, some of the fans at HoHoKam Park in Mesa started singing "O, Canada" in my honor. Later that inning, I showed my legs were feeling pretty good by going from first to third on a single by Leon Durham. The next day I was in the starting lineup. By the end of spring training, I was hitting .373 with six homers and 18 RBIs.

The second phase of my life and career were about to begin.

• • •

In 1987, the game became fun again. Some of my baseball cards that season pictured me in an Expos uniform, but from day one in Chicago, I was a Cub through and through.

After the drama of the previous winter, I entered the 1987 season in an unusual position. As a 10-year major league veteran, I didn't feel like I had anything to prove. But at the same time, Chicago represented a fresh start. If I wanted to remain with the Cubs past the 1987 season, I needed to make a good showing. And the key to that was staying healthy.

Vanessa and I got an apartment near the Navy Pier in a high-rise called Lake Point Towers. Even in Montreal, we had never gone overboard setting up house during the season. Miami was our home, and the apartments we leased in Montreal were designed for six-month stays. We'd always rent furnishings and take enough clothing to get through the season. My one-year arrangement with the Cubs added to the sense that we might only be making a temporary stopover in Chicago.

Maybe I was pressing a little too hard out of the gates, because a couple weeks into the season, I was hitting just .167. But with one swing of the bat, my season turned around. It happened on April 22 with the Cubs trailing their archrival Cardinals 3–1 at Busch Stadium. I came up with the bases loaded in the seventh inning against St. Louis closer Todd Worrell, who had just entered the game early to try to preserve the lead. I didn't wait to see what Worrell had to offer. I swung at his first pitch and hit it over the left-field wall for a grand slam, the third of my career. The Cubs went on to win 5–4.

A *Chicago Tribune* story about the home run described my bat as a ticking time bomb that exploded in St. Louis.

The next stop for the Cubs after St. Louis was Montreal. It was my first trip back to Olympic Stadium as an opposing player, and I was surprised by the negative reception I got. Based on the loud boos each time my name was announced, it was clear that Expos fans harbored a grudge against me. I think I knew why. Several stories in the local press had suggested I wanted out of Montreal at all costs. That just wasn't the truth. In reality, management was trying to *contain* costs in a way that was unfair to me. The fans were under the impression I had abandoned them. It was a shame because in many ways they had come a long way as baseball fans. Unfortunately, it seemed they still lacked an understanding of how management had been treating free agents the past couple seasons.

The negative reaction I got in Olympic Stadium helped motivate me during the series. In a three-game sweep of the Expos, I went 7-for-12 and hit two home runs in the final game of the set. Our dismantling of the Expos turned out to be one of the few low points in 1987 for Montreal, which finished with a 91–71 record and in third place, a surprisingly strong performance that earned Buck Rodgers Manager of the Year.

I had a lot of good memories of playing in Montreal. But those days were behind me. I was exactly where I wanted to be now, wearing a Chicago Cubs uniform.

• • •

During my time there, Montreal had at times felt like a baseball town, and by that I mean when the Expos were winning. In a city and country that were crazy about hockey, baseball always played second fiddle.

That wasn't the case in Chicago.

When I arrived in the Windy City, the Bulls were drawing some of the biggest crowds in the NBA thanks to a newcomer named Michael Jordan. And Mike Ditka's Bears, with a Super Bowl championship under their belts, had established themselves as one of the premier teams in the NFL. But Chicago fans had a special passion for baseball, so much so that one team wasn't enough for the city. Most of the North Side rooted for the Cubs, while residents of the South Side pulled for the White Sox.

The Expos were only in their eighth year of existence when I joined the team at the end of the 1976 season. While it was exciting to try to build a baseball tradition in Montreal, it was an even greater thrill to join a team already steeped in history, even if a lot of it centered on losing. The Cubs were the oldest franchise in baseball and hadn't won a World Series since 1908, a drought that would eventually exceed the 100-year mark.

Some considered the epic dry spell a curse. And every season the Cubs came up short had a story attached to it. There was one about a billy goat, another about a black cat, and much later there was the sad tale of Steve Bartman.

I don't believe in curses. I was more inclined to think that all the day games in Chicago took a toll on players over the course of a 162-game season. The fact that Wrigley Field was the only ballpark without lights well into the 1980s was a plus for me because I always liked hitting in natural settings. But during my time with the Expos, I had seen the Cubs race out to great starts only to fade during the warm summer months.

My theory on the whole thing was simple—baseball is a game of breaks, and the Cubs just hadn't had very many over the years.

The curse, or whatever it was, did not dampen the enthusiasm of fans who came out to watch ballgames at the "Friendly Confines" or who followed the team on the Chicago Superstation that broadcast the games all over the country. If anything, the hunger of Cubs fans for a championship grew with each passing year. I saw this as a visiting player, but I experienced this when I put on a Cubs uniform with the No. 8 on the back.

The Expos had no retired jerseys or legends, past or present, when I played there. The Cubs family featured former players such as Ernie Banks and Billy Williams, who was the team's first-base coach when I arrived. Ernie was Mr. Cub, and his mere presence around Wrigley provided a link to decades of baseball history. Both Ernie and Billy were part of the 1969 team that had been cruising to a division title before a late-season collapse allowed the Mets to overtake them. Nearly 20 years later, the heartbreak of that season was still felt.

The 1984 season had only compounded that collective pain. That was the year the Cubs won the National League East but lost a best-of-five League Championship Series to the Padres after winning the first two games.

Leon "Bull" Durham was the face of the 1984 loss. His fielding error late in the deciding game tilted things in San Diego's favor. The play didn't become as much a part of baseball history as Bill Buckner's error in the 1986 World Series against the Mets, but in many ways it ended up defining Leon's career. That's a shame because Bull was one of the team's most steady players throughout the 1984 season. Having played alongside him in Chicago, I know he wanted to win a title as much as anyone in the Cubs organization. I remember him as the guy who would be on the top step of the dugout pumping his arm after big hits.

Despite the bitter end to the team's most recent playoff run, I got the sense upon arriving in Chicago that it had created a fondness and closeness among the players, as well as a belief within the organization that it could reach the highest level.

I hoped I could help the team and its fan base create some new and more pleasant memories so that legendary Cubs broadcaster Harry Caray might one day during a World Series get to shout his signature line, "Cubs win! Cubs win!" Only three years removed from postseason play, I felt the team had enough talent to get back to the playoffs in the very near future. Dallas Green was a shrewd baseball man who had made a lot of moves that helped improve the team.

I think the fans believed that, too.

It didn't take long for me to develop a special relationship with the Bleacher Bums who sat beyond the right-field wall. The same fans who invented the ritual of throwing back home run balls hit by opposing players took to "salaaming" me by bowing down with outstretched hands. The ritual started slowly on Opening Day 1987 and built momentum as the season went on. I had never seen anything like it before, and neither had any of my teammates. This outpouring of support from the fans was a daily reminder of how special they were, and it strengthened my resolve not to let them down. My wife got a kick out of all the adulation. When I got home from the ballpark after our first game, Vanessa bowed to me and asked what I wanted for dinner!

• • •

The 1987 season got better and better.

As I vowed to do, I dedicated the season to my grandmother, who had passed away earlier that year. A lot of times, both on and off the field, I caught myself talking to her. At night, I prayed she was looking down on me. As I found my rhythm at the plate, it felt like a light was shining down on me. I felt I was being guided.

I followed up my strong series against the Expos with a 5-for-5 game at home against San Francisco in which I hit for the cycle. That performance only accelerated the salaams coming from the bleachers. Greg Maddux, a young pitcher who came into the game with a record of 0–2, got his first win of the season that day. He'd have a lot more during what assuredly was a Hall of Fame career.

Even better than my bat coming alive was the fact that the Cubs held down first place in early May.

As I had hoped, my knees felt a lot better on the Wrigley Field grass. The natural surface versus the artificial turf was the difference between night and day. I didn't fully grasp that until the Cubs hit the road for back-to-back series in stadiums with Astroturf. A few games into those series, the same discomfort I felt in Montreal started to return.

I loved the feel of the soft grass under my feet in Wrigley. It was also exciting to learn the quirks of the ballpark. A matter of inches separated a foul ball in the stands from a fair ball down the line. I learned the hard way about another unusual Wrigley Field feature. There wasn't much foul ground to begin with, but on top of that both the home and visiting teams' bullpens were in playable foul territory. On one occasion, in pursuit of a pop foul, I tripped over the visitors' mound and went hurtling toward the wall. Fortunately, I was able to brace myself as I went into the wall feet first.

And of course there was the ivy on the outfield wall. In the years I played for the Cubs, a couple balls hit my way rolled into the ivy and never returned. Every outfielder knows in that situation to throw up his hands in the air to signal that the ivy has eaten the ball. When that happens, a runner is awarded a double instead of the triple or inside-the-park home run he might have gotten while the outfielder searched helplessly through the leaves. The other interesting thing about the outfield is the wire basket at the top of the outfield wall. It protrudes over the playing field and sometimes catches balls that appeared to be about to fall into your glove.

My body felt great, and I found myself returning to the defensive form that won me six Gold Gloves in Montreal.

I really liked playing for Gene, whose nickname was "Stick" because he was tall and thin. He recognized how much I hated to be out of the lineup and never unilaterally decided to give me a day off. To this day, every time I see him, he jokes about how he was responsible for my big year in 1987, the only year he was my manager.

Everything in Chicago, not just my knees and my relationship with Gene, felt comfortable. I had gotten along pretty well with the Montreal media, who had a challenging job of writing for an audience less entrenched in baseball knowledge than their counterparts in the United States. The whole media culture was different in Chicago. The town took its sports very seriously and scrutiny of the Cubs was fairly intense. I quickly came to respect the beat writers who covered the team. A lot of times they'd stand by my locker after games, waiting for me to finish getting treatment on my knees. Even though they had deadlines, they never pressured me to talk before I had a chance to tend to my body.

Throughout my career, I had always been asked why I didn't smile more and often looked so mean. I'd respond, "Because I tend to be deep in thought, especially when I'm out on the field. It's a look of focus and concentration." I'm not sure that answer satisfied everyone. But in Chicago, the press and public didn't get too caught up in my facial expressions. They had come to know a lot of players with a lot of different personalities. And in my case, they took the time to get to know the person behind the scowl. Once they did that, I think they realized I could be a rather cuddly personality.

My mom and my wife knew me better than anyone, and they both noticed a change in my general attitude toward life in 1987. "There's just a different sound in his voice," my mom told Fred Mitchell of the *Chicago Tribune*. "He wasn't smiling in Montreal. He said, 'I gave them 10 years of my life, and they pushed me around. I'll play for nothing if I have to, just to prove myself to people. I'll leave it in the hands of the Lord.'"

My big season in 1987 put a Band-Aid on the wounds I felt after clashing with management in Montreal and then losing my grandmother.

As I later learned, I had some issues I should have confronted during this time. But instead I ignored them. That would cause a lot of grief later.

• • •

There were only a few times during my career when I felt a pitcher had intentionally tried to hit me with a pitch. I thought Marty Bystrom of the Phillies was guilty of that in the early 1980s. And Bill Dawley of the Cardinals was another guy I thought purposely knocked me down.

Whether you're talking about a pitcher or a position player, it's sometimes hard to distinguish hard-nosed play from dirty play. Early in my career, Bill Madlock of the Pirates was a guy who would try to take out infielders at second base on close plays. Don Baylor played the game that way, too. Mike Scioscia, when he caught for the Dodgers, was notorious for blocking home plate without having the ball. I recall a play in Montreal where I felt he stuck out his foot as I was about to touch the plate.

Those are the plays that occasionally turn baseball into a contact sport. But there's no greater weapon in baseball than the ball itself. What Eric Show of the Padres did to me on July 7, 1987, crossed a line from the aggressive to the dangerous. And I felt I had no choice but to take action.

To that point, Show was probably best known for yielding Pete Rose's 4,192nd hit, the one that broke Ty Cobb's all-time record. He had a reputation for being a bit of an oddball. After giving up Rose's historic hit, Show sat down on the mound as Pete and his teammates celebrated around him. Show's association with the conservative John Birch Society earned him some headlines, too.

He had also established himself as a pretty decent right-handed pitcher for the Padres. It was Show who started the decisive Game 5 of the 1984 National League Championship Series against the Cubs.

For a while, I really struggled to hit Show. Eventually, however, I made an adjustment that allowed me to get ahead in the count against him. In the first inning of the game in July 1987, I took Show deep, which gave me home runs in six of my last eight games against the Padres. The blast off Show came a day after I hit two homers in the opening game of the series.

My exploits had prompted Padres manager Larry Bowa to tell reporters that his pitchers needed to back me off the plate. Bowa had been one of those hard-nosed players, and that was still his style as a manager. He didn't say his pitchers should knock me down or throw at me. He just wanted his staff to reclaim the inside part of the plate.

Well, there's a fine line between pitching in and throwing at somebody. Most pitchers can hit a batter any time they want to. Only a handful of major league hurlers are wild to the point they can't control where the ball is going.

Coming into the game, Show had a record of 4–9. I think frustration got the better of him that day. His sinking fastball had a natural tendency to ride in on right-handed hitters, though he still had command over its location. Unlike four-seam fastballs that can be picked up right away, Show's two-seamers fell into a momentary blind spot that reduced reaction time. If one of those 90 mph pitches came at your head, you could easily find yourself in a world of trouble.

And that's what happened to me in my second at-bat that day. I had no time to react when Show's 1–1 pitch drilled me in the head.

The first thing I heard was a loud explosion in my ears. Then everything went black. As hard as I tried, I just couldn't open my eyes. I heard a lot of commotion around me, but I was unable to move. I had been struck in the helmet before and escaped injury. This time, however, my face took the brunt of the impact. In the first moments after the beaning, I thought, "Am I okay?" For what seemed like a couple minutes, I just kept repeating that to myself. Then I heard Leon Durham, who hit in front of me in the lineup, say, "Man, look at the guy's face!" It was then that I pried open my eyes and saw blood dripping down onto my uniform.

Anger immediately swelled up inside me. There was no doubt in my mind that Show intentionally hit me. And by doing so, he had put my livelihood at risk. I was mindful of what happened to my former Expos teammate Ellis Valentine, who took a pitch to the face in 1980 and was never the same ballplayer again. Another player, Dickie Thon of the Astros, didn't fully recover from being hit in the eye with a pitch in 1984.

The only thing I wanted to do at that point was get on my feet and find Show.

Some of my teammates were several steps ahead of me. Led by Sutcliffe, they charged out of the dugout and toward Show, and they chased him around the infield for a while. By the time I got to my feet, Show was well on his way to being whisked off the field. That didn't keep me from trying to track him down in the Padres dugout. I never did get to him, though.

The cuts on my face required quite a few stitches, but I only missed a few games.

A few days later, I got a handwritten letter that I later found out Show had composed in the Padres clubhouse immediately after his ejection. In the note, he apologized and claimed the pitch had simply gotten away from him. He said he'd be praying for me and hoped I'd be okay.

Despite the letter, I had some harsh words in the press for Show in the days after the incident. I went as far as to warn the Padres against pitching him the next time we faced them.

When we went out to San Diego a couple weeks later, the media prodded me to keep talking about the incident. I didn't take the bait. "That's in the past,"

I told them. "I don't have any more comments about it." That wasn't a good enough answer in their eyes. A San Diego reporter kept pestering me to make a comment. Things got pretty heated between us, and he had to be escorted out of the clubhouse.

I went 4-for-12 with a home run in the series. Show did not pitch.

I never wrote back to Show, nor did I ever speak to him about what transpired that July day at Wrigley. I didn't hold a grudge, but at the same time I felt no need to reconcile with him, either privately or publicly. He remained a productive pitcher for another season before personal troubles started to consume him. He died of a drug overdose in 1994 at the age of 37.

• • •

On the day I got beaned by Show, I gained huge admiration for Greg Maddux, who at the time was the youngest player in the National League and getting roughed up in his first full season in the majors. After I left the game and went to the hospital, Maddux retaliated by throwing a pitch that hit Benito Santiago of the Padres. Because both benches had been warned about escalating the situation, Maddux was ejected. Later in the game, Scott Sanderson tried to do the same thing and got kicked out, too.

Many years after the fact, Maddux said he was happy to help out. "As a young player, you're always trying to be accepted by your teammates. It was an opportunity for me to gain their trust. You can always say you care about the guys on your team, but you have to take advantage of opportunities to show it. Talk is cheap. Show me, don't tell me. It was the right thing to do. I was just glad I didn't miss Santiago. That would have been the worst thing."

Maddux finished the season with a 6–14 record and an ERA of 5.61. Did I think based on that first year that he'd eventually become one of the greatest pitchers of all time? Probably not. But I could tell that his combination of intelligence and pinpoint control would allow him to rebound from that rocky start. He studied hitters better than anybody, which made it only a matter of time before he figured out how to get the upper hand.

And well before he established himself as a great player, Greg Maddux showed he was a great teammate.

For a lot of people, that game against San Diego was one of the most memorable of my career. They remember how scary the incident was, that it happened during a dream season for me, and that my teammates had my back. They also remember how a very good season turned into a great one in the weeks and months that followed.

I didn't think too much about it at the time, but I believe the incident fueled me for the rest of the season.

From the time I broke into the majors, I vowed not to let anyone intimidate me. If a pitcher brushed me back or drilled me, I responded by inching up closer to the plate. All future at-bats against that pitcher now became personal. When Dawley of the Cardinals threw at me, I hit his next offering into the upper deck. From then on, he had a hard time getting me out. I was 7-for-17 with four home runs against him during my career, a stat line that included a very special home run in 1987, my last of the season at Wrigley Field.

I think the incident against San Diego had the effect of making at-bats against *every* pitcher personal for the remainder of the season.

A week after the beaning, I was in the lineup for my fourth All-Star Game, my first since 1983. A day before the game, I competed in the Home Run Derby against George Bell of the Blue Jays, Ozzie Virgil Jr. of the Braves, and a skinnier Mark McGwire of the A's. It was a scaled-back version of an event that has grown in size and popularity over the years. I won the derby with seven home runs. In the All-Star Game at the Oakland Coliseum, I went 1-for-3. My teammate Lee Smith got the win, and my former teammate Tim Raines was named MVP. My selection to the game and the fact that I hadn't gone on the disabled list before the All-Star break allowed me to cash $200,000 in bonus money from the Cubs.

Coming off the beaning, I suppose I could have skipped the All-Star Game, but that possibility never entered my mind. The All-Star experience never got old for me. It's disappointing to me how in recent years a lot of players selected to the game have chosen to skip it. The All-Star Game is the fans' game. The fans want to see the players they voted in, and the players owe it to them to make every effort to participate. I realize that injuries prevent some guys from playing, but the notion that a healthy player would rather have three days off than represent his league in the Midsummer Classic is crazy to me. At the very least, a player should travel to the host city and tip his cap during introductions.

• • •

August 1987 was by far the best month of my career. It started in Chicago with a three-home-run game, a feat I had accomplished once before as an Expo at, you guessed it, Wrigley Field. My long balls prompted three separate curtain calls and accounted for all our runs in a 5–3 win over the Phillies. I followed up that big day with three more two-home-run games that month. I hit 15 home runs in August, the most ever in a month by a Cub, breaking the record of 14 previously held by Hack Wilson and Ernie Banks. I also knocked in 28 runs.

Shawon Dunston, the team's starting shortstop, was in my batting practice group. He would remark that opposing players would stand around and watch me hit. Shawon would yell out, "He ain't no god. He's just Andre." Then to show them I was human, I guess, he'd come up and start punching me in the back. That left me no choice but to chase him around the batting cage.

Unfortunately, after posting a 47–41 record at the All-Star break, we struggled to win games in the second half of the season.

Our team's mediocre performance put Stick on the hot seat. He resigned with a month left in the season and the team at .500. Frank Lucchesi became interim manager in September. Even though we were well out of contention by that time, the fans at Wrigley still backed us as if we were world-beaters.

I wanted to show my gratitude to them by going out on a high note.

Our last home series of the season was against the Cardinals, who were battling the Mets and Expos for the National League East crown. Entering the three-game set, I hadn't hit a home run at Wrigley in nearly a month. But in the first inning of the series opener, I connected off Bob Forsch for my 46th homer of the season.

A couple days later, I came to the plate for what was likely going to be my last at-bat of the season at home. We had a 6–3 lead in the eighth inning. As I made my way from the on-deck circle to the batter's box, the crowd rose as one and started chanting, "M-V-P! M-V-P!"

Dawley, an old nemesis of mine, was pitching for the Cardinals. I was picking up his pitches really well and worked the count to 3–1. Then he came in with a change-up that broke right over the plate. I put a good swing on the ball and hit it out onto Waveland Avenue. After I circled the bases, the fans continued to scream and chant until I emerged from the dugout for a curtain call. The cheering continued a while longer. As I stood before the fans, I hope I conveyed that the admiration they felt toward me was mutual.

The home run was a fitting end to a magical season. I finished with 49 home runs, which shattered my previous career high of 32. The Cubs finished in the cellar of the National League East, however, with a 76–85 record. My batting average in the games we won was nearly twice as high as in the games we lost.

There was a lot of speculation that the baseballs used in the majors were livelier or "juiced" in 1987. More balls than ever before left parks that season, a record that stood until 1996, when the idea of juicing took on a whole new meaning. It's true that a lot of players, including me, set career highs in home runs in '87. And without getting defensive about it, I'll just say that a lot of the homers I hit that season were tape-measure shots. The grand slam against St. Louis early in the season put me in a groove that never ended.

I knew it was going to be a tough call that year for the writers who cast MVP votes. Dale Murphy of the Braves, who beat me out in 1983 for the award, had a good year, and Jack Clark and Ozzie Smith of the Cardinals starred for a team that made it to the World Series. There was debate over whether a player on a last-place team deserved MVP recognition. To that point, it had never happened.

I was home in Miami when I got a call from the Cubs informing me that I had won the award. I immediately flew to Chicago for a press conference. A seventh Gold Glove award soon followed.

From a team standpoint, that gave the Cubs two out of the previous four MVP winners. Ryne Sandberg took home the award in 1984. Rick Sutcliffe, who won the Cy Young in '84, was runner-up for that award in 1987. These performances gave Cubs fans hope that the team was ready to compete for a pennant again.

10

THE CUBBIES

IF 1987 WAS AN AUDITION WITH THE CUBS, THEN I FELT PRETTY confident I had won the part. Unfortunately, the casting director split town before my agent and I could discuss a contract extension. Dallas Green resigned as general manager after the 1987 season and resurfaced a couple years later as manager of the Yankees.

I entered the off-season in a very different bargaining position than the year before. Without Dallas around, new general manager Jim Frey and team vice president Don Grenesko represented the team in negotiations.

I was asking for $2 million for the 1988 season. The Cubs countered by offering $1.85 million. Those figures were pretty close, and it seemed to me we should have been able to work something out. But when we didn't, we moved to salary arbitration, in which a third-party determines which amount is more appropriate. The arbitrator decided in favor of the team, making me the second-highest-paid Cub behind pitcher Rick Sutcliffe. A few weeks later, the Cubs went ahead and extended my contract an additional two years at $2 million a year. Did that make a lot of sense to me? Not really.

Around this time, major league owners agreed to pay a total of $280 million to players affected by collusion from 1985 to 1987. My portion of that settlement ended up being more than $1.5 million.

One of the greatest honors bestowed upon me after my MVP season came from the City of South Miami when it chose to rename a street I used to live on after me. It was a very touching day that drove home how far I had come since playing on the old neighborhood sandlots. Don Zimmer, who took over as Cubs manager during the off-season, came down for the dedication ceremony, which was also attended by my family, representatives from my alma mater Southwest Miami High School, and children in the neighborhood. From that day forward, SW 58th Place was known as Andre Dawson Drive. My mom lived on that street until her death in 2006.

My MVP award, combined with the fact I was playing in one of the biggest markets in the country, elevated me to a new level of celebrity.

In Chicago, I felt more pressure than in Montreal to be a public figure. I did some charity work for Alzheimer's research and picked up several endorsement deals. I also rubbed elbows with Chicago sports royalty when I joined Michael Jordan and Walter Payton for a magazine shoot. It was the first time I had met either of them. In addition to being the African American faces of Chicago's most popular teams, we also became good friends.

I had never been too aware of racial politics during my career. In Montreal, a couple of black players grumbled that the organization treated whites better. But I never had firsthand experience with that. The Expos always had an abundance of black players, and I never felt we were treated any differently than white players. I was bitter about management's handling of my contract situation in Montreal, but I don't think that had anything to do with the color of my skin. The only remotely racial incident I experienced in Montreal was at a department store when an undercover police officer put a gun to my head in a case of mistaken identity.

In Chicago, playing for a team whose icons included Ernie Banks, Billy Williams, and Fergie Jenkins, I felt that I was in a place that was very hospitable to black players.

Still, I understood the country as a whole was still dealing with lingering racial biases. And baseball wasn't immune to that. At the start of the 1987 season, Dodgers general manager Al Campanis appeared on *Nightline*, which happened to be my favorite program at the time, to talk about the 40th anniversary of Jackie Robinson's debut with the Dodgers. During the interview, host Ted Koppel asked Campanis why so few managing and front-office jobs in the major leagues were occupied by blacks. Campanis proceeded to explain that he thought blacks lacked "some of the necessities" required for leadership positions in baseball.

I was stunned that someone who had been a friend and minor league teammate of Jackie would say something so farfetched. I had always thought Major League Baseball could help set an example for the country in terms of being a place of equal opportunity. I knew that if given a chance, minorities would do a commendable job in the dugout or front office.

I didn't see myself as a political person, but I also understood there were times you had to stand up and be proud of your heritage. That's why I sent a campaign contribution to Jesse Jackson, a civil rights activist with Chicago ties, who was attempting to win the Democratic Party's nomination for president in 1988. He was the first black politician to make a serious bid for the presidency, and I felt it was important to recognize that.

• • •

In Chicago, I had the pleasure of playing with some great teammates. Ryne Sandberg was at the top of the list. My relationship with Ryno was defined by mutual respect. Here is how Ryno describes the Cubs teams we played on. "In a lot of ways, Andre and myself and Rick Sutcliffe kept an eye on the clubhouse to make sure it was professional and that we had the right atmosphere to win baseball games. Andre's influence in the clubhouse was unique. He didn't have to say a lot to get his points across. When he spoke, people listened."

I could easily have said the same thing about Ryno.

I also played alongside two of the best closers of all time: Lee Smith and Goose Gossage.

Smitty was a Louisiana native who had a laid-back, comedic way about him. He was known for taking naps in the clubhouse during games that sometimes lasted until the seventh inning. As the crowd sang "Take Me Out to the Ballgame," Smitty would make his way to the bullpen and wait for a chance to close out a win.

Considering that Smitty made his living throwing heat in the late innings of tight ballgames, I wouldn't have expected him to take batting practice so seriously. As a closer, he didn't often get a chance to swing the bat in games, and when he did, the results weren't very good. In his career with the Cubs, he was 3-for-60, which translated to a .050 batting average. Most of his at-bats came during the seasons he started games.

When Smitty swung, he swung for the fences. In fact, one of his three career hits with the Cubs came in 1982 when he connected for a home run off Braves knuckleballer Phil Niekro.

Smitty loved my bats and decided they were the only ones he could use for batting practice. He'd go through every bat in the box and then pick out the piece of lumber he considered best. Every so often, he'd pick a different one.

"How do you decide which one to use?" I asked him.

"I pick the one that feels good in my hands," he replied.

Then he'd go to the cage and try to hit balls onto Waveland Avenue.

After the 1987 season, Smitty was traded to the Red Sox for pitchers Calvin Schiraldi and Al Nipper. He had some great seasons in Chicago, but his best years came later in his career with St. Louis. As one of the most dominant closers of all time, I believe he deserves a place in Cooperstown.

Goose Gossage, who was inducted into the Hall of Fame in 2008, got his 300th career save with the Cubs after coming over from San Diego to replace Smitty. His stay with the Cubs was short but very memorable for me. As intimidating as he and his walrus mustache were to opposing hitters, Goose was completely different off the field. He was similar to Smitty in that regard. I joked during my Hall of Fame induction speech that Goose was the only person I knew who could finish off a case of beer on a flight from St. Louis to Chicago. I might have been exaggerating the truth just a bit, but no one could dispute that the man drank a lot of beer! I can still picture him sitting behind the card players in the clubhouse, telling stories and jokes with his can of beer. Unfortunately, Goose's only season with the Cubs was a disappointing one. He saved only 13 games and was released prior to the 1989 season. Desperately in need of a closer, the Cubs traded Rafael Palmeiro and two other players to the Texas Rangers for, amongst others, Mitch Williams, who filled that role.

In addition to sharing a clubhouse with two great closers, I also got to play for a time alongside two of the brightest young offensive talents—Palmeiro and Mark Grace.

Palmeiro, a first baseman for most of his career, primarily played left field for the Cubs while Grace was groomed as the team's first baseman of the future. Grace's emergence in his rookie season of 1988 prompted the team to trade

Leon Durham to the Reds a month into the season. It wasn't long thereafter that Palmeiro was dealt, too.

Prior to the 1989 season, I was called into Zimmer's office to discuss comments I made to the *Chicago Tribune* after Palmeiro's off-season trade to the Rangers. The reporter asked me whether I thought the team should have held onto Raffy and traded Grace. I praised both players' ability to hit for average but added that Palmeiro had the ability to play both infield and outfield. I was asked a question, and I gave an honest answer. I never said that the Cubs should have traded Grace, but the article made it seem that way. That didn't sit well with Gracie, who had finished second in Rookie of the Year voting the previous season.

Grace felt I should apologize for my comments. If that was the reason Zim wanted to talk to me, I suggested we both go back to what we were doing because I wasn't going to apologize for something I considered kind of petty. "I'm appalled that I'd be asked to apologize to a player who barely has his feet wet in the big leagues," I told my manager. "I told the reporter that Gracie was a good hitter, and I believe that."

Unlike other rookies, Gracie wasn't a wallflower. He was chirpy and media-friendly. And with his Hollywood good looks, the cameras gravitated to him. The word "cocky" was thrown around a lot with him. Ironically, it was some things *he* said to a reporter prior to his rookie season that helped him gain that reputation. At the time, he and Durham were competing to be the Cubs starting first baseman. Mark hinted that Leon hadn't come to spring training in great shape and that Leon would have to fight to keep his job. Some of the veterans on the team gave Gracie a tough time about that. To his credit, Gracie quickly learned to be gracious. All anybody wanted was for him to let his natural ability do the talking. And that's what he did. After Durham's trade, Gracie's quotes demonstrated he had learned a lesson. "I owe a lot to the veterans," he told a reporter. "I've had a lot of help since I came up."

The meeting in Zim's office ended peacefully. I didn't apologize, and I think Gracie was happy to hear I respected his talents and valued him as a teammate.

So how does the Palmeiro trade look more than 20 years later?

At the outset of their careers, Grace and Palmeiro had a lot of the same skills. Both were left-handed contact hitters with incredibly sweet swings. In his only full season with the Cubs, Palmeiro hit .307 with eight home runs. But after going to the American League, Raffy became a different type of hitter. He still hit for a high average, but his power numbers jumped in a way few people would have ever expected. He hit more than 35 home runs in 10 different seasons with Texas and Baltimore and ended up with far more career homers than I did. Grace collected a lot of hits but never had more than 17 home runs in a season. They were similar players, but I guess you could say Raffy made an off-the-field decision that took him down a different path.

In 2005, when Congress held a hearing to address the use of performance-enhancing drugs in baseball, Palmeiro flatly denied ever having used banned substances. A few months later, however, shortly after picking up his 3,000th career hit, he tested positive for steroids. That was very disappointing to me for a couple reasons. Not only did he take steroids, but he wasn't truthful about it, either.

Even though Raffy is one of only four players in major league history to have 500 career home runs and 3,000 career hits, he fell well short of making the Hall of Fame in his first year of eligibility in 2011. Many question whether his association with steroids will permanently keep him out.

In my Hall of Fame speech, I expressed my feelings about players who used steroids. "Baseball will from time to time, and like anything else in life, fall victim to mistakes that people make. Those mistakes have hurt the game and taken a toll on all of us. Individuals have chosen the wrong road and have chosen that as their legacy."

• • •

Because of my introverted nature, I often got to know teammates through my wife, who was more outgoing and quickly befriended other spouses. I'd then tag along on a double date. One of the guys I got to know that way was shortstop Shawon Dunston.

The Cubs took Shawon with the first overall pick of the 1982 draft. When I competed against him in his early years in the majors, I immediately noticed how hard he played the game. And he immediately noticed that I wasn't the most gregarious person in the world.

He likes telling the story of our first encounter, which came during his rookie season in 1985. I was standing on second base for the Expos, and he came over to the bag and said, "How ya doin', Mr. Dawson?" I guess I was caught off guard by the question because I just stared at him for a while before grunting an answer. Shawon said he went back to his shortstop position wondering, "What did I do wrong?" He had apparently admired me for some time. While in the minors, he tried to convince teammates I was the best player in the National League. At one point, he put his money where his mouth was and bet a few of them I would win the 1983 MVP award. I came in second to Dale Murphy of the Braves, but that didn't keep Shawon from continuing to sing my praises.

After our wives hit it off, Shawon found the opening he needed to continue the conversation he tried to start at second base a few years earlier. As Shawon tells it, "We were going to be friends no matter what. He was going to have to talk to me whether he liked it or not." Well, lucky for me, I guess, I did like it.

Shawon enjoyed every moment he spent on the field and played with a tremendous amount of energy. There was never a dull moment when he was around. When an opposing batter hit a ball to left field, he'd take off sprinting from his shortstop position in an attempt to catch it. He and Ryne Sandberg were the Cubs' double-play combination for many years. Ryno was as cool as Shawon was high-strung. If a fly ball went to right field, Ryno would take a few steps onto the outfield grass, make sure the ball was deep enough to reach the outfield, and then point his index finger in the air to help the right fielder find it. Ryno's was the standard way of doing things. Shawon's was the Shawon way.

I wasn't privy to the conversations that took place during late-game infield meetings on the mound, but from what I hear, they were pretty entertaining. Zim would come out and encourage the pitcher to bear down and get the final out or outs. He'd then say, "Make them hit it to Ryno. If you can't do that, make them hit it to Grace. If that doesn't work, make them hit a pop up to Shawon." Zim's instructions didn't offend Shawon, who knew he had problems with easy ground balls. He was great at fielding balls hit in the hole or up the middle, but he often turned routine plays into adventures.

Shawon had a rocket arm, but the accuracy of his throws often left something to be desired. A throw from Shawon intended for the first baseman's mitt might end up in the fifth row of the stands. Some people wondered what a pitch from Shawon Dunston might look like. But for the safety of hitters and the ego of guys who pitched for a living, he was never tempted to try it. "I wouldn't have wanted to show off by going out there and throwing harder than pitchers," he said, only half joking. "I might have been able to get it up there around 98 or 99 mph but I wouldn't have known where the ball was going."

I'll say this about Shawon—In contrast to my good friend Timmy Raines, whose locker was next to mine in Montreal, Shawon was probably the tidiest guy I ever dressed alongside. Most players are real messy, but Shawon was very particular about having everything neatly in its place. His locker was between Ryno's and mine. Shawon liked to comment on how Ryno and I only said 10 words a day. That was okay because Shawon did enough talking for all of us.

I said during my Hall of Fame speech I had a lot of funny Shawon Dunston stories. Here are a couple of my favorites:

Shawon, like a lot of hitters, hated facing Nolan Ryan. When Ryan was on the mound, Shawon went up and took his hacks in the hopes of just putting the ball in play. One night when we were facing Ryan in Houston, a couple of us teased Shawon by telling him Ryan was upset with him and was going to pitch him inside.

During the game, with Shawon batting, our then-manager, Gene Michael, came out of the dugout to ask the umpire to check whether Ryan was scuffing the baseball. This wasn't part of the joke, but it might as well have been. The timing was perfect. Gene had thought for some time that Ryan and teammate Dave Smith were doctoring balls. But he chose this opportunity to act on his suspicion.

Shawon looked at the umpire and said, "Hell no, blue, forget that, let's play ball!" He then turned to our manager and said, "Sit down, Gene! Go back to the bench!" Obviously, Shawon didn't want to further "upset" Ryan. Three pitches later, he was back on the bench explaining to the manager why he had shooed him away.

Shawon and I went out to dinner a lot. When we did, without fail, he'd tell the server, "This is my grandpa. Give him the check." And if he felt I left too much tip money on the table, he'd say, "No, no, no. You're overdoing it." Then he'd take what he wanted from the tip and pocket it. Of course he didn't object when I reached back in my wallet to replace the money he swiped. This was before he signed a big contract with the Cubs. And it might have been Shawon's payback for losing his bet that I would win the MVP award in 1983! His former Cubs teammates kid him that long after leaving the organization, he still has a pocketful of unspent meal money. In his defense, he did pick up the cab fares to and from the restaurants.

He liked to kid me about my age. I told Shawon, who was about 10 years younger than me, "Have your fun now, but you're going to be old one day, too." He seemed to think that was never going to happen. But sure enough, when he hit 35, his teammates started calling him "old man" and "grandpa." He also developed a fear of flying as he got older, something that prevented him from attending my Hall of Fame induction ceremony in 2010. This was ironic considering the way he behaved on a bumpy flight the Cubs once took into Atlanta. The turbulence was pretty bad, and everybody was getting a little nervous. Some of the coaches were sweating through their shirts. But Shawon wasn't worried at all. In fact, he was laughing like a kid on a roller coaster.

Shawon and I also had serious moments when we talked about our craft. He realized he needed to learn patience at the plate if he wanted to reach his maximum potential.

He'd say, "I'm in a rush. I want things to happen now."

"You can't be in a rush, Shawon," I'd tell him. "You just have to calm everything down and let things happen."

"But I'm ready for things to happen."

"I know you are, Shawon. And they will."

I didn't take a lot of walks, but Shawon redefined the meaning of "free swinger." In 1990, he walked only 15 times in 573 plate appearances. But that was his game. Despite a rash of injuries later in his career, he played 18 seasons. He may never have developed patience, but he did learn what it means to be resilient.

• • •

Shawon was my best friend on the team, but there were a lot of guys I enjoyed being around.

The team featured a couple of young pitchers who went on to enjoy long and successful careers. One of them was Jamie Moyer. Back in his early years in Chicago, he was mostly known as the guy who was dating the daughter of legendary Notre Dame basketball coach Digger Phelps. Jamie was never overpowering, but he was a master at changing speeds to keep hitters off balance.

I had been out of the game for over a decade when Moyer was still having very good seasons. As a 45-year-old with the Phillies, he had particular mastery over the Marlins, the team I worked for in an advisory role. Game after game, I watched as the young Marlins hitters failed to adjust to what Jamie was doing. I took a few players aside and said, "This guy isn't going to come in on the inner half of the plate so that you can hurt him. You have to be patient with him. If you're overly aggressive, he's just going to make you look worse." Finally, when Jamie was 46 years old, the Marlins started hitting him!

The most impressive performance on the team in 1988 belonged to Greg Maddux, who bounced back from a dismal season to post a 15–3 record at the All-Star break. He finished the season with 18 wins, but his first half was indicative of the pitcher he would become. It was amazing how quickly he adapted to pitching in the majors.

Here is how Maddux described his quick maturation as a pitcher: "When you first get to the majors, you're just trying to fit in. You're not sure if you even belong there. You don't know the league. You don't know the hitters. You're not even sure how to find the entrances to certain stadiums! There are just a lot of things you're not prepared for during your first year. One of the things I most struggled with on the mound was pitching 'slow.' I worked hard on my breaking ball and change-up in winter ball after my rookie season, and then good things started happening."

Mad Dog Maddux was quiet and unassuming his rookie year. Before long, however, he emerged as one of the biggest practical jokers on the team.

One particular gag really stands out in my memory. I was among a group of players soaking in the clubhouse hot tub before a game. The other players in the tub were also black. Well, Mad Dog walked into the room with a mischievous grin on his face and said, "Hey, have any of you guys ever seen one white dude make four black dudes run away?" We thought he was about to tell a joke, but he didn't say another word. Instead, he took a few steps toward us, unzipped his pants, and proceeded to urinate into the hot tub. And just like that, one white dude succeeded in making four black dudes run away!

There wasn't a racist bone in Mad Dog's body. He just liked a good laugh, and in this case, he got one from everybody except the team trainer.

"I thought it'd be okay to piss in it, because I knew the chlorine would take care of it," Maddux said about the incident. "There were a lot of stories about how I used to take dumps in the hot tub. Those weren't true. That would just be wrong."

He was a joker off the field and a genius on it. His nicknames, Mad Dog and the Professor, both very much applied.

I was proud to have shared a field with Mad Dog, whose stellar career included 355 wins, the eighth-most in the history of the game.

• • •

Don Zimmer, who took over the team in 1988, was a baseball lifer who had previously managed in Boston, San Diego, and Texas. He enjoyed some successes with those teams but never led any of them to a division title. For the previous four seasons, he had been a bench coach for the Cubs.

In the four years Zim managed the Cubs, I grew closer to him than any other skipper I played for during my career. He had his own unique way of dealing with players. If you got to the ballpark on time and gave maximum effort, you never had a problem with him. He largely kept his emotions under control, but when he got into it with an umpire, he knew how to blow off steam. He didn't often berate his players, however. One time after a tough loss, he walked into the clubhouse, took his cap off, rubbed his fleshy head and said, "Hell, I don't know what to tell you guys. It's not that we're playing bad baseball. We just need a break here and there. Go out and have a beer and come back tomorrow ready to win a ballgame." Other times, he'd use more colorful language to describe his displeasure with us losing games. As I said during my Hall of Fame speech, "I thought I knew every curse word, but Zim made up some new ones." In Boston especially he had clashed with certain players. But I think from the very beginning, he had the respect of the clubhouse in Chicago.

It was clear Zim and the coaching staff valued my contributions to the team. With the Eric Show beanball incident from the season before still fresh in everyone's minds, Cubs pitching coach Dick Pole warned opposing teams during spring training in 1988 not to vent their frustrations by throwing at me.

Nearly a year after the brawl with the Padres, Bob Ojeda of the Mets threw a high and inside pitch that hit me in the wrist. This came right after Palmeiro hit a home run off him. I pointed my bat at Ojeda and let him know I wasn't happy with his actions. Ojeda tossed his glove aside and challenged me to come out and do something about it. I took a few steps toward the mound before Gary Carter, my former Expos teammate who was catching for the Mets, grabbed me and held me back. Did I overreact? I don't think so. It's one thing for a pitcher to try to claim the inside of the plate, but it's another when a pitcher uses a hitter for target practice. I had hoped the league now knew I didn't tolerate that kind of thing.

By far the biggest news of the 1988 season was that after more than 70 years, the days of day-only baseball at Wrigley Field came to an end.

The decision to play night games at Wrigley wasn't without controversy. The Tribune Company, which purchased the Cubs in the early 1980s, had long been interested in putting up lights. But over the years, local and state politicians had passed laws and ordinances to block that from happening. In doing so, they felt they were reflecting the will of the people.

The 1984 playoffs had a big impact on public opinion. Peter Ueberroth, the commissioner of baseball at the time, told the Cubs they risked losing future home playoff games if nighttime baseball didn't come to the north side of Chicago. It got even more interesting from there, with the Cubs at one point saying they'd be forced to vacate Wrigley for a suburban stadium if state law forbade them from building lights. Major League Baseball chimed in by informing the Cubs in 1986 that they'd have to play possible home playoff games at Busch Stadium in St. Louis! Finally, in 1987, a compromise was reached. For the foreseeable future, the Cubs were to play 18 of their 81 home games under the lights, as well as any postseason games.

From a player's standpoint, I felt playing a limited slate of night games would help the team. It was always hard to return late at night from a road trip and then have a day game about 12 hours later. And if Major League Baseball was going to ban the Cubs from staging day playoff games, well, that was another reason to build lights. I loved the history of Wrigley Field, and the addition of lights guaranteed the Cubs wouldn't be moving to a new ballpark anytime soon. During my career, I had always hit better during the day, but ironically, 1988 was one of the few seasons when I had a higher nighttime average.

It took me a little time to adjust to the lights at Wrigley when playing outfield. They weren't as high as the lights in some other ballparks, and sometimes the ball appeared to soar above them.

Two weeks before the lights went on for the first night game, 3,000 people attended an evening team practice. Technically speaking, I hit the first home run under the lights, a batting-practice bomb into the bleachers in left field. The ball I hit was sent to the Hall of Fame.

On August 8, 1988, we played the Phillies in what was supposed to be the first night game. It was a star-studded event. The governor, the mayor, the commissioner, and the National League president were all there. Phil Bradley of the Phillies appeared to earn the distinction of hitting the first home run in a night game. But then rain started to pour down, and the game was called before it became official. To entertain the crowd, some of my teammates, including Mad Dog, went out and slid on the wet tarp during the rain delay.

The next night, in the first official game under the lights, we beat the first-place Mets 6–4. I had a single and two RBIs in the win. Lenny Dykstra of the Mets had the first home run.

My power numbers in 1988, though team-leading, were a far cry from those of the year before. I hit 24 home runs and knocked in 79 runs, a decrease of 25 and 58, respectively. On a positive note, I hit .303, my highest average in eight seasons.

As a team, we showed little progress compared to 1987, finishing 77–85 and in fourth place behind the Mets, Pirates, and Expos. But there were signs of hope. The 1988 team had been built from the ground up, with 12 players on the roster coming from within the Cubs organization. That group, which included Dunston, Grace, and Maddux, meshed well with the veterans who had come from other organizations, including myself, Sandberg, and Sutcliffe. In a repeat of what happened in my third season with Montreal, the Cubs were about to put together a special season my third year there.

• • •

I wouldn't be telling the whole story of my time in Chicago if I failed to mention some things that were happening in my personal life while I was there.

From the outside, it may have appeared that everything in my life was perfect. I was a year removed from an MVP award, playing in a city I loved, and my knees were feeling good.

Although things at the ballpark were going well, my home life was a different story. Off the field, I was a human being struggling with the same stresses, troubles, and dark moments as everyone else.

I had always prided myself on my self-discipline. I wasn't a drinker, smoker, or partygoer. I always tried to conduct myself in a professional manner. I was someone who teammates often turned to for support when they were experiencing personal turmoil.

There came a time in Chicago, however, when I stopped doing the things necessary to make sure my marriage was on solid ground. As I later learned, healthy relationships are based on communication. In retrospect, I should have devoted the same energy and commitment to communicating with my wife as I did to the game. While I was always focused when it came to baseball, I started to lose focus on life.

After 10 years of marriage, I had closed myself off to Vanessa. We'd even stopped talking about having kids, which had been a goal of ours for a long time.

In the year or so that followed my acrimonious parting with the Expos and the death of my grandmother, I retreated within myself. My MVP year in Chicago helped heal some of the hurt I was feeling, but clearly I was still dealing with some lingering emotional pain.

It was during this time that I engaged in extramarital relations and fathered two children by two different women, both of whom worked in the airline industry.

I remember talking to Timmy Raines in the early 1980s about how confusion in his life led him to behave in uncharacteristic ways. In his case, he got involved with drugs. In mine, I got involved with other women.

I didn't hide the truth from Vanessa. Telling her about my indiscretions was the hardest thing I ever had to do. She demanded an explanation, but I had none to offer. All I could tell her was that the relationships weren't long-term affairs, but rather the result of selfishness and getting caught up in the moment. I knew that sounded kind of feeble, so I spent most of my time just apologizing.

I could see how hurt Vanessa was. And for a while my confession caused the rift between us to grow even bigger. I considered seeking professional help but decided against it. I didn't need anybody telling me what I already knew—I needed to work on my marriage.

The whole ordeal caused us to take steps that saved our marriage. I knew in my heart that Vanessa was the only woman I loved, and I wanted to do whatever was necessary to share the joys of parenthood with her.

I also realized I had a responsibility to the two children I had fathered, a girl named Krystal and a boy named John Christian. I felt, however, that their mothers were demanding too much of me financially. The child-support issue ended up in the courts. Over the years, I developed a relationship with both children, especially with John Christian, whose mother moved to Florida. Most of my contact with Krystal came over the phone because she and her mom lived in the Houston area. I am proud of John Christian and Krystal, who both graduated college in 2011.

As for Vanessa and me, it took a lot of hard work and rebuilding of trust to mend our relationship. It took two people believing in each other and in God. And I thank God that Vanessa stood by me.

11

PARENTHOOD AND PLAYOFFS

DURING THE DIFFICULTIES IN OUR MARRIAGE, VANESSA AND I HAD stopped trying to find out why she couldn't get pregnant. In the wake of my affairs, we resolved to do whatever was necessary to identify the cause of the problem.

Vanessa's forgiveness required a lot of patience and understanding. And I emerged from the whole ordeal with a renewed commitment to my marriage. Above all, I wanted to start a family with Vanessa.

In the fall of 1988, Vanessa went in for a pelvic examination that revealed she had fibroid tumors on her uterus. The tumors were preventing her eggs from being fertilized. Based on that diagnosis, the doctor told us her chances of getting pregnant weren't good at all.

That news was hard to accept. But we didn't give up. We were determined to explore every medical option at our disposal.

Our research on the subject led us to an in vitro fertilization clinic operated by Dr. William LeMaire at the University of Miami's Jackson Memorial Hospital. We scheduled a consultation with Dr. LeMaire to learn what, if anything, he could do to help us. He was honest with us. He said the in vitro procedure was relatively new and had a success rate of only about 15 percent.

We prayed on it for a couple days before telling the doctor we wanted to give it a try.

To start Vanessa off, Dr. LeMaire prescribed her Lupron, a drug frequently used to treat men with prostate cancer. The medication helped shrink her tumors. That was a big first step.

Then it was on to the in vitro process. The odds were still very much against us, but we tried to stay positive. Three embryos were placed in Vanessa's uterus, one at a time. About 10 days later, Vanessa took a pregnancy test. It was positive!

We didn't realize we still had some very tough days ahead of us. Early on in her pregnancy, Vanessa nearly miscarried. For several weeks after that, she was on bed rest.

An ultrasound let us know we were expecting a son, and I prayed for his and his mother's health during some nerve-wracking weeks. Vanessa needed a lot of rest, and I tried to help by giving her doctor-prescribed vitamin shots in her hip to make sure she didn't lose the baby.

Amid one of the worst hitting slumps of my career, I got the most welcome distraction of my life on August 12, 1989. On the day Vanessa went into labor, I called my manager, Don Zimmer, to let him know the news. He told me to get to the hospital and not worry about that day's game.

You never know when major events in your life are going to take place. When you're a major league player, you just hope things concerning your family don't happen when you're on the road. Luckily, that wasn't the case this time. It seemed like God had a plan, and the plan was for me to be there to welcome 7 lb. 14 oz. Darius deAndre Dawson into the world. Vanessa and I named our son after King Darius in the Bible.

It was an amazing and eye-opening experience to witness the birth of my son. Despite the difficulties we had getting to that point, it all worked out in the most beautiful way possible. After 10 years of marriage, Vanessa and I were finally parents.

Following Darius' birth, it seemed like every restaurant in Chicago was sending over food platters to our apartment. Vanessa commented that she felt like the Queen of Sheba.

Our marriage had survived the ultimate test. I vowed to make sure that communication between Vanessa and me never broke down again.

• • •

Amid all that was happening in my personal life, I still had a job to do. But injuries made 1989 a very challenging season.

At the end of spring training and then again a couple weeks into the season, I had fluid drained from my right knee. With medication and treatment, I was able to play, but by early May I couldn't ignore the pain any longer. The team scheduled me for arthroscopic surgery, which meant I was going to miss a lot of games for the first time in my career. At least I departed the lineup on a high note. In the games before my operation, I went 11-for-16, which included a stretch where I got hits in eight straight at-bats. At that point in the season, I was hitting .305 with five home runs in 105 at-bats.

The surgery caused me to miss 33 games. When I went on the disabled list, the Cubs were one game out of first place. When I returned to the team in mid-June, they were a half game up. A lot of people had picked the Cubs to finish last in the National League East in 1989. We were out to prove them wrong.

A big reason for the team's success was the play of rookie outfielders Jerome Walton and Dwight Smith, the first teammates in more than 30 years to finish first and second in National League Rookie of the Year voting. Early that season, Jerome, who we called "Juice," had predicted this would happen. He said to Dwight, "We're gonna finish one and two for Rookie of the Year…me one and you two!" From then on, they maintained a friendly competition with each other, which helped both themselves and the team.

Juice and Smitty had incredible ability for young guys, and I was impressed by how they made an immediate impact. In that respect, they reminded me of Warren Cromartie and me during our rookie seasons in Montreal in 1977. They played the same positions as Cro and me and, like us, were friends with very different personalities. Juice was serious-minded while Dwight was kind of a comedian. Smitty's talents went beyond playing baseball. Before a game that season, he actually performed the national anthem at Wrigley Field!

Our talented rookies were indispensable to the team's success. Jerome's season, which included a .293 batting average and 24 stolen bases, also featured a 30-game hitting streak. Dwight hit .324 to lead the team in batting. The Cubs got a lot of bang for the buck out of guys who were both earning the major league minimum of $68,000 for the year.

It wasn't my style to take fellow outfielders aside and talk their heads off about the finer points of the game. I did, however, make an overt gesture toward Smitty that season. I offered him a glove with a gold patch that Rawlings had sent me for winning a Gold Glove in 1988. The knock on Smitty was he didn't play good defense. I had heard that about myself early in my career . In Smitty, I saw someone with all the skills necessary to be a solid outfielder. When I handed him the glove, I told him, "Here, use this, and you'll win one of your own before long." He took the glove and said with a smile, "I can't use this—but I'd love to put it on my mantel!"

Smitty improved his defensive performance in 1989. I remember one game in particular against the Astros when he threw out Rafael Ramirez at the plate to help us pull out a game we had trailed 9–0.

Regrettably, neither Dwight nor Jerome was able to duplicate the success of his rookie season. Jerome developed hamstring problems that kept him out of action for long periods and led to a premature end to his career. He averaged only about 150 at-bats a year over the course of 10 seasons with six different teams before playing his final major league game when he was only 32. Dwight's 343 at-bats in his rookie season were the most in any season he played. After leaving the Cubs at the end of the 1993 season, his playing time continued to decrease. He played as a backup on a World Series championship team with Atlanta in 1995 before he too was out of the big leagues at 32.

The 1989 team had its share of big names, but contributions from players like Juice and Smitty were what elevated the Cubs to the next level. Another guy who quietly helped the team win ballgames was third baseman Vance Law, who had also been a teammate of mine in Montreal. His career year had come the previous season when he drove in 78 runs and hit .293 for the Cubs. Though his numbers slipped in 1989, he came up big at some important times. He played his best baseball in late May when we won 10 out of 12 games to stay competitive in the National League East.

Vance, whose nickname was "Vinnie," wasn't like most players. As a practicing Mormon, he didn't drink, swear, or act up. And when I say he didn't drink, that means I never saw him with a beer or a caffeinated beverage. When he was around, other players tried to keep their language clean. Vinnie's idea of swearing was using the phrase "jeezo peezo." That's what he'd say when he was struggling at the plate, as in, "Jeezo peezo, I can't buy a hit right now!" In Montreal, Tim Raines used to get on him about that. Timmy would tell him, "Vinnie, it'll work a lot better if you just say, 'Goddamn, I need a hit!'"

I had a lot of respect for how Vinnie carried himself, and he was an important part of the Cubs teams of the late 1980s.

• • •

I didn't like missing so much of the 1989 season and wanted to get back on the field as quickly as I could. In the weeks following my surgery, I worked out in the clubhouse and then took a seat on the bench to watch my teammates do battle. It was a frustrating time to say the least.

The decision that I was ready to play came after I started feeling comfortable running and taking batting practice. But that didn't prepare me for game situations. This was before the days when teams sent players to the minor leagues for rehab assignments as often as they do now. I can understand why it's done that way today. Seeing game action prior to coming off the disabled list helps ease players back into things.

When I returned to the Cubs in mid-June, I started off slow. My play was starting to improve when I again started feeling discomfort in my right knee. I went to have it checked out and learned a cyst was causing fluid to accumulate. The team doctor told me I'd likely need additional surgery in the off-season.

Zim, who was a proponent of keeping players fresh by giving them days off, saw my condition and kept me out of the lineup for certain games. I respected his judgment and didn't question his decisions. Overall, I thought he was doing a great job.

And so did the Cubs, who rewarded him with a two-year contract extension at the All-Star break in 1989. At that point we were in second place and 1½ games behind the Expos.

My selection to the All-Star team as a reserve that season came as a surprise. I had missed a big chunk of the first half of the season and entering the day the reserves were announced, I was only hitting .253 with seven home runs and 28 RBIs. But Dodgers manager Tommy Lasorda still chose me. My first reaction to hearing the news was, "Who doesn't want to go? Who got hurt?" In explaining his decision, Lasorda told the *Chicago Sun-Times*, "I want Dawson playing for me. That's the reason I took him. I want to win the game." Unfortunately, I couldn't do much to help the National League in the game, which was played in Anaheim. I went 0-for-1, and the National League lost 5–3.

My knee pain didn't subside in the second half of the season, and it affected my play. During a stretch that lasted from late July to the middle of August, I became mired in a 6-for-63 slump that dropped my average into the .230s. It was enough to make me want to shout, "Jeezo peezo!" I'm sure I used more colorful language to express my frustration, however. It also caused Zim to experiment with inserting Mark Grace into the cleanup spot in the lineup while dropping me down in the order.

As bad as that month was on the field, it was also the month Darius was born, so I didn't let myself get too down.

My struggles aside, the team continued to play well. Greg Maddux and Rick Sutcliffe were very good. And Grace, Ryne Sandberg, and Shawon Dunston gave us balance throughout the lineup. According to many sportswriters, we were overachieving. That may have been a nice way of saying they thought we were a fluke. But Zim kept us focused, and I could feel the confidence of the team growing with each passing month.

Walton and Smith were pleasant surprises in the outfield, and so was Mike Bielecki on the mound. Coming into the year, Bielecki had pitched five years with the Pirates and Cubs, never winning more than six games in a season. In 1989, he went 18–7. Some of his success was attributed to a nasty forkball he developed while playing winter ball in Venezuela. Whatever the reason, he really turned it up a notch that season. He was dominating at times, particularly on the West Coast, where he shut out the Dodgers and Padres. Three of his four career shutouts came in 1989. Like Walton and Smith, it was a special year for Bielecki.

A team can win without significant contributions from role players, but it makes things a lot easier when versatile position players can step in and make the most of their starts. For the 1989 Cubs, Lloyd McClendon filled that role by playing a lot of left field and first base and turning in career highs in home runs and RBIs.

The Cubs also had a strong presence at the back end of the bullpen.

Mitch Williams had inherited the closer's role previously occupied by Lee Smith and Goose Gossage. Mitch was known as "Wild Thing," and he lived up to his nickname. Every time he entered a game, players and fans alike prepared for an intense finish. It wasn't uncommon for him to walk the bases loaded before getting out of the jam. He threw the ball hard, not always knowing where it was going. But like his predecessors, he wanted to be on the mound in crucial situations. And more often than not, he found a way to get the job done during a season in which he saved 36 games.

In early August, we were tied with the Expos going into a three-game home series against Montreal. We swept the series behind great outings from Maddux, Bielecki, and Sutcliffe, who yielded a total of just four runs.

Now we needed to hold first place.

So many players had stepped up to put us on the inside track to a division title, but I felt the team needed contributions from me if we wanted to ensure a playoff spot. In an effort to help the team, I may have tried to force things by swinging at too many bad pitches.

I had my moments, however. A few days after the birth of my son, I broke out of my horrendous slump by hitting home runs in back-to-back games against the Reds. We won both contests to extend our first-place lead over the Mets, Expos, and Cardinals, who were all bunched together behind us.

A couple nights later, in a tough loss to the Astros, I collected the 2,000th hit of my career, a second-inning single at the Astrodome off Jim Clancy. It wasn't a milestone I heard much discussion about until it actually happened. A lot of guys reach 2,000 hits. It's the 3,000-hit mark that separates the great players from everyone else. It's similar to the way 300 wins gets a pitcher into the Hall of Fame, while 200 wins doesn't. In a year when I already had one surgery and was scheduled for another after the season, I had more pressing concerns than whether I'd make it to 3,000 hits.

After playing up-and-down baseball for several weeks, our lead over second-place St. Louis was trimmed to half a game following a home loss to the Cardinals on September 8. The Mets and Expos were also both within three games of first place. But over the course of the next week, we won six straight at Wrigley against St. Louis, Montreal, and Pittsburgh to put some distance between us. That was an exciting period. The fans were coming out in droves in hopes that the Cubs would make it back to the playoffs.

On September 25, I had two home runs in a game against Montreal, the second of which was probably the strangest of my career. I smacked a deep fly ball to center fielder Dave Martinez, who dove to the turf in an attempt to catch it. The umpire ruled "no catch," so I kept running. It was later revealed that Martinez may have caught the ball. But because the umpiring crew signaled the ball was live, I made my way around the bases for an inside-the-park home run, the first and only of my career.

The next night, we clinched the division. It would have been nice to do it at Wrigley, but punching our ticket to the playoffs in Montreal was exciting, too. I didn't do a lot of jumping up and down, though. I'm not sure my knee would have withstood that. It was just a relief to be playoff-bound after everything Vanessa and I had experienced. The rough patch in our marriage, the early difficulties in her pregnancy, the joy of the birth of our child, my knee surgery, and my struggles after returning to the diamond all made for an interesting year.

We finished the 1989 season with a record of 93–69, six games better than the second-place Mets. It was time to get ready for the postseason.

• • •

For the first time in five years, not very long by Cubs standards, the team was making a trip to the National League Championship Series. In the half-decade between playoff appearances, a lot had changed. Sandberg, Sutcliffe, and Scott Sanderson were the only players who remained from the 1984 team. Zim was the third-base coach for the Cubs when they fell to the Padres in the five-game NLCS that year.

I was about to break a personal playoff drought of eight years. I hadn't played in the postseason since the strike-shortened 1981 season when the Expos beat the Phillies in a division series to reach the NLCS. Ever since the Expos lost to the Dodgers on "Blue Monday" in Montreal, I had yearned for the chance to return to the postseason.

Our opponent in 1989 was the San Francisco Giants, a team that tallied one fewer win than us during the regular season. I felt we matched up well against them. In Kevin Mitchell and Will Clark, who would go on to finish first and second in National League MVP voting, respectively, they had two tremendous bats in the middle of the lineup. But top to bottom, I thought we were capable of outslugging the Giants. And on paper, we appeared to have a pitching edge over Roger Craig's team. San Francisco's ace, 40-year-old Rick Reuschel, was a former Cub coming off an outstanding 17-win season. But I liked the depth of our pitching staff that included three guys who won at least 16 games.

Before the start of the playoffs, the Cubs announced that, despite my uncertain health, they were picking up my $2.1 million option for the 1990 season. That vote of confidence gave me added incentive to go out and have a memorable postseason.

And it was memorable—just not in the way I had hoped.

The best-of-seven series opened under the lights at Wrigley Field with Maddux taking the mound against Scott Garrelts. Both were coming off very strong seasons, but Game 1 of the NLCS belonged to the offenses. After the first inning, the Giants led 3–2. Clark's grand slam off Maddux in the fourth inning, his second home run of the game, gave the Giants an 8–3 lead. After the game, Zim faced criticism for leaving Maddux in too long. Mitchell added a three-run home run in the eighth to make the final score 11–3. Clark and Mitchell were a two-man wrecking crew that went a combined 6-for-9 with three home runs and nine RBIs. Hitting fifth in the lineup, I went 0-for-3 with a walk.

In Game 2 the next night, we tried to send an early signal that we wouldn't be going to San Francisco down 2–0 in the series. We jumped all over Reuschel by scoring six runs in the first inning en route to a 9–5 win. Grace and Walton each had three hits to fuel the offense. I was 0-for-4 with three strikeouts, making me the only player on either team to have started both of the first two games without getting a hit. In the first inning of Game 2, Reuschel hung me a breaking ball that I crushed down the left-field line. On a normal day, the ball would have landed out on the street for a home run. It started out 10' into fair territory, but the wind pushed it foul. Following the near-miss, I struck out.

That at-bat symbolized my entire series. I was happy we had salvaged the split at home and hoped my bat would finally come alive at Candlestick Park. I knew from experience that a hot streak was sometimes just a swing away. So did Zim. Asked by reporters whether I was healthy enough to play, he acknowledged my struggles but added, "I'm not going to take him out of the lineup. You never know when he's going to come out of it and pop a three-run homer."

As was usually the case, Zim and I were on the same wavelength. I told him, "I didn't come this far *not* to play in the postseason. I'm going to be out on the field even if I have to crawl out there."

We went to San Francisco for the middle part of the series knowing we had to win at least one to guarantee another game in Chicago.

My single in the first inning of Game 3 plated the first two runs of the night. It was a short-lived lead, however. The Giants scored three times in the bottom half of the inning to go on top.

Sandberg broke a 3–3 tie in the seventh with a sacrifice fly. But a two-run homer by Robbie Thompson off Les Lancaster put the Giants back on top 5–4. Thompson's home run, his second off Lancaster in the series, proved the difference in the game. Our best chance to even the score came in the eighth after Grace led off with a single. But he was thrown out trying to advance to second on a deep fly out that I hit to left.

Of the game-winning home run he yielded to Thompson, Lancaster later said he thought the count was 3–0 instead of 2–0 when he threw a fastball down the middle. "If I knew it was 2–0, I would have thrown another off-speed pitch," he said after the game. "I'm making him look like the MVP right now."

Things were falling into place for the Giants. If stars like Mitchell and Clark weren't killing us, role players like Thompson or Matt Williams were. That has always been a recipe for postseason success. Still, I thought it was still shaping up to be a tight series. A few close calls on the bases had Roger Craig advocating for the use of instant replay in baseball. I think he and everyone else believed the series could turn on a bang-bang play.

My two-out double in the fifth inning of Game 4 scored Grace and tied the score at 4–4. It also chased Garrelts, the starting pitcher, from the game. Maddux had already left the game after giving up four runs.

The Giants answered quickly with a two-run home run by Williams in the bottom of the inning to retake the lead 6–4. After the game, Zim again had to answer to critics who said left-hander Steve Wilson should have intentionally walked the right-handed Williams with first base open. Williams finished the NLCS with nine RBIs, a huge contribution from someone who spent much of the season in the minors and hit only .202 while with San Francisco. The combination of Clark, Mitchell, and Williams proved too much for our pitchers in that series.

Zim's unorthodox managerial style was on full display against the Giants. He was famous for making decisions based on hunches. I was quoted that season as saying, "I've been around a long time, but I've never played for a manager quite like Zim. I've seen him hit-and-run with the bases loaded." In fact, he was the only manager I had ever seen do that.

Some of the team's frustration bubbled to the surface in the sixth inning of Game 4 when Dunston, who had reached base on a bloop single, started jawing with Clark. Both benches cleared, but everything calmed down quickly.

We entered the ninth inning still trailing 6–4.

Giants reliever Kelly Downs got two quick outs to start the ninth before giving up a single to Sandberg. Craig then replaced Downs, who had already pitched four innings, with closer Steve Bedrosian. Lloyd McClendon singled to put runners on first and third. Bedrosian then walked Grace on five pitches to load the bases.

I walked in from the on-deck circle for what I would later call "the biggest at-bat of my life." The stage was set. With one big hit, I could break out of my slump and help us tie the series at 2–2.

A single would have plated a couple runs, but I was looking for something more. In other words, I was trying to do too much. And I think Bedrosian sensed it. He started me off with a slider that I whiffed at. The only fastball he threw during the at-bat wasn't where I could reach it. With the count 1–2, I swung through another slider. Game over.

Steve Wilson was in tears after the game, and I wasn't feeling so great myself. Zim tried to keep our morale up, using the old Yogi Berra line, "It ain't over 'til it's over."

Trailing the series 3–1, our backs were up against the wall. Game 5 was the first pitchers' duel of the series with Bielecki and Reuschel both pitching extremely well.

We led 1–0 in the seventh inning when Will Clark lined a ball to right field that grazed off my glove and went for a triple. It was a ball I normally would have speared, but I was having difficulty running and bending my knees. That made it hard to get my glove down to catch the ball. Clark scored on a Mitchell sacrifice fly.

With the game tied 1–1 in the eighth, Walton walked and advanced to third on a sacrifice and a ground out. Grace, the hottest hitter on the team, came up with a chance to break the deadlock.

Only he never had a chance to swing the bat.

Very rarely in my career did pitchers intentionally walk hitters to get to me. More often than not, I was on the receiving end of an intentional pass. Now for the second time in the NLCS, the Giants opted to put the left-handed-hitting Grace on in front of me. Even though I realized the move created a more advantageous matchup for the right-handed-throwing Reuschel, it still amounted to the Giants saying they'd rather face me than Grace. Based on our respective performances in the series, I can't say they made the wrong choice. Grace ended up hitting .647 against the Giants.

But any time someone is intentionally walked ahead of you, you take it personally.

In this crucial spot in a must-win game, I came to the plate with runners on first and third for another of the biggest at-bats of my life. This time I made contact, but the ball rolled just 60' into Reuschel's glove. The ground-out ended the rally and my postseason.

I wasn't even in the game when the Giants clinched the series. After making the final out of the eighth inning, I was removed as part of a double-switch that put Mitch Webster in right field.

We went down fighting. With two outs in the ninth, Bedrosian gave up three consecutive singles to Curtis Wilkerson, Webster, and Walton. With the score 3–2 and the tying run on second base, Sandberg grounded out to end the game and series.

I felt terrible. And so did Vanessa. During the series, she had witnessed Cubs fans booing me and saying unflattering things. She knew me well enough to see I was overcompensating for my struggles by trying to come up with a big hit that might turn the series around. After we lost Game 5, she broke down in tears on a bus back to the hotel, an outburst she later attributed to postpartum mood swings.

A coach's wife tried to console her. "It'll be okay," she said. "This is nothing new. This is what happens to the Cubs."

In 1981 with the Expos, my teammates and I had our bags packed for the World Series when the Dodgers came up with a late run to beat us in the decisive game in the NLCS. That was hard to swallow. But so was 1989. Though we won only one game against San Francisco, it felt like the series could have shifted in our favor on several occasions. While the loss in 1981 boiled down to a single "what if" moment, the loss in 1989 had many such moments. And I had the whole off-season to dwell on every one of them.

Why did we lose? I needed only to look in the mirror to see one of the reasons why. I was 2-for-19 with three RBIs in the series. I was the main reason Grace scored only three runs despite going 11-for-17 with four walks.

The media went after several of us, including Zim. That was fine. Part of their job was to second-guess. But I think they realized the Giants won the series more so than we lost it. And though Zim was criticized for some of his moves during the NLCS, he still won National League Manager of the Year.

I became a Cub the first moment I heard the cheers of fans when I stepped onto the Wrigley Field grass in 1987. But in a strange way, following the loss to the Giants, I reached another level of belonging with the organization. I now shared the heartbreak of coming agonizingly close to competing for a championship. There was the collapse of 1969, the playoff loss of 1984, and now the disappointment of 1989. Of course, a lot more heartbreak over the years would only add to the Cubs' reputation as Lovable Losers.

I had my second knee surgery of 1989 the day the Giants and A's were scheduled to play Game 3 of the World Series at Candlestick Park. When I woke up from the operation, I found out the game had been called off because of a major earthquake in the Bay Area. The news gave me perspective. There were more important things than the Cubs losing in the playoffs or my knee problems. The A's ended up sweeping the Giants in a series that was overshadowed by the quake.

I spent a couple months in Chicago rehabilitating from the fifth knee surgery of my major league career and sixth of my life. I had a cast on for six weeks. When I returned home to Miami, I got to spend the first extended period of time with my son. That helped soothe the double dose of pain I was feeling from my knee and the way the season had ended. Several days a week, I drove to the University of Miami to do additional rehab on my knee. By mid-January, I was finally able to return to baseball-related activities.

As tempting as it was to dwell on the past, there was no time for that. I had another comeback to tend to.

12

FIGHTING BACK

COMING OFF TWO RECENT KNEE SURGERIES, I KNEW I HAD A LOT OF hard work ahead of me. During spring training in 1990, I spent more time with Cubs trainer John Fierro than with any of my teammates. When I talked to the media, I sometimes sounded like a trainer myself, using terms like "muscle definition" and "arthritic changes" to discuss how my knees were feeling and when I thought I'd be ready to play. I understood why the reporters were so curious about my health. At 35, I was at a turning point. No one was publicly saying my career was on the downturn, but I'm sure a few people—some with notebooks and tape recorders and others with office space in Wrigley Field— were thinking it might be a possibility.

I knew I was far from done. And with each passing day, I could feel my leg getting stronger.

I accepted the reality that I would always experience some degree of discomfort in my knees. After so many surgeries and games, it was inevitable. Playing with discomfort was the easy part. Playing with pain took a little more resolve. What was the difference? I defined "discomfort" as the nagging injuries that are always in the back of your mind when you play, the type of ailments you can work through. To me, "pain" was more than just the physical sensation of a body part hurting. It also included a psychological element in which you were never sure if your body was going to do the things you were asking it to do.

In today's game, players generally sit out when they're feeling pain. The decision whether to play or not isn't even in their hands most of the time. Advanced medical technology decides for them. I didn't have my first MRI until my playing days were almost over. For most of my career, there weren't MRIs that yielded an immediate medical diagnosis. So I tried to gauge things on my own and play with discomfort and pain. I just asked that my body hold up for the three hours a day that I was on the field.

Cubs manager Don Zimmer wasn't confident that I would be ready for Opening Day in 1990, especially after a 32-day lockout ate a big chunk out of spring training.

Zim was right … but just barely. I missed the team's season opener but came back to hit a two-run homer against the Phillies in the second game.

By the end of April, I was hitting .339 with four home runs and 15 RBIs. I was off and running, achy knees and all.

A real test of my health came in May when we went to Houston for a four-game series. To that point, I had defied a lot of expectations by playing in 31 of the team's 33 games. But the Houston trip meant four games on the hard Astroturf. I don't think Zim intended for me to play the entire series, but I was adamant about not taking a day off. I got eight hits against the Astros, which helped us win three of four. I also stole my fourth base in four attempts so far that year.

When we left Houston to return to Chicago for a 10-game home stand, I led the National League in home runs, RBIs, and slugging percentage. Zim told reporters he was stunned by my performance. "I can't believe it. After what I saw in spring training and last year, I can't believe this is happening."

My contract was due to expire at the end of the season, and based on my early-season success, the Cubs appeared ready to discuss an extension.

I also received affirmation I had regained my reputation as a feared hitter. I was taking batting practice before a May 22 game against Cincinnati when my former Montreal teammate Tony Perez, who was a coach with the Reds, approached me and said, "You're not going to beat us tonight. We're not even going to give you that chance."

Sure enough, with first base open in the first inning, Cincinnati manager Lou Piniella instructed starting pitcher Tom Browning to intentionally walk me. The game was tied 0–0 in the eighth inning when Browning gave me another free pass. Still scoreless, the game went into extra innings. In the 11th, I singled and was part of a successful double steal, but we still couldn't push a run across.

The next inning, I was walked intentionally again. Both teams scored a run in the 13th to extend the game. We finally won 2–1 on a 16th inning single by Dave Clark that came on the heels of my fifth intentional walk of the game, a major league record.

I caught up with Tony after the game and joked, "Well, that didn't really work out for you, did it? You should have just pitched to me."

I think Piniella's strategy that day raised some eyebrows, but nobody was questioning his judgment by the end of the season. In his first year as manager after taking over for Pete Rose, he led the Reds to a World Series sweep over the favored A's.

• • •

It was nice to be performing at a high level and to have the respect of the league again. The only thing missing from the 1990 season was that the team wasn't playing nearly as well as it had in 1989. At the All-Star break, we were 15 games behind the first-place Pirates and stuck in the cellar with St. Louis. The Cardinals' struggles prompted the resignation of manager Whitey Herzog.

The 1990 season had featured a lot of the unexpected. Home runs around the majors were up, yet there were five no-hitters pitched before the All-Star break.

The Cubs' losing record was another of the surprises, especially considering my strong play and the fact Ryne Sandberg was having an MVP-caliber season.

From a personnel standpoint, we weren't much different than the team that had just won the National League East by six games. But things weren't falling into place like they had before. Mike Bielecki, who won 18 games in 1989, had a 3–8 record at the break and was on the verge of losing his spot in the starting rotation. Our other ace, Greg Maddux, was also struggling. Jerome Walton and Dwight Smith, two outfielders coming off outstanding rookie seasons, were experiencing sophomore slumps. On top of all that, we were dealing with injuries to starting pitcher Rick Sutcliffe, closer Mitch Williams, and catcher Damon Berryhill.

It was unrealistic to think we could leapfrog four teams to come back and win the division, but I at least hoped we could play respectably in the second half of the season.

The good news for me was the Cubs were now convinced I was worth keeping around a while longer. On July 10, 1990, which happened to be my 36th birthday, I became the highest-paid player in Cubs history when I signed a one-year, $3.3 million contract for the 1991 season. The contract contained a clause that guaranteed a second year at the same amount if I played 140 or more games in 1991. In signing the deal, I became the 13th player in the majors to make more than $3 million a year, a list that included Will Clark, Kirby Puckett, Rickey Henderson, and Jose Canseco.

In what was one of the most memorable days of my career, only hours after signing my contract extension, I was in the lineup as the starting National League right fielder in an All-Star Game played under the lights at Wrigley Field. Sandberg and Shawon Dunston also represented the Cubs.

Before the game, I was asked whether the media and others had tried to write me off after my poor performance in the '89 playoffs. My response was, "The same people who build you up will try to knock you down. I don't let the critics affect me."

It seemed the national baseball writers had more doubts about my future than the local ones, so it was gratifying to sign the contract with all the writers in town for the All-Star Game.

And I felt I still had the support of the fans.

My goal remained to retire in a Cubs uniform. Even during my struggles, most of the Wrigley faithful never wavered in their support of me. At the All-Star Game, I got an enormous ovation when my name was announced and again when I took the field. The fans didn't have too much to cheer about during the rain-delayed game, however, as the National League was held to two hits in a 2–0 loss.

I entered the All-Star break batting .324 with a modest three-game hitting streak. Two-and-a-half weeks later, my average was up to .333 after I hit safely in my 15th straight game. I came back to earth in August but still finished the season with a career-high average of .310 to go along with 27 home runs and 100 RBIs. I also stole 16 bases in 18 attempts, my highest total in four years and an indication I still had mileage left in my legs.

My last stolen base of the season gave me 300 for my career, making me the only player at the time other than Willie Mays to have career totals of 2,000 hits, 300 home runs, and 300 stolen bases. Among the other bright spots of the season was that Sandberg hit 40 home runs to become the first second baseman in several decades to win the National League home-run title.

The team finished in fourth place with a record of 77–85. Unfortunately, this is the level of play we'd have to live with for the next couple of seasons, a period when we just couldn't get over the hump.

By the time we played our last game of the season in Philadelphia, I think Zim was ready to shake things up a little. I had joked during a pregame meeting in the clubhouse that because I wasn't in the lineup that day, I would instead manage the finale. I meant no disrespect toward Zim. He wasn't the reason we couldn't duplicate our playoff run from the year before. In fact, he had led us to a winning record in the second half of the season. He knew I was kidding around but agreed to let me have his job for one night. To make sure I didn't do anything too rash, however, he sat next to me the entire game.

With the Cubs leading 4–3 through eight innings, Greg Maddux was doing everything in his power to make my unofficial managerial debut successful. He had given up three unearned runs and helped his cause by hitting an RBI single. My biggest decision of the night was whether to let Mad Dog complete the game or to bring in a reliever to pitch the ninth. Zim seemed to think I should go to the bullpen.

"Aren't you going to get Mitch up?" he asked, referring to our closer Mitch Williams.

"Nah," I replied. "You gave me the day off. I'm going to give Mitch the day off, too."

A promise was a promise. I was in charge. Zim bit his tongue as I opted to bring in Paul Assenmacher. Fortunately, Paul closed out a 4–3 win. After the game I sat at Zim's desk, taking questions from reporters.

I guess that day in Chicago raises the question of whether I've ever considered trying my hand at managing a club. I'll say this—the idea has crossed my mind a few times but not to the point where I've acted on it. I've never been offered a job as manager, either. At the end of the day, managers are hired to be fired. In my career, I saw that happen to a lot of fine ones, including Dick Williams and Don Zimmer. I'm not sure I'd like having my decisions put under a microscope. Then there's the challenge of dealing with 25 egos in the clubhouse, not to mention a sometimes impatient front office. I have to think managers are constantly looking over their shoulders, wondering whether they're one game away from the unemployment line. On top of that, I adhere to a lot of old-school principles that may not be in style anymore. For example, I'm a big proponent of players taking infield practice before games.

All of that said, I think I could be a really good manager. I know how to show tough love, and I think I'd relate as well to the 25th man on the roster as the star player.

Maybe the best way for me to test whether I have what it takes to manage would be by trying it out on an interim basis. I don't know if that opportunity will ever arise, but if it does, I'd consider it.

• • •

To this day, my MVP year in 1987 remains the biggest part of my legacy in Chicago. The way in which collusion kept teams from signing me and how a blank contract got me to the Cubs made the story of my breakout season all the more compelling. I also view that season as my most memorable. But 1990 was special, too. Coming off a subpar and injury-riddled season, the pressure was on to show I could still perform at a high level. If I had failed to regain my old form, I'm sure a lot of people would have written me off. Fortunately, I worked hard to rehabilitate my injuries and went on to have a great season.

My health was still very much on the minds of Cubs management, however. Fearing I might tweak an injury, they denied my request to play for a major league All-Star team that toured Japan after the 1990 season. "We can't take a chance that he'll hurt his knees playing for someone other than the Chicago Cubs," team president Don Grenesko told reporters. "Andre Dawson is too valuable to us as a player."

I regretted not making the Asia trip and wished I had been told earlier that I couldn't go. But at the same time, it was good to hear I was considered a valuable member of the team.

After the season, Vanessa and I got some good—and unexpected—news. She was pregnant again! It came as a wonderful surprise. Following the birth of our son, Darius, we were told she'd almost certainly never have another baby. But the first pregnancy had somehow made it easier for her to conceive again.

We were overjoyed when we welcomed our daughter, Amber, into the world on September 5, 1991. I was in San Diego with the team as Vanessa neared her due date. I hoped we would return from the road trip in time to witness the birth. Our plane landed at about 5:30 AM, and I went immediately to the hospital. Later that morning, Vanessa went into labor. I experienced a lot of exciting situations in my playing career, but nothing compared to the time I spent by my wife's bedside as she gave birth to our children.

Before Amber was born, Vanessa and I moved from our downtown, high-rise apartment overlooking Lake Michigan to a building within walking distance of Wrigley Field. The new location allowed Vanessa to push a stroller to the ballpark. It also made our home a popular hang-out for my teammates and their wives. Vanessa started referring to our home as Grand Central Station. My mom came to town pretty often to see her grandbabies, and she cooked for everyone who stopped by. Those were special times.

• • •

During the off-season, the Cubs signed free agent George Bell, a former American League MVP who had enjoyed some good seasons in Toronto. With Bell's bat added to the lineup, we had the potential to score a lot of runs. Many people predicted we'd recapture the magic of the 1989 season and win our division again.

We had our moments in the early part of the 1991 season, including when Chico Walker and I hit late-inning home runs to fuel a come-from-behind victory against the Braves. My homer came as a pinch hitter; I didn't start the game because my lifetime average against Braves starter John Smoltz was less than .100. As I rounded the bases after my homer off Kent Mercker, I pumped my arm a couple times in a rare display of celebration. At that point in the season, I was hitting .295 with eight home runs in 122 at-bats.

That was a good night, but a lack of consistency kept us from establishing ourselves as the team to beat in the National League East. And 37 games into the season, with our record at 18–19, Zim paid the price for our mediocrity.

Zim was a joy to be around, and it was tough watching him clean out his office. It was also frustrating. The bottom line was my teammates and I hadn't played well enough to save his job. We were hitting a lot of long balls, but that was about the extent of our offensive game. Our bullpen and starting pitching were also shaky. I think most of us agreed Zim deserved at least another couple months to see if he could turn things around.

Shawon Dunston took the news harder than anybody. When Zim was the team's third-base coach in Shawon's rookie year, Zim took a liking to Shawon and helped with his transition from the minors. They had some personal wars because Shawon sometimes did things on the field that caught Zim off guard. But Zim loved him to death. Their relationship really blossomed early in the 1989 season when Zim showed patience in Shawon at a time when his struggles at the plate led to calls for him to be benched. Shawon turned things around that season and helped us make the playoffs. When he got the news of Zim's firing, Shawon told reporters, "I'm taking this personally because he's my friend, not just my manager."

Grenesko had a simple explanation for the move. "There is too much talent here not to at least be a contender."

The Cubs promoted Jim Essian, who had been managing the organization's Triple A affiliate in Iowa. At 40, Essian became the youngest manager in the majors. We won our first five games under him. But we couldn't sustain that level of play. In June, we dropped 12 out of 13 games to fall 12½ games out of first place.

I was having another strong season, hitting .289 with 15 home runs and 52 RBIs at the break. My numbers helped earn me another trip to the All-Star Game.

My second at-bat of the game, held in Toronto's SkyDome, came against fire-balling Roger Clemens of the Red Sox. I had never faced Clemens before, not even in spring training. Roger was throwing hard that night, and after getting ahead of me in the count, he threw a high and tight fastball that I had to fall to the ground to avoid. I got up, dusted myself off, and prepared for Roger to come at me with another fastball. It was a classic power-vs.-power matchup. When he gunned a fastball right down the middle of the plate, I connected and hit it over the wall in straightaway center field.

It was my first home run in eight All-Star appearances. I'm glad I had that experience because it turned out to be my last trip to the All-Star Game.

• • •

Through the first 15-plus years of my career, I had played more than 2,000 major league games and been ejected only one time. That came in 1987 when I went after Eric Show of the Padres after he hit me in the face with a pitch. That incident aside, I was known for my stoic demeanor on and off the field.

Generally speaking, I was on pretty good terms with umpires. Sure, I disagreed with calls from time to time, but I never let myself get too worked up, even if I felt an ump made a blatant mistake.

Well, there's a first time for everything.

On July 23, 1991, during a game against the Reds at Wrigley Field, I had a run-in with home-plate umpire Joe West that led to an uncharacteristic tantrum on my part. The whole thing started in the seventh inning after West rang me up on a Norm Charlton breaking pitch I thought was clearly off the plate.

It's common for players and umps to exchange a few words in these situations, so I gave Joe a piece of my mind while standing at home plate. I was about to head back to the dugout when he yelled, "Go sit down!" and tossed me from the game. I turned around and noticed he had a big smirk on his face. That set me off. I didn't see anything funny about the situation. I took a couple steps toward Joe and inadvertently bumped his chest. That was a definite no-no in player-umpire relations, and I knew I'd be hearing from the league office for the indiscretion.

As I walked back to the dugout, I saw West was still smirking. I thought to myself, "Okay, if I'm getting kicked out and fined anyway, I'm going to get my money's worth." I went back to the dugout and started tossing bats onto the field. I noticed West counting the number of bats I threw, so I decided to see how high he could count. In the end, there were 15 pieces of lumber on the field. While I was heaving bats, Essian was out on the field throwing a fit of his own.

Finally, I went to the clubhouse to cool off. I watched the still-unfolding events on an overhead monitor. For several minutes play was halted because fans were showering the field with cups and other items.

When the game resumed, more craziness took place. Doug Dascenzo laid down a squeeze bunt toward first base against Reds reliever Rob Dibble in the eighth inning. Dibble fielded the ball, but instead of tossing it to the first baseman, he threw a fastball at Dascenzo's legs. West, a busy man that night, immediately ejected Dibble. I had never seen a pitcher do something like that before. Needless to say, the actions of Dawson and Dibble overshadowed an 8–5 Cubs victory.

A few days later, the league office fined me $1,000 and handed me a one-game suspension for "nearly inciting a riot." Maybe worst of all, I got scolded by my mom, who called me after the incident to ask, "What the hell's your problem?!"

My problem was that West had blown the call. On the memo line of the check to National League President Bill White I wrote, "Donation to the blind."

• • •

We finished the 1991 season 77–83 and 20 games behind the first-place Pirates.

Zim wasn't the only casualty of the disappointing season. General manager Jim Frey lost his job at the end of the year. And the Cubs let Essian go, hiring Jim Lefebvre to replace him.

The months that followed the season also represented an abrupt and unpleasant shift in my relationship with Cubs management. The problems started when the team named Larry Himes general manager, a position he had previously held with the White Sox.

I played 149 games in 1991, which meant the Cubs had to pick up my option for the following year. But we were looking beyond that point. Before the season, my agent, Dick Moss, started negotiating with Himes on a contract extension for me. We were looking for a two-year deal that would enable me to play for the Cubs through the 1994 season, when I would turn 40. Himes didn't seem interested in discussing it, however. We couldn't help but notice he seemed to be spending a lot of time trying to court free-agent Bobby Bonilla, who had played third base and right field for the Pirates. The Cubs may have had a need for a solid third baseman, but as far as I was concerned, I was still the team's best option in right for several years to come.

To be fair, Himes did have other things on his plate. Before the season, the Cubs made Ryno the highest-paid player in baseball at the time by signing him to a four-year, $28.4 million deal.

My problems with Himes, at least at first, had nothing to do with contract talks.

Dating back to his days with the White Sox, Himes insisted his players abide by a set of rules that included a dress code requiring players to wear suits or at least shirts and ties while traveling with the team. I never in a million years would have guessed I'd get on his wrong side based on how I dressed. One of my favorite things was clothes shopping, and I had always taken great pride in my appearance. After the 1991 season, a tailor in Chicago made me several lapel-less blazers that I planned to wear with mock turtlenecks when it was chilly in Chicago early in the season. They were expensive and sharp-looking jackets. I was mindful of Himes' shirt-and-tie rule but didn't think he'd have a problem if I occasionally wore one of these outfits.

Larry never approached me directly with his displeasure at my choice of attire. Instead, he had Lefebvre convey the message for him. I told Jim I had a real problem with Larry's overly strict interpretation of what made a player look "presentable."

"Look around the clubhouse, Jim," I said. "You've got guys who wear ties with jeans and cowboy boots. You're telling me that's acceptable but how I dress isn't?"

Some of my teammates openly mocked the dress code. One went as far as to wear a tie that was designed to look like a penis. Nothing in Larry's code of conduct forbade a player from wearing a phallic tie, so nothing was said or done about it.

Jim understood my point, but he knew Larry was too stuck in his ways to change anything about his dress code.

By the time this flare-up occurred, the weather was getting warmer, and there wasn't much need for my custom-made suits anymore. But a rift had apparently developed between Larry and me. I noticed he was acting distant toward me. He'd come into the clubhouse and say hello to everyone around me but not to me. It got to the point where my teammates picked up on it. "What's going on between you two?" Shawon asked after he saw Larry give me the cold shoulder. On another occasion, Larry walked into the clubhouse and saw just two people: a reporter he didn't care for and me. Which of us did he go up and speak to? I'll give you a hint—it wasn't me.

Larry's feelings toward me became evident at a team function the Cubs held for potential sponsors. Every player was put at a table with members of the business community. My table in the banquet hall was near a small stage where Larry and others planned to address the audience. As the room filled up, I noticed every table had about 10 people at it. But not mine. I was sitting alone with my wife, normally something I enjoyed but not exactly the purpose of the evening in question. I looked at Vanessa and said, "You know what's going on, don't you? We should just get up and leave." She didn't want to make a scene and encouraged me to stay. I agreed to stay put for the time being, but it crossed my mind to bolt at the very moment Larry went on stage to speak. Vanessa whispered to me, "Can we just grin and bear it and get through it?" She was right. By remaining there, I hope I showed who was the bigger man.

On top of the personal beef Larry apparently had with me, Dick wasn't getting anywhere with contract negotiations, even though he had made it clear he was willing to talk about an extension during the 1992 season.

I recall the situation emotionally affecting me to the point that I carried negative feelings onto the playing field. My body language let those closest to me know that something was bothering me.

"What's wrong, Pudgy?" my mom asked me on the phone one day early in the season.

"Nothing, Mom," I told her. "You know how this game can be sometimes."

I never clashed with any of the many managers I played for, but for whatever reason, I had problems with two general managers, Murray Cook of the Expos and Himes, both of whom didn't seem to have a high opinion of me. My run-ins with Cook in 1986 came during the height of baseball's collusion era when hostilities between players and management were common. Himes' attitude toward me didn't have the same historical context.

When I perceived someone was mistreating me, rather than rebel, I'd retreat. And I suppose that only increased the tension level. I wish Cook and Himes had simply approached me and told me what was the problem. Yes, I had a reputation for being intimidating, but these were grown men and front-office executives who should have at least communicated their feelings.

Ultimately, I was able to block out the silliness with Himes after a woman who worked in the Cubs front office took me aside for a private conversation.

"Try not to let what Larry's doing to you affect you," she told me. "He doesn't like the fact that the front office respects you more than they do him."

All of a sudden, it was clear to me. Larry's feelings of insecurity had led him to pick on me.

And he refused to stop.

When Hurricane Andrew hit Florida in August 1992, I had a hard time reaching family members to check on their safety. I heard reports of how the Category 5 storm was ravaging the Miami area, and I was understandably worried. I asked Jim Lefebvre for a few days off to go check on things. He had no problem with my request and encouraged me to go.

While I was gone, an unnamed front-office source was quoted in the paper as saying I had abandoned the team.

This time around, I wasn't going to let anything Larry or anyone else said bother me. I had enough to deal with when I got home to Miami. Following the hurricane, it looked like a bomb had been dropped on the area. My old neighborhood wasn't in the evacuation zone, but it got hit pretty hard. The wind had ripped a lot of roofs off homes. My Uncle John told me how he held a mattress against his front door to keep the wind from blowing it out. The roof of my brother-in-law's home collapsed, and his family was forced to hang onto an iron gate in the front yard as the storm raged. Some families huddled in cars, fearing they might get hit by flying glass or other debris if they stayed in their homes. My mom's house became an unofficial shelter for hurricane victims in the neighborhood.

Not for a second did I regret my decision to go down to Florida and help my family recover.

I was swinging a hot bat before my trip home, and upon my return to the team in early September, I banged out five hits in a 14-inning loss to the Padres. That came during a stretch in the season where I went 21-for-37 and raised my average from .258 to .283.

As the season wound down, I guess Himes decided it was time to try and make peace with me. When a reporter asked him about a September call-up who was struggling in the majors, he said, "I wanted him here to see a big-league clubhouse and hang around a guy like Andre Dawson." Around this time, Larry even started relaxing his dress code a bit.

For me, 1992 was another solid season. But the team again stumbled to a fourth-place finish in the division. The highlight of the year was seeing Maddux elevate himself to one of the best pitchers in the game. He finished with a 20–11 record and won his first Cy Young Award.

The Toronto Blue Jays won their first of back-to-back World Series in 1992. That wasn't a surprise from a talent standpoint. The Blue Jays were absolutely loaded with top-flight players such as Jack Morris, Paul Molitor, and Roberto Alomar. But if you had told me during my time with the Expos that Toronto would be the first Canadian team to win a title, neither I nor anyone else in the country would have believed it. For several years, the Expos were Canada's only team. Even after Toronto got an expansion team in 1977, the Blue Jays took a back seat to their National League counterparts. But entering the 1990s, the Blue Jays were the superior team, both in performance and popularity. The times were changing.

• • •

One of the most enjoyable parts of the 1992 season was getting to know a new teammate named Sammy Sosa. Although Sammy had struggled in his first three seasons with the Rangers and White Sox, I felt he had the potential to become a great hitter. The Cubs shared that opinion, so they traded George Bell to the White Sox for Sosa. Unfortunately, Sammy was injured for much of his first season with the Cubs.

On top of having enormous talent, Sammy was a genuinely nice guy. We got along well, and I tried to take him under my wing.

One time, I even saved him from running afoul of Himes' code of conduct. We were playing in Montreal when he realized he didn't have a suit to wear on the team plane. I told him not to worry, that I had a friend from my Expos days who owned a clothing store downtown near the team hotel.

"It's my treat, Sammy," I said. "Find a suit you like, and I'll take care of it later."

On my way to the stadium the next day, I stopped by the store to see if Sammy had taken me up on my offer. He had. My friend handed me the bill for Sammy's purchase—the $2,500 bill!

"He selected the best suit I had in the store," my friend told me.

When I got to the ballpark, I went right over to Sammy's locker.

"You realize you could have bought three or four very nice suits for the price of the one you got, right?"

Before answering, Sammy took a garment bag out of his locker and unzipped it to reveal a beautiful silk suit.

"One-hundred percent silky, me likey!" he said with the awe of a child as he slowly ran his hand down the suit jacket.

I wish I would have had the opportunity to play a few more years with Sammy.

As it stood, my days in Chicago were coming to an end, so the last week of the 1992 season was meaningful and emotional for me. I wanted to make sure I conveyed to the fans how thankful I was for my time there. I took a little more time making eye contact with the Bleacher Bums.

I came into the final day of the 1992 season with 398 career home runs. In the third inning of a game against the Expos, I sent a Mark Gardner pitch through a brisk wind and over the left-field wall. I had a couple opportunities to hit my 400th homer at Wrigley Field as a Cub. Unfortunately, I couldn't write a storybook ending and finished up the game with a single and a strikeout.

As I feared, the Cubs and I never really got close on the terms of a new deal. Their offers included a 10-year, $10 million contract that would have kept me in the organization after my playing days were over. I wasn't ready to contemplate my post-career plans, so that wasn't acceptable to me. I was looking for a two-year deal that the Cubs weren't willing to offer.

The team had its hands full that off-season because Maddux's contract was also expiring. Mad Dog was trying to find a way to stay in Chicago where he had spent his first six seasons, but Himes and the Cubs didn't make it worth his while. He ended up signing a five-year, $28 million deal with the Braves. Himes brushed off Maddux's departure by touting the Cubs' free-agent signing of Jose Guzman, who was coming off a 16-win season in Texas. Guzman would win just 14 more games in his major league career.

Before declaring for free agency, I went to Northwestern Memorial Hospital for tune-up surgery that involved removing debris from my left knee.

When it came time to look for another place to play, there were two more options than the year before. The Florida Marlins and Colorado Rockies were joining the National League as expansion teams for the 1993 season. The Marlins were set to become the first major league team in my hometown of Miami. I was intrigued with the possibility of returning home to continue my career, but I realized the Marlins were going to be a young team that would experience a lot of growing pains in their first years. I wanted to be a regular on a team I felt could compete for a championship.

The first team to call with a contract offer was the Boston Red Sox, who were coming off a season in which they finished dead last in the American League East. They were a team in desperate need of offensive help. In 1992, outfielder Tom Brunansky had led the team in home runs and RBIs with 15 and 74, respectively. The top batting average on the team belonged to center fielder Bob Zupcic and reserves Scott Cooper and John Valentin, who all hit just .276. I trusted, however, that Red Sox management was committed to taking the team in the right direction.

After the Red Sox expressed interest in me, a lot of thoughts went through my mind in a short period of time. Since I signed with the Cubs in 1987, I had always resisted the idea of going to the American League and serving primarily as a designated hitter. Was I ready now to do that? And after growing so fond of Chicago, did I feel up to learning a new league, a new ballpark, and new cities this late in my career?

Boston general manager Lou Gorman put to rest any doubts I may have had about making those transitions. He made it clear he badly wanted to see me in a Red Sox uniform. That carried a lot of weight with me. Lou was a warm man and a native New Englander who struck me as honest and straightforward. On December 9, 1992, I signed a two-year contract with Boston that was worth more than $9 million. In doing so, I became the team's highest-paid player in 1993.

Nearly a decade earlier, my Expos teammate Warren Cromartie was reluctant to negotiate with the Red Sox because he felt they weren't the best choice for a black player. Cro ended up going to Japan instead. I had no firsthand knowledge that Boston was hostile to blacks. And more importantly, I needed to go to the place that offered me the best opportunity to continue my career.

With that in mind, I said goodbye to Wrigley Field and hello to Fenway Park.

13

BEANTOWN

I WAS FORTUNATE THROUGHOUT MY CAREER TO HAVE BUILT CLOSE AND trusting relationships with several teammates. I've never been the most outgoing person, so I appreciated guys like Timmy Raines in Montreal and Shawon Dunston in Chicago who took the time to get to know me.

Shawon was as loyal a friend as I've ever known, and he wasn't happy that the Cubs didn't do more to keep me. After I signed with Boston, he hugged me and said, "Things around here won't be the same without you."

But Shawon was also facing an uncertain future in Chicago. Having missed nearly all of the 1992 season with back problems, he was set to embark on a rigorous rehabilitation program. He told the *Chicago Tribune* before the 1993 season he was committed to working hard to get back on the field. He said he would try to emulate my routine for coming back from injuries. Though we had never specifically discussed my regimen, he had ample opportunity to observe the hours I spent in the conditioning room trying to get game-ready. It was gratifying to know I had rubbed off on him. Shawon's rehabilitation caused him to miss almost all of the '93 season, as well, but he bounced back strong the following year.

I knew I'd miss Shawon and the other guys on the Cubs, especially at spring training where we had some of our best times. When I reported to Red Sox camp in Fort Myers, Florida, I looked around and realized I knew hardly anyone. Outfielder Billy Hatcher and I had some mutual friends. I had faced pitcher Danny Darwin when he pitched for the Astros. And I had played against Red Sox hitting coach Mike Easler when he was with Pittsburgh. But that was about it.

There was a lot to process when I arrived at spring training. As I joked to a reporter at the time, "I'm getting too old for massive changes." To help myself adjust to the new setting, I grabbed a locker next to Jack Clark, who had come to the Red Sox a couple years earlier after spending 15 out of 16 years in the National League. Unfortunately, Jack was cut before camp was over.

The transition was also hard on my family.

Vanessa had grown to love everything about Chicago. It's where our children were born, where my MVP was won, and where our marriage had survived some rocky times. But as she said when Red Sox general manager Lou Gorman called with a lucrative offer the Cubs weren't willing to match, "It's nice to be wanted."

She was right. I recognized I was in the twilight of my career, but I was in no way, shape, or form contemplating retirement. On the brink of a season in which I would turn 39, I felt I had some good years still ahead of me. We got a comfortable house in the suburb of Brookline and set out to enjoy our New England experience.

Vanessa still had one minor concern about the change of scenery.

During our first 15 years of marriage, she evolved from someone with little interest in baseball to a real expert on the game, or at least of the National League. She worried she'd have a hard time learning new teams and players in the American League. I explained to her that in terms of baseball, Boston and Chicago had a lot of similarities.

"They both play in old ballparks in front of great fans, and neither of them has won anything in a while," I told her.

Even our son, Darius, who wasn't yet four years old, found it difficult to leave Chicago behind. Shortly after arriving in Boston, we went to the Fenway Park gift shop to get him a Red Sox hat. As we browsed the store, we found ourselves in front of a display of team caps from around the majors. Darius saw a blue cap emblazoned with a red "C" and pointed up to it. "No, you have one of those already," I told him, and brought over a navy blue Red Sox cap for his inspection. He stared at me blankly and pointed again at the Cubs cap. To keep my son happy, we left the store with both caps.

A highlight of our early weeks in Boston was the discovery of a terrific soul food restaurant called Bob the Chef's. The owner of the place, Darryl Settles, noticed my family and me eating there on a regular basis and decided to host a welcoming party for me. It was a nice way to get to know some people in the community.

Prior to joining the Red Sox, the only previous time I had stepped foot in Fenway Park was for an exhibition game between Boston and Montreal. I liked the idea of trying to hit balls into or over the Green Monster in left field.

The change of leagues also offered me a great opportunity to play for the first time in other American League ballparks, including Yankee Stadium. Dating back to childhood, I had always associated myself with the National League, but as I got older, I realized I wanted to be able to say I played in the House that Ruth Built. I got only one hit in 21 at-bats in Yankee Stadium, but the experience of playing there was still special.

I was penciled in as the Red Sox everyday right fielder with the understanding I'd see time at designated hitter whenever my legs needed rest. Our manager, Butch Hobson, was only a few years older than me. He was extremely laid-back compared to a lot of other managers. Butch let me know he was happy to have me on the team and was going to get me as much playing time as possible.

For the team, there was nowhere to go but up. I was one of the few new faces in a clubhouse that included Roger Clemens, who had won three Cy Young Awards at that time; and Mo Vaughn, a 25-year-old first baseman on the verge of becoming one of the game's best hitters. The pitching staff also featured veterans Danny Darwin and Frank Viola.

Somewhat to my surprise, once I got to know him, I discovered Clemens was a very down-to-earth guy. My only previous contact with Roger came in the 1991 All-Star Game when I hit a home run off him. By the early 1990s, the guy was a bona fide superstar. But he was also a very hard worker who didn't take his success for granted.

I liked Roger, just as I liked former teammates Pete Rose, Rafael Palmeiro, and Sammy Sosa. Away from the field, I can say without hesitation they are all good human beings. The same can be said about Alex Rodriguez. Shortly after A-Rod broke into the majors in 1994, he came to the batting cages in Miami where I took swings. He asked me a lot of questions about how I played the game. I was impressed with his attitude and his desire to fulfill his vast potential. I'm aware all have received harsh judgments in the court of public opinion. Pete's career was tarnished by gambling on baseball. The others were implicated in the use of performance-enhancing drugs. Let me be clear—I don't condone their actions, and I don't think the court of public opinion is necessarily wrong. But I'd also argue, as with so many things, the cover-up is worse than the crime. Engaging in certain behavior is one thing, but lying about it is another. What I would have liked to see is more honesty from these and other players who broke rules or violated the public's trust. That's the reason the handful of players who owned up to their mistakes, including Jason Giambi and Andy Pettitte, are seen in a less harsh light than some of their peers.

• • •

Coming off a last-place finish, Red Sox fans couldn't have been blamed for having low expectations for their team in 1993. But one thing I learned when I got to Boston is their fans never have low expectations. That was one difference between Cubs and Red Sox fans. In some ways, there was little pressure to win in Chicago. Losing had become such a part of the team's DNA that fans didn't get too bent out of shape after a losing season or a winning one that ended with heartbreak. Red Sox fans, on the other hand, were dying to win. Maybe this was because of their rivalry with the Yankees, a team that had steamrolled Boston and everyone else in their path for decades. Sure, the Cubs had a rivalry with the Cardinals, but it was much less hostile than the Red Sox/Yankees relationship. As a Cub, I had actually been cheered in St. Louis after making nice plays. Would Red Sox fans have cheered Reggie Jackson? No way. Would Yankees fans have clapped for Dwight Evans? Not a chance.

I hoped to hear plenty of cheers from the Fenway faithful, but before I even had a chance to play a game there, I suffered an injury that affected my first few months in Boston.

It came in the fourth game of the season at Texas after I hit my second double of the night off 46-year-old Nolan Ryan, who was in the final season of his great career. As I tried to advance to third on a Ryan wild pitch, I had a moment of indecision about whether or not to slide. As I approached the bag, I made an awkward slide and wrenched my knee.

The good news was that I was safe. The bad news was that I was in pain. I shrugged it off and stayed in the game, however. My previous knee problems had all stemmed from general deterioration, not from a specific on-the-field incident. I didn't want a base-running mishap this early in my time with Boston to lead to my third-ever trip to the disabled list.

I was eager to get acclimated to American League pitching. During my years in the National League, I had kept notes on the tendencies of most pitchers I faced. Now that notebook was as good as useless. I tried to learn on the fly what pitchers in this league were trying to do to me. Early on, it became clear they wanted to work me inside and jam me. That explained why I got hit by four pitches in April.

I made a good impression on the home fans in my first two series at chilly Fenway Park.

My first home run in a Red Sox uniform happened to be the 400th of my career. It was also my first ever as a designated hitter. The homer came in the second inning of an April 15 game against the Indians. A cut fastball from Jose Mesa got too much of the middle of the plate, and I stroked it over the wall in left field, up in the direction of the famous Citgo sign, to become the 25th player in major league history to reach the 400 home run mark. A groundskeeper at Fenway Park saw to it that the home run ball was retrieved and given to me.

My new teammates streamed out of the dugout to greet me as I crossed home plate. Then I experienced another first—a curtain call at Fenway Park. I got to savor the events of the evening for several more hours as we beat Cleveland 4–3 in 13 innings.

The ovation in Boston meant a lot to me. I had only played a few games there, but I already felt warmly embraced by Red Sox Nation. Nothing in baseball compares to the roar of a stadium crowd. I had always appreciated the support of the fans in Montreal and especially Chicago. I would have gladly played out my career in either place had I been offered the contract extensions I deserved. Even though I wasn't going to retire as an Expo or Cub, I felt my legacies in Montreal and Chicago were well established.

Or maybe that wasn't the case in Montreal.

In 1993, I found out my jersey number was going to be retired at Olympic Stadium in Montreal. The only problem was the Expos were retiring No. 10 not in my honor but because of Rusty Staub, who wore the number when he played in Montreal from 1969 to 1971. By contrast, I had played 11 seasons with the Expos. Rusty's uniform was the first the Expos had ever retired. Later in 1993, Gary Carter, who finished up his career in Montreal after the 1992 season, also received the honor.

I was in the middle of a season and didn't have time to dwell on the slight.

My milestone home run at Fenway came during a seven-game homestand in which I got a hit in each of the six games I played and knocked in seven runs. Even better, the Red Sox won six of seven games.

But the injury I suffered in Texas didn't go away on its own. In fact, it worsened to the point where there was no choice but to have another surgery. On May 6, I had cartilage removed from my right knee. The nature of the procedure surprised me because after seven previous operations I didn't think I had any cartilage left in my knee!

Around the time of the operation, the *Boston Herald* called me "the 38-year-old with the 25-year-old build and the 75-year-old knees." That about summed it up.

I was expected to miss up to six weeks, but instead I returned in less than three. I wanted to get back to the task of helping the Red Sox compete for a division crown. No team was taking control of the American League East, and thanks to an outstanding home record, we were right in the hunt. Even a dismal stretch in May and June when we lost 16-of-19 games didn't put us out of the race. We were 13 games out of first place on June 20, but in the next month or so, we strung together separate winning streaks of seven, five, and 10 games to climb into a three-way tie for first with the Yankees and Blue Jays.

Mo Vaughn was the offensive catalyst during that stretch. He finished the season with a team-high 29 home runs and 101 RBIs. He also hit .297.

I raised my batting average 53 points during the team's incredible early summer turnaround. My improved performance was partly due to the fact that I was becoming increasingly comfortable in the designated-hitter role.

After my May surgery, it was a no-brainer I was going to see time at DH until my knee felt good enough to roam the field again. That role took some getting used to. In spring training, I'd view a day at DH almost as a day off. The whole rhythm of the game is different when you're not playing defense. And I didn't care for that at first. But I looked at it as a challenge I wanted to conquer. I learned to keep myself occupied and sharp between at-bats by taking swings in the stadium batting cage.

My 1993 season ended on a down note. I missed nearly three weeks in September, not because of my knee, but because a pitch from Tim Belcher of the White Sox fractured my right wrist. It was the 12th time that season I had been hit by a pitch, the most since I led the National League in that category in 1978. At the time I went on the disabled list, we were six games out of first place and barely clinging to life. Even though the fracture hadn't completely healed, I returned for the final week of a season that ended with the Red Sox 15 games behind the division-winning Blue Jays. That was the year Joe Carter's dramatic home run in Game 6 of the World Series against the Phillies gave Toronto back-to-back titles.

Despite missing a good portion of the season due to the knee and wrist injuries, I finished with 13 home runs and 67 RBIs, which put me among the team leaders in both categories. Every game I started, I hit either third or fourth in the batting order.

With one year left on my contract in Boston, I looked forward to a special 1994 season. And that's exactly what it turned out to be—for all the wrong reasons.

• • •

When spring training rolled around, sportswriters in Boston and around the country started posing the question, "Is this the last hurrah for Dawson?"

I sought Vanessa's opinion on the matter. She told me I should play as long as I felt I could contribute to a team. Whether that meant playing beyond 1994 remained to be seen. I planned to end my career on my own terms and not because of injury or poor performance. I wanted to return the uniform, not have it taken away from me.

I was prepared for the possibility of retiring after the 1994 season, but I in no way had made up my mind. My body had taken a beating over the years, but I still possessed the determination and bat speed to be a productive hitter. If called upon, I also felt I could still play right field on a semi-regular basis. It may have been wishful thinking, but I hoped my last season—whenever that came— would be uninterrupted and injury-free.

Unfortunately, 1994 was neither.

There was a lot of uncertainty going into the season, and only some of it had to do with my own personal situation. The bigger issue was that a strike loomed over a proposal by baseball owners to enact a salary cap for major league teams. The plan required approval of our union, which was vehemently opposed to the idea of limiting the earning power of players. I agreed wholeheartedly with the union.

In addition to that drama, 1994 was also the year Major League Baseball went to a three-division format in each league and added a wild-card playoff team. I viewed that as one more opportunity for me to get back to the playoffs.

I had the support of my manager, who during spring training made a lofty statement about my upcoming season. "Hawk's one of those guys, he'll get hot and for three weeks he'll carry your club," Butch said. "He'll get 100 RBIs this season, just you watch."

Butch's prediction looked good after we opened the season with a three-game sweep of the Tigers at Fenway. In that series, I hit two home runs and knocked in five runs.

A strained hamstring sidelined me for a couple games later in April, but I returned to finish the month with five home runs and 15 RBIs, the type of numbers I had put up during the prime of my career.

Then, on cue, I went down with another knee ailment.

The injury occurred in a game against Cleveland. I was running out a ground ball when my left knee started making a crunching and grinding sound I had never heard before. It was a noise you'd expect to hear from a car transmission, not a human body! I was placed on the 15-day disabled list and underwent surgery at UMass Medical Center in Worcester. Dr. Arthur Pappas, who was the Red Sox physician as well as a part-owner of the team, estimated I'd miss six weeks.

I was hitting just .246 when I went on the DL, but my 10 home runs and 27 RBIs at just past the quarter-mark of the season put me on pace for close to 40 home runs and 100 RBIs. I now had no chance of attaining those numbers, but I still felt I had good production left in me. I had been through post-surgery rehabilitation enough times to know how it went. I decided to create my own rehab plan.

A few weeks later, I went to see Butch in his office.

"I'm ready to play," I told him.

"Ready to play?" he asked with surprise. "Aren't you supposed to be a few weeks away?"

He called in the team trainer, who watched me run through a series of agility exercises. Despite my fluid movements, they still seemed unconvinced that I could have gotten myself back into game shape that quickly.

Nonetheless, Butch played me at DH that night and I got three hits against the Orioles. A couple weeks later I hit two home runs and had four RBIs in a game against the Brewers.

I felt good again—for a while.

When my knee acted up yet again, I realized that more surgery was inevitable. For obvious reasons, I preferred not to have another in-season surgery. But with a strike looking more and more likely, I figured I'd just go ahead and do it. I didn't feel that procedure fixed my problem, so I had another in Miami in December. That meant the same year I turned 40, I had three knee operations in the span of eight months.

After the second surgery of the season, I started to seriously consider whether it might be time to call it quits. I even met with new Red Sox general manager Dan Duquette to discuss the possibility of taking a job with the organization if I decided to retire.

Then the season took another turn for the worse.

For the second time in my career, baseball experienced a midseason strike. The players walked out on August 12, 1994. At the time, the Red Sox were 54–61 and 17 games out of first place. About a month later, the rest of the season was cancelled, postseason and all. For the first time in 90 years, there was no World Series.

The strike couldn't have come at a less opportune time, just as pennant races were heating up.

I had monitored the fortunes of the Expos ever since I left the team in 1987. I had played on some good Montreal teams in the late 1970s and early 1980s, but the team managed by Felipe Alou in 1994 played the best baseball in franchise history. The lineup, featuring Marquis Grissom, Larry Walker, and Felipe's son Moises Alou was potent from top to bottom. Pedro Martinez and Ken Hill anchored a strong pitching rotation. At 74–40, the Expos had the best record in the majors and appeared to be cruising toward their first playoff appearance since 1981.

The cancellation of the remainder of the 1994 season wiped out the Expos' chances of competing for their first World Series. The strike was also blamed for sending the organization into a decade-long tailspin in attendance that hurt its financial health and eventually led the franchise to relocate to Washington, D.C.

Baseball lost a lot of fans due to the 1994 strike. I think owners were caught off guard by the public's anger at the game stopping at such a pivotal time in the season. I supported the union's goals, but in my opinion, the dispute between players and owners never should have gotten to the point it did. The business of baseball was getting increasingly complex, and for a player like me, a little distasteful. As a kid, you had to tear me away from the field. Nothing came between me and the game I loved. In the twilight of my career, I started to wonder if money hadn't become more important than the game itself.

The strike dragged on throughout the winter. By spring 1995, with no resolution in sight, teams brought in previously unsigned players to spring training. This angered a lot of major leaguers, who considered "replacement player" a kinder word for "scab." I didn't make that big a deal about it. On the one hand, I realized the presence of these players was undermining the objectives of the players union. But I also realized the replacements were thinking in terms of their careers and trying to fulfill a dream of playing in the big leagues.

That situation was defused when the strike finally came to an end in early April 1995.

By that time, my contract with Boston had expired and I was again a free agent. A few months before the strike ended, the Florida Marlins contacted me to let me know they were interested in my services.

I didn't want my career to end with a season in which I experienced multiple injuries and baseball experienced an historic strike.

I hadn't contacted the Marlins when I was looking for a team two years earlier because the Red Sox seemed like a better fit. But now the time was right to play in Florida.

A few days after the strike ended, I signed a one-year deal worth $500,000 with the Marlins. It was an ideal situation for me. I would get to play in front of family and friends and sleep at my house in Miami.

After almost 20 years in Canada, the Midwest, and New England, Vanessa and I were going home.

14

HOME AGAIN

WHEN I PLAYED AT FLORIDA A&M UNIVERSITY IN THE EARLY 1970S, I HAD a teammate named Charles Johnson. With the Marlins, I played alongside his son, Charles Jr. In my first two seasons with the Expos, one of my teammates was utility player Jose Morales. In Florida, Jose was my hitting coach. I was two years older than Marlins general manager Dave Dombrowski. And except for 34-year-old Terry Pendleton, I was at least 10 years older than every player in my new team's Opening Day starting lineup.

I knew I would play a limited role with the Marlins in 1995. My job was to be ready whenever manager Rene Lachemann called on me for a spot start or a pinch-hitting appearance. Beyond that, I was expected to provide veteran leadership in the clubhouse.

For a franchise with just one full season under its belt, the Marlins had built a pretty good nucleus. Jeff Conine, Gary Sheffield, and the newly acquired Pendleton looked ready to lead the offense. And the pitching staff featured former 22-game winner John Burkett.

Because the strike didn't get resolved until early April, the 1995 season started late and was abbreviated to 144 games.

Lach didn't waste any time before testing my pinch-hitting skills. In two close games against the Dodgers to open the season, he sent me up in the ninth inning. I failed to come through either time, and the Marlins lost both games.

For the second time since leaving the Cubs, I found myself trying to get used to an unfamiliar role. In Boston, it had taken me awhile to adjust to being a designated hitter. But that was nothing compared to what I faced in Florida as

Lach's go-to pinch-hitter. As a DH, I got several at-bats a game, which helped me establish rhythm at the plate. I underestimated how difficult it would be to come off the bench for a single at-bat, usually with a game on the line and the opponent's flame-throwing closer on the mound. It was a few weeks before I got my first pinch-hit of the season. This experience with the Marlins helped me appreciate guys who thrive in this role. They are a special breed.

My struggles off the bench carried over to the occasional games Lach put me in the starting lineup. Unlike the everyday player who has numerous chances to break out of a slump, as a part-timer I felt added pressure to get a hit each time I came to the plate.

With the team off to a terrible start and my average at .182 in mid-May, I vented my frustration on an umpire and earned myself the fourth ejection of my career. The incident came after I questioned a strike call by home plate umpire Angel Hernandez.

I had pledged to continue playing as long as I felt I could help a team win. After my slow start, I started to wonder if I was an asset or liability to the Marlins.

After discussing the situation with Vanessa, I decided to play out the season and then announce my retirement. I didn't reveal my intentions to the team or media, however. Instead, when asked about my possible retirement, I focused my answer on how I was playing. "I'm not at all pleased with my performance," I told reporters. "You can go as far as saying it's embarrassing."

After 61 at-bats with the Marlins, I had yet to hit a home run.

On June 16, 1995, I finally connected for my 400th career National League home run. It came off David West in the fourth inning of a game in Philadelphia. The fans at Veterans Stadium gave me a nice ovation as I crossed home plate. That positive reception was short-lived, however. Later in the game, when I dropped a fly ball for a two-base error, I heard a guy yell, "What's the matter, Dawson, forget how to catch a baseball?" It was good to know Philadelphia fans hadn't changed a bit during my two years in the American League.

I may have followed through on my plan to retire if it hadn't been for a thumb injury to Sheffield that landed him on the disabled list for a couple months in 1995. With Gary out of the lineup, I saw a lot of starts in the outfield. And I took advantage of the unexpected playing time.

The home run in Philly got me going a little bit. Over the next week, I hit three more homers. In the final two weeks of June, I had 11 RBIs.

All of a sudden, the season wasn't looking so bleak anymore.

But then I ran into some bad luck—literally.

I missed nearly all of July with a strained hip flexor muscle, an injury I suffered when I slid into Expos catcher Darrin Fletcher during a play at the plate.

Before rejoining the Marlins, I went down to Single A Brevard County for a rehabilitation stint. It marked the first time I had played in the minors since 1976. In what I still believed would be my last season in the majors, things were coming full circle.

Sheffield was still on the disabled list when I returned from my injury in early August. For a month, it was just like old times as I held down the starting job in right field. I collected 25 hits in 26 games that month. In a game at Atlanta-Fulton County Stadium, the scene of my first major league home run in 1977, I hit two home runs, including a grand slam. My other home run that night came off Pedro Borbon Jr., whose father I homered against during my rookie season.

Sheffield was slated to return at the end of August. In order to allow me to continue playing right field, Gary volunteered to move to center, a position he had never played before. "I respect him as an individual and a ballplayer," Gary told reporters. "He deserves a good farewell, if this is going to be it."

Even though Lach declined the offer, Gary's willingness to make the switch showed me he was a quality individual. One of my few at-bats in early September came off Greg Maddux of the Braves, who got me to hit into a rally-ending double play. It was the only time in my career I faced Mad Dog.

With my playing time diminished again, I was at peace with the fact that I was about to embark on the final month of my major league career. That's not to say I didn't face an internal conflict. As much as I hated to end my career when things were going bad, how could I retire at a time when I was playing well?

Then there was the team.

The Marlins were showing signs of becoming a good ballclub in the second half of the season. After going 8–24 in April and May, the team went 59–52 the rest of the way. We posted a winning record in games I started. It wasn't out of the question that the team could compete for a division title—or at least a wild-card berth—the following season. If possible, I wanted to be part of that.

As I was trying to decide my future, I faced an unwelcome distraction during a series in Denver against the Rockies. I was leaving a team party when I got hit in the face with a G-string outside our hotel. I thought the hotel valet threw the garment, and I went to confront him. I wound up getting charged with assault, even though I never touched the guy. The case was eventually dismissed. At a court hearing, the judge told me, "I will wish you good luck, despite being a Rockies fan."

I finished the season with eight home runs and 37 RBIs in only 226 at-bats.

Dombrowski knew I was contemplating retirement and approached me in September with an offer. He said he was pleased with my play and felt I earned a chance to return to the team.

"We'd like to bring you back, if you're willing to come back," Dave told me.

I followed my heart and decided to return to the Marlins with little doubt 1996 would be my last go-around.

• • •

If I didn't feel I could contribute to the Marlins, I wouldn't have come back for another season at the age of 41.

Lach agreed I could still help the team. He went as far as to say that, if it wasn't for my knee problems, I could probably play until I was 50. That was a big if, of course.

An early sign I had something left in the tank came during the 20th spring training of my major league career. We had lost our first 10 exhibition games in 1996, but I helped break the losing streak by hitting two doubles and knocking in four runs in a win against the Expos.

I also took advantage of opportunities to mentor younger teammates. I had always been reluctant to approach anyone with unsolicited advice because you never know how a guy will take that. But if someone came to me with a question or in need of guidance, I was happy to help in any way I could.

During my time with the Marlins, I spent a good deal of time with a young outfielder named Darrell Whitmore, who had starred in baseball and football at West Virginia University. In 1993 at Triple A Edmonton, he hit .355 with 62 RBIs in only 273 at-bats. Unfortunately, he couldn't duplicate that success when he was called up to the Marlins. He had battled a lot of injuries in his young career.

Darrell and I worked out together over the winter before the 1996 season at a park near my childhood home in South Miami. During those weeks, Darrell got to know my wife, kids, and mom. I think my mom made the biggest impression on him with the meals she prepared for us. Darrell told the *South Florida Sun Sentinel* how attached he became to her. "No matter how down you are, you walk into her house, she brings you up, just joking around and having fun with you. I told Andre, I don't see it. I don't see how he got to be so quiet. They're like night and day. But they're both class, all the way."

Darrell got off to a good start at spring training but started the year back in the minors and never again got the call to the big leagues. He was a talented player, but sometimes talent only gets you so far. Darrell would have benefited from the opportunity to play on a regular basis, but he never got that chance.

I entered the 1996 season as the oldest player in the National League. In my first start, which came in the sixth game of the year, I got four hits in a 14–7 home loss to the Giants. After I knocked in two runs with a ninth-inning single, some fans started to "salaam" me by bowing down with outstretched arms. For a day, it was like I was back at Wrigley Field!

In a late April game at San Francisco, Barry Bonds of the Giants homered against us to become the fourth player in major league history to reach career marks of 300 home runs and 300 stolen bases. It was an eventful night for Barry, who went on to hit a second home run and get ejected for arguing balls and strikes. The three other members of the 300–300 club, Barry's father, Bobby; his godfather, Willie Mays; and I were all on hand to see him accomplish the feat. Before the following day's game, we all posed for a picture together.

I was closer in age to Bobby than Barry, and by that point in my career I had hit just about all the home runs I was going to hit. Barry, on the other hand, wasn't even halfway to his career total of 762.

When I played against him, I viewed Barry as a player poised to build upon a very successful first 10 years in the big leagues. He was a consistent .300 hitter who I believed would continue hitting at least 30 home runs a season.

Technically, I was right. I just never would have guessed that there would come a season when he hit his 30th home run *on June 4*. But that's what happened in 2001, the year Barry hit 73 homers.

• • •

Though our careers overlapped, I guess you could say Barry and I played in different eras.

A lot of what took place behind the scenes in the steroid era was revealed after my career ended. The details of what players did to enhance their performance came as a surprise to me. That's not to say I didn't know something peculiar was going on. The signs were hard to miss. In 1996, Brady Anderson of the Orioles exploded for 50 home runs. Anderson was a small guy whose previous season-high in homers was 21. Meanwhile, I was seeing players like Lenny Dykstra of the Phillies put on an incredible amount of muscle mass in a short period of time. I was looking at it from the vantage point of someone who worked out a lot and tried to hit home runs for a living. When I saw the ease with which some players were bulking up and going deep, I suspected they had found a shortcut.

Like the rest of the country, I observed the 1998 season from a seat in a ballpark or from the comfort of my living room.

The home run chase between Mark McGwire and Sammy Sosa generated a lot of excitement in a game that was still experiencing the backlash of a strike that, among other things, led to the cancellation of the 1994 World Series. The competition between McGwire and Sosa provided great drama throughout the season. After each broke Roger Maris' single-season record of 61 home runs, they engaged in a head-to-head battle to see who would be the new record-holder. The country really embraced the personalities of both guys. More importantly, the two players developed a friendly relationship with each other as McGwire went on to hit 70 home runs, four more than Sammy.

Amid all the hoopla and hype surrounding the competition, little was said about the role of performance-enhancing drugs.

It's generally accepted that Barry sought a chemical advantage on the field because he craved the same level of notoriety that McGwire and Sosa had achieved in 1998. That suggests Barry was insecure. All I'll say is the Barry I got to know was supremely confident and had a high opinion of his own abilities. He got the attention he wanted when he broke the single-season home run record in 2001. Of course, that performance took place under a huge cloud of suspicion.

I've made it clear that players who took performance-enhancing drugs have to live with the legacy of their decisions.

But there's enough blame to go around.

As I told *The Boston Globe* in 2006, "The players who used performance-enhancement substances knew they were illegal, but Major League Baseball is to blame for it, too. They let something like this [slip] through the cracks. If they had not been so sold on how many fans were coming through the turnstiles, they might have responded sooner. Now baseball is left with a bad scar, and we've got to deal with it."

• • •

I got increasingly fragile with age, but it wasn't because of any drug I had put in my system. During the 1996 season, I started to break down all on my own.

I played sparingly in the first weeks of the season, starting only a handful of games. The Marlins were already 9½ games out of first place by the second week of May, which also happened to be the week I was shelved with more knee problems.

The Marlins' hopes of competing for a playoff spot hinged on whether we could muster enough offense to help support a very solid pitching rotation headed by newcomers Kevin Brown and Al Leiter. Unfortunately, only Sheffield and Conine hit well in 1996, meaning the Marlins were a year and a few big bats away from making real noise in the division.

In July, the Marlins fired Lach and replaced him with John Boles, the organization's vice president of player development whose only previous managerial experience had come in the minors a decade earlier. It was a surprising hire, similar to the one the Expos made when they brought down Jim Fanning from the front office in 1981. The explanation for Boles' hiring was the team lacked discipline under Lach, and Boles was considered someone who could bring more order to the clubhouse. John posted a winning record during his tenure as manager but wasn't brought back for the 1997 season. He did, however, return to manage the team in 1999.

On the same day Leiter threw the first no-hitter in Marlins history, I had the 11th knee surgery of my career. Any lingering thoughts I might have had of coming back for another season disappeared at that point. I realized my body had been through enough.

I also realized I wanted to spend more time with my family and continue working to make my marriage solid.

While I was on the disabled list, one of the women with whom I fathered a child in the late 1980s sued me for increased child-support payments. The media picked up on the story and sought my reaction. I declined comment because I didn't think this part of my personal life needed to play out in public. I was committed to making sure the children, Krystal and John Christian, were provided for. That's what was important.

Vanessa and I had spent a long time trying to heal the wounds caused by my extramarital relationships. Our kids, Darius and Amber, were six and four at the time that lawsuit was filed. I knew the day would come when I would tell them about the whole situation.

I decided to announce my retirement after the season. The reason for that was simple—I wanted to walk away from the game quietly, and I felt a formal announcement during the season would lead to fanfare.

What I didn't factor in to the equation was the frequency with which reporters were going to ask me about my plans. It was an awkward situation. I didn't want to reveal my intentions, but I didn't want to lie, either.

After an inflamed knee put me on the disabled list for a second time in 1996, I had no choice but to put an end to the speculation. The Marlins called a press conference for August 14, 1996, so I could announce my retirement. My original plan was to leave the team on that day, but the Marlins convinced me to stick around for a farewell tour around the league.

I had a hard time sleeping the night before the news conference at Joe Robbie Stadium. So many things were swirling in my head. When morning came, I was anxious to just get it over with. I had jotted down some notes but didn't plan any kind of speech.

When I got to the podium, no words came out. As flash bulbs popped and TV cameras rolled, I stood there speechless. I glanced down at my notes and tried to compose myself. But when I looked up, I still couldn't form any words. I was at peace with my decision to retire, but I guess my heart and brain were conspiring to give me one last chance to change my mind. I just couldn't picture it was all over.

Finally, Darius walked up, tugged on my pants leg, and said, "It's okay, Dad." With my son's words of reassurance, I was finally able to address the room, though I faltered a few times during my address. Thankfully, Vanessa was at my side to help me get through it.

"I've been blessed with a wonderful career," I said. "Through the years, I've gained the respect of both current and former players of the game, and I'm most appreciative. But mostly, I'm appreciative of the fans. I want to thank the teams that believed in me, the Montreal Expos, Chicago Cubs, and Boston Red Sox, for giving me the opportunity to play the game. And I would especially like to thank the Florida Marlins, who not only believed in me but gave me the opportunity to play in front of my family."

One of the first stops on my farewell tour was Wrigley Field. I was still hurt and didn't get to play in the series against the Cubs, but prior to the last game, I walked onto the field through a gate in right field and hobbled around the stadium, waving to the fans. I'm sure it wasn't a pretty sight watching me run. I saw a lot of tears in the bleachers. When I got to home plate, my former Cubs teammates Ryne Sandberg, Mark Grace, and Ed Lynch, who had become the team's general manager, were waiting for me. They presented me with gifts that included blades of grass from Wrigley and a section of wood from the right-field bleachers.

The Marlins also made a trip to Montreal in September. The Expos organized a modest ceremony for me. I viewed that as either a slap in the face or, more likely, a sign they had something special planned for me once I was officially retired.

There was also a ceremony at Veterans Stadium, the scene of my first major league hit in 1976 and a ballpark I got to know well during my career. Garry Maddox, who I considered the best center fielder of my era, was on hand for the festivities and presented me with gifts.

As I entered my final month in the majors, the *South Florida Sun Sentinel* asked me to compile an All-Star team of players I competed with and against during my two decades in the majors. It was a difficult task because I had seen a lot of greats in my career. But after giving it some thought, these were my answers: Catcher: Johnny Bench; First baseman: Willie Stargell; Second baseman: Ryne Sandberg; Shortstop: Ozzie Smith; Third baseman: Mike Schmidt; Center fielder: Garry Maddox; Right fielder: Ken Griffey Jr.; Left fielder: Barry Bonds; Left-handed pitcher: Steve Carlton; Right-handed pitcher: Tom Seaver.

If I had been asked at any point to name the two players who most reminded me of myself, I would have answered Eric Davis and Torii Hunter.

• • •

Reminders of my longevity were all around me as I prepared for my swan song. I was 42. The combined age of Edgar Renteria and Luis Castillo, the Marlins' double-play combination in September 1996, was 41.

I was ready—or as ready as I was going to be—to come off the disabled list in late August, but based on things I'd read and heard, I knew the Marlins had a young outfielder named Billy McMillon who they wanted to keep on the big league roster. To make the decision easier for the team, I approached Boles and told him what I thought he should do.

"Don't worry about me, John," I said. "My career is pretty much over. Don't waste a spot on me if you want to take a look at a young player. Keep me on the DL, and I'll come off in September."

And that's what happened. I was activated when the roster expanded to 40 players. I entered the majors in 1976 as a September call-up and wound down my career in a somewhat similar way.

My first start for the Marlins since April came on Andre Dawson Day at the ballpark. In the clubhouse, I got a shot of cortisone in my knee to make sure I could play. Prior to the game, my family and I rode around the field in a Rolls-Royce as fireworks exploded over the ballpark.

In recognition of my lifelong love of fishing, the Marlins gave me some wonderful fishing-related gifts. Then many of the people who had been most influential in my life paraded onto the field. My former high school coach Paul Comeau was there. So was Costa "Pop" Kittles, who coached me in college. Three of my former managers in Montreal showed up: Dick Williams, Jim Fanning, and Buck Rodgers. And Shawon Dunston, Warren Cromartie, Gary Carter, and Tony Perez represented the hundreds of players I had called teammates. There were videotaped messages on the JumboTron from Sandberg, Dusty Baker, Don Zimmer, Dallas Green, Mark Grace, Harry Caray, and Buck O'Neil. Add to that all the family and friends at the ceremony and it was close to a perfect night.

The only thing that took away from it was my 0-for-3 performance at the plate against the Astros.

It turned out I was a day late in providing everyone, including myself, with a lasting memory.

In the final game of the Houston series, I came in to pinch-hit against Xavier Hernandez with two runners on base in the eighth inning. I didn't know if it was going to be my last at-bat at home, so I decided to do something special if I reached base. If I got a base hit, I was going to ask to be lifted for a pinch-runner. Then, as I jogged off the field, I planned to take off my uniform shirt and toss it into the stands.

That was the plan, at least.

I put a good swing on a 3–1 fastball from Hernandez and smacked it down the left-field line. As the ball soared toward the foul pole, I stood at home plate and leaned my body to the right in an attempt to will the ball fair. It curled inside the foul pole for a home run.

I circled the bases and then went back to the bench. I guess I was acting from muscle memory. I had hit 437 home runs prior to this one, and for a moment, I completely forgot my plan to do something special. Castillo, the next hitter in the lineup, had already started his at-bat when I heard the cheers of the crowd and came out of the dugout to tip my cap.

A fan in the left-field stands came away with the home run ball. He later gave it to me in exchange for an autographed ball and a handshake.

It turned out that wasn't my last at-bat in Florida, but I wasn't complaining. Boles wanted to give me an opportunity to start the Marlins' last home game of the season. Hitting in the cleanup spot against the Braves, I went 3-for-4 with three singles off Atlanta pitcher Denny Neagle. Considering I had 16 hits all season, that was a pretty big night.

I was going to let that game be my last, but Boles asked me to join the team on its final road trip of the season to Houston. Figuring I wouldn't see any action, I sat in the clubhouse for most of the first game of the series. When I was called on to pinch-hit in the ninth inning, I struck out against Todd Jones. I think Boles wanted me to end my career with a hit, so he sent me up to face flame-throwing reliever Billy Wagner in the second game of the series. Wagner threw me a fastball away, which I popped up to second base. The last at-bat of my career came as a pinch-hitter in the sixth inning of the final game of the season. I fouled out to the third-base side against Doug Brocail.

And with that, my playing days were over.

• • •

A few weeks after the season, Dave Dombrowski offered me a job as his special assistant. I thanked him for the opportunity but told him I needed a year or so away from the game to let my body heal, and more importantly, to give my family some quality time. He understood and said the position would be waiting for me whenever I was ready.

My first year out of baseball was an eventful one.

In July 1997, the Expos held a ceremony for me at which they retired my jersey number—for a second time. They had originally retired No. 10 in 1993 for Rusty Staub, who wore it during the franchise's first few seasons. I was told this wasn't the first time a team had retired the same number twice. The Yankees did it for both Bill Dickey and Yogi Berra. Despite the odd circumstances, I considered it a great honor to have my number retired. I harbored a lot of resentment toward the Expos when I left the team after the 1986 season. The ceremony at Olympic Stadium, which was attended by a lot of former teammates, helped me once and for all put those negative feelings behind me.

I'm glad I made peace with the franchise before Montreal lost its team following the 2004 season. That was a sad development, but like a lot of business decisions, it had everything to do with financial stability. I felt worst for the team's fans, many of whom remembered when the Expos came into existence in 1969. By the time the team left for Washington, D.C., and became the Nationals, those fans had likely turned their children and grandchildren into Expos fans. While baseball had always enjoyed an up-and-down relationship in hockey-crazy Montreal, I truly felt the sport had caught on in a way that made its departure all the more disappointing. It helped that the Expos played competitive baseball in the 1990s and 2000s despite being run on a shoestring budget. On a personal level, I had to accept the fact that baseball was no longer going to be played in a city and stadium where I experienced a lot of great moments.

The Expos left Montreal quietly. Former players weren't brought back for a ceremony. And despite some nice stories in Canadian newspapers about the

Expos' legacy, nobody really seemed too upset about what was happening. In an ironic twist, Jeffrey Loria, whose sale of the Expos to Major League Baseball in 2002 prompted their departure, ended up buying the Marlins at the same time. Jeffrey later became my boss after I came to work for the Marlins.

Two of the clubs I played for during my career—the Cubs and Red Sox—boasted as much tradition as any other team in the majors. The other two—the Expos and Marlins—were baseball newbies. The demise of the Expos marked the end of a 35-year attempt to build a lasting baseball tradition in Montreal.

If winning helps build tradition, then the 1997 Marlins took a major step in the right direction. And I was sorry I wasn't around to be part of it.

Under new manager Jim Leyland, the team won 92 games, 12 more than the season before, and secured a wild-card berth in the playoffs. The acquisitions of outfielder Moises Alou, third baseman Bobby Bonilla, and starting pitcher Alex Fernandez gave the Marlins some additional pieces that turned them from a mediocre team into a very good one in only their fifth year of existence.

The Marlins swept the Giants in the National League Division Series and then bested the Braves, who had won 101 games during the regular season, to advance to the World Series against the Indians. Most people expected the Indians, who were making their second World Series appearance in three years, to end Florida's Cinderella season.

As a Marlins season-ticket holder with seats right behind home plate, I had gotten a firsthand view of the special season. How did I feel about the team making a World Series run the season after my retirement? The fact that the team differed significantly from the one I played on kept me from engaging in too many "what if" scenarios. That said, both Vanessa and I found the whole thing somewhat bittersweet, especially because I never played in a World Series.

The Marlins-Indians series turned out to be one of the best in recent years. Two wins by 22-year-old Livan Hernandez helped put the Marlins on the brink of a title. But a Cleveland victory on the road in Game 6 forced a deciding game in Miami.

With the Indians two outs away from a championship, the Marlins got a sacrifice fly from Craig Counsell to tie the score at 2–2.

Darius, Amber, and I were among the more than 67,000 people at the game. When it went into extra innings, we left because the kids had school the next day.

192 IF YOU LOVE THIS GAME

That may have seemed like an odd thing to do, but I know my grandmother, who instilled in me the importance of education, would have approved.

At home, we watched on television as Edgar Renteria ripped a single up the middle in the 11th inning to score Counsell with the winning run.

For a moment, I thought about driving back to the stadium to join in the celebration. Then I realized with all the traffic and commotion, I'd have little chance of getting back into the ballpark.

I continued to watch on television as champagne flowed in the Marlins clubhouse.

15

LIFE, LOSS, AND ALWAYS BASEBALL

I THOUGHT AFTER A YEAR AWAY FROM THE GAME I'D TAKE UP MARLINS general manager Dave Dombrowski on his offer to become a special assistant for the team. But it turned out I needed a while longer. Only after retiring did I realize how much time I'd been away from Vanessa, Darius, and Amber during my playing career. I wanted to make up for my absences at birthday parties, school events, and other special occasions by spending as much quality time as possible with them.

After three years of being a stay-at-home dad, I think Vanessa was starting to get tired of looking at me! With her blessing, I called Dave and told him I was ready to come and work for the Marlins.

I've held the special assistant's job for all but one season since 2000. It's offered the best of both worlds in terms of keeping me involved in the game without giving me all the responsibilities of a coach or manager. My duties with the Marlins have included assisting the coaching staff during spring training, giving talks to the team on certain aspects of the game, and doing community outreach.

Above all, I've enjoyed my one-on-one interactions with players. I'm very comfortable in an official role of adviser and mentor, probably because it's a natural extension of what I did with younger teammates during my playing days. I also love being at the ballpark, where I have a locker in the coaches' quarters.

In my first year as an executive with the Marlins, I worked with Cliff Floyd, a Chicago native who was a high school freshman when I got to the Cubs in 1987. He remembered coming home from school and watching most of the Cubs home games on television. Cliff had a lot of talent, and most of our conversations dealt with his general outlook on the game. His last two-and-a-half seasons with the Marlins were among the best of his career, both offensively and defensively. I took pride in watching him further fulfill his potential.

The difference between my early years on the job and now is that I'm no longer mistaken as somebody who might still be able to play the game at its highest level.

For a while, Tony Perez, a friend and former teammate who managed the Marlins for part of the 2001 season, would see me in the clubhouse and ask, "Hey Hawk, are you starting in the outfield today?"

From the outside, it looked like I could still compete. But appearances can be deceiving. In the years following my retirement, I developed arthritis in both knees and was nearing the time when I would need double knee replacement surgery.

I wanted to keep my own body parts for as long as I possibly could, and I figured my body would let me know when there was no choice but to have that procedure. It reached that point in 2006 when the pain in my left knee became more than I could tolerate. The replacement process involved two surgeries followed by several months of strenuous physical therapy. After a while, the replacement knee became stronger than my natural one. I anticipate the day will come when I'll need my right knee replaced, as well. But that hasn't happened yet.

Despite my creaky body, I'm still fanatical about my workouts.

It was gratifying to read a 2007 feature story about my cardio and weight training in *The Wall Street Journal*.

• • •

My first chance to experience a World Series came as a special assistant with the Marlins in 2003. The Marlins' Game 6 victory at Yankee Stadium was absolutely thrilling, but I think most people remember that year's playoffs for events that occurred in the National League Championship Series against the Cubs.

We entered Game 6 at Wrigley Field trailing the series 3–2. Everyone on the team, the executives included, had overpacked for the trip to Chicago in hopes that we would win two games at Wrigley and then travel on to New York for the start of the World Series.

It looked like we'd have to lug our heavy suitcases home the same day we arrived. The Cubs were cruising 3–0 behind starting pitcher Mark Prior and needed just five outs to qualify for their first World Series since 1945.

As we all know, that didn't happen.

Thanks to that game, every baseball fan knows Steve Bartman, the young man who may or may not have prevented Cubs left fielder Moises Alou from catching a foul ball off the bat of Luis Castillo. If Alou had caught the ball, it would have been the second out of the eighth inning. Instead, Castillo walked on a wild pitch that put runners on first and third base.

From my vantage point in the Marlins suite, it seemed the Cubs still had the game well under control.

Then they fell apart.

Before the inning was over, the Marlins had scored eight runs. And much of Chicago blamed Bartman's actions for causing the disaster. But it wasn't Bartman who committed a crucial error on a potential double-play ball that inning. It was Cubs shortstop Alex Gonzalez. It wasn't Bartman who couldn't get anyone out after that. It was Prior and a couple of Cubs relievers. And it wasn't Bartman who came up with a string of clutch hits. It was the Marlins.

I saw the Bartman play. To me, it was simply a foul ball. Only later did I become aware of the controversy. I had never experienced anything similar when I played right field at Wrigley, so I couldn't say with certainty that Alou had no chance of catching the ball. But my opinion is that Bartman didn't keep him from making the play.

On my walk back to the Marlins clubhouse after Florida finished off the 8–3 win to force Game 7, several Cubs fans recognized me and yelled out, "Traitor!" I shrugged it off.

I had played in front of Cubs fans hundreds of times, but I had never witnessed their jubilation so quickly turn to agony. When the final out of Game 6 was recorded, I looked around the ballpark and saw a lot of pain. The place was dead quiet. I tried to put myself in their shoes. When I contemplated how long they had waited for a shot at the World Series, I just couldn't bring myself to cheer their loss.

There was still a game left in the series, but the Cubs seemed deflated by the crushing defeat. The Marlins came from behind to win Game 7 by a score of

9–6. Like the night before, I waited to celebrate the win until I was in the visitors' clubhouse.

The young Marlins were hungry and on a roll when they faced the Yankees. They weren't the least bit intimidated by the more experienced and talent-laden Yankees. Josh Beckett and the other starting pitchers felt they were destined to win the World Series. That's what I admired most about that team. I don't think many people expected the Marlins to be competitive in the series, much less to clinch the championship in the Bronx.

The 2003 Marlins differed from the 1997 championship team that captured the organization's first World Series title. The '97 team was full of veterans, like Bobby Bonilla and Darren Daulton, who had been brought in to help the team win right away. That team disintegrated the following season. The '03 team was built from the ground up, which was a testament to the Marlins player development system.

I enjoyed finally being part of a World Series champion. As I said after Game 6, "It was worth the wait."

As for the Cubs, I wonder, like everyone else, what it will take to end their generations-old drought. They had a great shot in 2003 behind Prior and Kerry Wood. It didn't hurt having Sammy Sosa in the lineup, either. But the key to the Cubs' chances of finally breaking through and winning a championship is starting pitching. In my opinion, they've spent too much money in recent years giving big contracts to the wrong players. Maybe new president of baseball operations Theo Epstein will help turn things around.

I still enjoy Wrigley Field. I go back almost every year when the Marlins play there. And when asked to, I'm always happy to sing "Take Me Out to the Ballgame" during the seventh-inning stretch. It's a special place with special fans, even if some of them called me a traitor and unfairly blamed Steve Bartman for a playoff loss. It's only a matter of time before the Cubs get over the hump. I believe the Ricketts family, led by team chairman Tom Ricketts, is committed to fielding a winning team. The day the Cubbies can again call themselves World Series champs will be a great day for a first-class organization and city.

• • •

My life since retirement has included projects that have had nothing to do with baseball.

Early in 2006, my brother, Vincent, and I got the idea to open a soul food eatery in Miami Gardens. We wanted to dedicate the restaurant to my mom, whose greatest passion and talent was cooking. She was retired at the time, and we thought she'd enjoy having a hand in operating the business.

The restaurant wasn't my first entrepreneurial venture. In 2001, I co-founded an independent record label called Acclaim that in retrospect was a big mistake. To help fund the label, I sold a valuable coin collection. The idea was to discover and develop young artists who might then get distribution deals from bigger labels. But the country and R&B artists we signed never took off. The experience helped show me the similarities between the sports and music industries. To succeed, both athletes and artists need incredible desire and dedication to reach a goal that millions dream about but only a few achieve.

I felt I was on much better footing with the restaurant.

But a few months before it was scheduled to open, my mom, who was 67, passed away when a blood clot in her lung caused a massive heart attack. Losing her was painful. She was very young when I was born, and she worked hard to make sure I was brought up right. Between working long hours and raising my siblings, she counted on my uncles and grandmother to help her with that task. But as my mother, her influence was special.

After her passing, I had a moment of doubt about whether to forge ahead with the restaurant. Then I realized it was the best way to honor her memory. As Vincent told *The Miami Herald* when The Mahogany Grille first opened, "You can get soul food anywhere in the city, but not like we prepare it. My mother is the essence and soul of Mahogany." The restaurant's specialties included waffles and Southern fried chicken, St. Louis ribs, and oxtail stew. Food critics gave it rave reviews. Unfortunately, after a few years, the business started to struggle. Part of that had to do with the nation's economic recession, which meant people were going out to eat less frequently. In 2011, Vincent and I made the difficult decision to close shop.

I had hoped the restaurant would become a fixture of the community. Despite that not happening, I'm glad we got to operate it for five years. I think my mom would have been proud.

I know she would have been proud to see me inducted into the Hall of Fame in 2010. She saw my disappointment at not having gotten in during my first few years of eligibility. She reassured me it would happen one day. And she was right.

In preparing for her funeral, I made the decision to invite the two children I had fathered in the late 1980s by women other than Vanessa. By this time, Krystal and John Christian were teenagers, as were Darius and Amber, who didn't know about the other children. I had wanted to wait to bring them together until they were old enough to understand the whole situation. I may have waited too long to take that step, but there was no ideal time or easy way to make the introduction. When my mom died, I realized I didn't want to keep this secret from Darius and Amber anymore.

I am proud of all four children. Krystal and John Christian graduated from college recently. And Darius and Amber are both finishing up their degrees. Each has been involved in sports in some way.

My father, Floyd, also came to my mom's funeral. For the most part, we've maintained a cordial relationship.

He visited me at my house in the summer of 2011, but it was hardly your typical father-son get together. I invited him over to discuss a lawsuit he had filed against me stemming from disputed ownership of a funeral parlor I had helped him get a loan for.

I couldn't understand why he was suing me, and our meeting was anything but amicable.

"I don't know what your mom told you, but I wasn't a deadbeat," he told me before I asked him to leave the house.

During a deposition in the case in 2010, he approached me in the hallway of the courthouse and offered his congratulations for my recent Hall of Fame induction. I nodded at him but didn't say anything.

"I said, 'Congratulations,'" he repeated.

I nodded again.

In the deposition room, Floyd, who was 75, blurted out, "He's just being vindictive because I wouldn't marry his mother."

I had to be restrained from going across the table and grabbing him.

• • •

Amid dramas in my life, I can always fall back on baseball.

I'm an optimist who thinks the sport has a bright future. It seems, however, that others don't share my opinion. Lately, there's been a lot of talk about shortening the regular season, finding ways to speed up games, and increasing the use of instant replay reviews. Commissioner Bud Selig formed a commission to look at these and other possible reforms.

I suppose these things are worth examining. The criticism of baseball is that it hasn't changed with the times, and for this reason, it has been surpassed in popularity by other more dynamic sports. In Miami, for example, LeBron James and Dwyane Wade have made NBA games must-see events. Low attendance in many major league ballparks and low television ratings for several recent World Series seemed to give credibility to this point of view.

I would argue, however, that baseball can thrive without sacrificing what has always made it special. The key to retaining existing fans and winning over new ones is making sure kids develop an early interest in the game. More affordable ticket prices to games would go a long way toward getting parents to bring their sons and daughters to the ballpark.

I believe it is incumbent upon today's major leaguers to be visible in the communities where they play. A lot of battles were fought before and during my playing days to ensure that players earn the money they deserve. They owe the fans who help pay their salaries a little loyalty.

I don't think baseball should appease the people who say the game's popularity would increase if the games had more scoring. We recently saw an era where offensive numbers were through the roof. And it wasn't natural. In fact, it stained the game. True fans appreciate a well-pitched game, and I'm excited by how much young, talented pitching there is in the majors today.

Baseball is what it is because of its long season. In the NFL, teams play 16 games a season, making each game a big event. The beauty of baseball is that its storylines play out over time. That's what makes it such a great game.

When I returned to Cooperstown as an enshrined member for the 2011 Hall of Fame induction ceremony, I was able to take a step back and enjoy a weekend that celebrated the game of baseball.

While there, I chatted with my former Expos manager Dick Williams, and we reminisced about our time together in Montreal. If you play, manage, or just watch baseball long enough, there is always plenty to talk about. I'm glad I had a chance to spend time with Dick before he passed away later in 2011.

That same year, the baseball community lost several people I got to know well during my playing days, including my former Expos teammate Charlie Lea, Hall of Famer and former Expos broadcaster Duke Snider, and former Cardinals and Astros right-hander Bob Forsch, who I faced more times in my career than any other pitcher. When I go to Cooperstown for the 2012 induction ceremony, I will pay respect to former Cubs third baseman Ran Santo, who will enter the Hall along with Barry Larkin. I got to know Ron pretty well when he was on the Cubs' radio broadcast team. Over the years, we stayed in touch and were rooting for each other to get into the Hall of Fame. Unfortunately, Ron, who battled diabetes, died in December 2010 before he could take the call telling him he had earned his place among baseball's all-time greats. Then, this year, we lost Gary Carter, a guy whose play and personality set him apart. Gary was a good teammate and a great friend.

• • •

The 2011 baseball season is winding down. Only a couple thousand fans look on as the Marlins play the Phillies in a Labor Day weekend series at Sun Life Stadium. The visiting team is on its way to the playoffs. The Marlins are counting down the days until we move into a new, baseball-only home for the 2012 season.

The fiery Ozzie Guillen would be hired later that month to manage the club. On this day, however, 80-year-old Jack McKeon, is in the dugout.

I'm sitting in the owner's box, the place I've watched Marlins games for the past decade. I'm studying how our hitters react to certain pitchers, looking at whether they make adjustments from one at-bat to the next. I'm watching the footwork of outfielders, too.

To my left is Tony Perez who, like me, is a special assistant to team president Jeffrey Loria. Tony is a link to my past. He and I played together in Montreal when I broke into the majors. Tony was a veteran who had come over from Cincinnati; I was just trying to make the team. We first met at spring training in Daytona Beach in 1977. I was eager to take batting practice, but Tony cut in line to take his swings. That prompted me to shout some angry words in his direction.

Life can be funny.

Despite our uncomfortable first encounter with each other, Tony became a mentor to me. Then he became a friend. Now we're both Hall of Famers. As we sit and watch the Marlins and Phillies, Tony's grandkids scamper around the room under the watchful eye of his wife, Pituka.

At times, Tony and I have been called on to try to adjust the attitude of players like talented shortstop Hanley Ramirez. In 2010, Hanley was benched for lack of effort. He then criticized his manager and teammates in the press. He had also turned his back on Loria when he tried to talk to him. The plan was for me to talk to Hanley in English and for Tony to follow up with him in Spanish. I approached Hanley in the clubhouse as news of the controversy blared from a TV monitor tuned to ESPN.

I told him I'd keep the conversation brief.

"If you say the wrong thing to me, then you might wind up on the floor on your rear end," I told Hanley.

Then I tried to sum up all I had learned in my decades as a player and executive: "This game will humble you, and it'll do it fast. You've got talent, and that's great, but talent sometimes only gets you so far. Nobody is bigger than the game."

I played tens of thousands of innings in the majors. Now I just observe, and when called upon, assist.

The Sunday afternoon game between the Marlins and Phillies goes into extra innings. For many, it's a meaningless September game on a hot and humid Miami day, finally won by the Marlins in the 14th. For me, there's no such thing as a baseball game without meaning. And there never has been.

INDEX

Uncle Theodore "Sugar Bo", 17
University of Miami, 13, 27, 30, 151
Unser, Del, 32

V

Valdosta State University, 30
Valentin, John, 168
Valentine, Ellis, 37, 40, 43, 56–57, 61–62, 67, 72, 78, 94, 117
Valenzuela, Fernando, 74–75, 79
Vaughn, Mo, 171, 174
Venezuela, 33–35, 39, 144
Veterans Stadium, 38, 73, 180, 187
Viola, Frank, 171
Virdon, Bill, 89–90, 95, 98
Virgil, Ozzie Jr., 52
Virgil, Ozzie Sr., 119

W

Wade, Dwyane, 199
Wagner, Billy, 189
Walker, Chico, 159
Walker, Larry, 177
Wallach, Tim, 89
Walton, Jerome, 141, 144, 147, 149–50, 155
Warthen, Dan, 38
Washington, U.L., 27, 169, 182
Watson, Cokes, 24, 29
Webster, Mitch, 150
Welch, Bob, 75
West, David, 180
West, Joe, 161–62
West Palm Beach, 6, 31, 33, 68
West Virginia University, 182

White, Bill, 162
White, Frank, 27
White, Jerry, 53, 75, 84
White Sox, 95, 100–111, 106, 154–55, 158, 166
Whitmore, Darrell, 182
Wilkerson, Curtis, 150
Williams, Billy, 112, 124
Williams, Dick, 39, 51, 70, 72–73, 80, 86–87, 98, 157, 188, 200
Williams, Matt, 148
Williams, Mitch, 126, 144, 155
Wilson, Hack, 120
Wilson, Steve, 148–49
Winfield, Dave, 7, 101
Winton, Wayman, 30
Wood, Kerry, 196
Worrell, Todd, 110
Wrigley Field, 43, 99–100, 102, 106, 109, 112, 114, 119–20, 134, 141, 147, 151, 153, 156, 159, 161, 167–68, 183, 187, 194, 196

Y

Yankee Stadium, 171, 194
Yankees, 34, 75, 78, 100–101, 123, 172, 174, 196
Young, Cy, 55, 61, 89, 121

Z

Zimmer, Don, 123, 127, 129, 133–34, 140, 143–44, 146–49, 151, 154, 157, 159–60, 162, 188
Zupcic, Bob, 168